Richard Hague's exquisite book of essays, *Earnest Occupations: Teaching, Writing, Gardening, & Other Local Work* is an exploration through layer upon layer of literary paleontology, anthropology, and archaeology. It begins with the very soil beneath our feet, "as we sift it through our fingers...we sift...a living and vividly present community astounding in its diversity and numbers." From the local quiet of "back doors and back yards" and "slouching and loafing places," Hague's writing expands out into a substantial volume that maintains that "the coalescing of atoms, molecules and movement into crickets, kremlins, moons, thrushes, earthworms, grocery stores, and [us]—is a set of stories." The vision here comes from Whitman and Thoreau and rises through such contemporaries as Wendell Berry and Gary Snyder. His poetic prose "includes wasps and lard and zeppelins, that makes [us]... weep—not sadly, not sentimentally, but reverentially, gratefully." Here in the words and memories of a poet, teacher, husband, and father is an excavation of time and place, bringing the reader, at last, from gravitas to grace.

—Christina Lovin, author of *Echo: Poems,* and
A Stirring in the Dark

ALSO BY RICHARD HAGUE

CHAPBOOKS
Crossings
A Bestiary
Greatest Hits
A Week of Nights Down River
Burst: Poems Quickly

POETRY
Ripening
Mill and Smoke Marrow
Possible Debris
Alive in Hard Country
Garden
The Time It Takes Light
Where Drunk Men Go
During the Recent Extinctions: New & Selected Poems 1984-2012
Beasts, River, Drunk Men, Garden, Burst, & Light:
Sequences and Long Poems
Studied Days: Poems Early & Late in Appalachia

PROSE
Milltown Natural: Essays & Stories from a Life
Learning How: Stories, Yarns, & Tales

MIXED GENRE
Lives of the Poem: Community & Connection in a Writing Life

BOTTOM DOG PRESS

HURON, OHIO

EARNEST OCCUPATIONS

TEACHING, WRITING, GARDENING, & OTHER LOCAL WORK

RICHARD HAGUE

HARMONY MEMOIR SERIES
BOTTOM DOG PRESS
HURON, OHIO

CREDITS:
General Editor: Larry Smith
Cover & Layout Design: Susanna Sharp-Schwacke
Assistant Copy Editor: Aimee Bounds
Cover Art: Elizabeth H. Murphy, www.illusionstudios.net

ACKNOWLEDGMENTS

Thanks to my wife Pam Korte, whose suggestions and remarks,
over the years during which these essays were written, have always
been insighful and useful. I am also grateful to the members of the
Southern Appalachian Writers Coop, who, during their annual meeting at Highlander Center, Tennessee, have been hearing and offering
comments on drafts of these essays for more than a decade. Jim Minick,
Pauletta Hansel, and Michael Henson have paid especially close attention to this book. Larry Smith and Bottom Dog Press have been indis-
pensable supporters of Appalachian and working writers for decades:
deepest thanks. And thanks to all of the other writers, most especially
Wendell Berry, who have fundamentally informed and deepened my
perceptions of my neighborhood, my region, and the connections (and
disconnections) between community, work, and place.

(Continued on page 191)

TABLE OF CONTENTS

FOREWORD 9

LOCAL 11
DIRT RICH 15
BACK DOORS 20
WILDING THE HOUSE 24
PENCIL TO THE PAGE 28
BREAKING IN 36
THE ELEGANT REDNECK 42
WORKING BACK TO THE OLD PLACE 46
ECLIPSE 50
WALKING THE TRACKS 51
SERMON IN THE STONE 56
SYCAMORE COUNTRY 59
SKIRMISHES AND SALLIES 64
SKIRMISHES AND SALLIES RECONSIDERED 66
VOLCANOES, GARDENS, AND RESURRECTION LILIES 69
LEARNING THE TONGUE, TEACHING THE EAR 72
THE ATMOSPHERE OF NAMES 79
NOT APPLES ENOUGH OR TIME 108
SEVEN TIMES SEVEN SONS 110
SMOKED 119
TROUBLE, MESS, DISASTER 125
GETTING URBANE AT THE ACADEMY 128
GUERILLA GARDENING 132
ICE TIME 147
A DAY AND A NIGHT ON THE LATE BIG BONE 151
THE COURSE OF THE RIVER 162
BOX TURTLE 170
GREAT WINDS 173
STILL LIFE WITH SHOVEL 180
WINTERING OVER 182
THAT TIME OF YEAR 184
EVENING IN THE GARDEN 186

ACKNOWLEDGMENTS CONTINUED 191
ABOUT THE AUTHOR 193

Mix sometimes your joys with your earnest occupations.
—Attributed to Carolus Linnaeus

...sailing, gardening, politics, and poetry... crafts of place:
they work by the light of local knowledge.
—Clifford Geertz

I was learning what John Muir, the American environmentalist,
observed a century ago: "When we try to pick out anything by
itself, we find it hitched to everything else in the universe."
—Dan Barber, *The Third Plate*

FOREWORD

I have tried more than once to compartmentalize these writings, sorting and organizing them into chapters, by subject. But it is no go. The epigraph from Linnaeus, the father of taxonomy, that highly categorizing science, nevertheless says, "Mix." Just as there is such a thing as a braided essay, intertwining one braid with another, one more memory-based, another more deeply researched, so this is a kind of braided book. The work of teaching and the work of writing become entwined; the work of gardening and the work of writing and the work of householding or neighboring complicate and inform one another. When Wendell Berry points out that eating is an agricultural act, he is suggesting such unavoidable intertwinings of realms. My wife says a typical day in our house is never one thing, but a number of things usually overlapping—gardening, cooking, reading, making pots, writing, housekeeping, neighboring—they are not regularly segregated. One thing may happen as another happens in time, or in close proximity to one another in space. We live within a few minutes of where I taught, within a few paces of where I garden, within the same house in which we prepare, preserve, and consume the things I grow in the garden, and within which we revise the things we write and in which we revise and think out the crop rotations annually. The rhythm of each day is alternation: and so I have tried to mix these joys and earnest occupations, to suggest the shifting of the mind and the body themselves, occupied this hour by one thing, this hour by another, this hour by a blending and enfolding of the several.

LOCAL

The four generations that preceded mine lived in "The Patch," a working-class neighborhood in Steubenville, just a stone's throw from the Pennsylvania Railroad tracks and the Ohio River. Of Irish and African ancestry, the neighbors of The Patch occupied frame houses with wide board fences in their backyards; in the generations before mine, there were small breweries here and there within a few blocks. My father's Aunt Kate lived there. Paul and Jack, my father's brothers, grew up there. I believe that at least for some of the time, my great-grandfather and namesake Richard — drinker, bon vivant, ward politician, and cobbler — called The Patch home.

They were all local people. By "local" I mean that they lived where they lived, steeping themselves in the lore and gossip and complex business, human and otherwise, of their neighborhood. They knew the people next door and down the street, knew the names and habits of the fish they caught from the river, knew what kinds of trees grew on their block, knew the names of the creeks that ran down the hollows to the Ohio. They rarely traveled far or long. Though my grandfather worked on the railroad, he often ate lunch at home, letting his switching engine idle on the siding just three doors down from the homestead. Our family's church, St. Peter's, was three blocks away, the grade school next to it, and my grandfather, for all the time I knew him, did not own a car. I was born in Gill Memorial Hospital about seven blocks from there, and lived a couple of miles away until I finished college and took up permanent residence in Cincinnati when I was twenty-one. My parents continued to live in our house for more than three decades until they finally joined the fringe of the Appalachian out-migration from eastern Ohio to Columbus.

I think this unusual in a time when the average American moves every five to seven years. I feel blessed in it all. It is true that there is much to say for a change of scene, for new challenges, new homes, new neighbors and friends. The mix of our culture is probably the richer for it. But we can be too rootless, too ready to pull up and move on, as if 21st Century America were still the wild and extravagant 19th, and Horace Greeley were still out there on the street corner urging us to Go West. A superficial and temporary connection to a place is unhealthy, leading to a sense of alienation and to a spiritual dislocation that spawns waste and irreverence. Not knowing—not even caring to know—about the history and meaning of local places allows us to dispose of them in ways which are not only ugly and vulgar, but self-destructive, even criminal.

This need not be the case. We can choose—deliberately and calmly—to be local in the best sense, and to live where we live with commitment and depth. Even when hemmed in by socioeconomic or other factors, we do not have to live like either prisoners or desperadoes. We can make virtues of necessities, and live with honor and dignity even though not totally free.

Such a way of living locally need not be provincial and narrow-minded, either. It can be as cosmopolitan (and as ecological, even cosmological) as our knowledge and imagination can make it. We can place ourselves wherever we are with much grace and purpose; or we can thoughtlessly stay here, relating to our house or apartment, our yard, our neighborhood as if it were nothing more meaningful than a motel or a roadside campground.

Wendell Berry, poet, essayist, novelist, farmer, and teacher, inhabits a farm bordering the Kentucky River about 50 miles from our home here in Madisonville, Ohio, a village which nearly borders the Little Miami River. Berry is making living locally a deep project, paying attention to his place with intensity and feeling. An anecdote he relates focuses for me the meaning and the blessings of being local, and points up the broader connections, the broader belongings, living locally can engender.

Remarking on the appearance of a pair of blue geese on his farm, he writes:

> My encounter with them cast a new charm on my sense of the place. They made me realize that the geography of this patch of riverbank takes in much of the geography of the world. It is under the influence of the Arctic, where winter birds go in summer, and of the tropics, where the summer birds go in winter. It is under the influence of forests and croplands and of strip mines in the Appalachians, and it feels the pull of the Gulf of Mexico... Here as well as any place I can look out my window and see the world. There are lights

that arrive here from deep in the universe. A man can be provincial only by being blind and deaf to his province.

Here Berry sees in a way that clearly puts the lie to any limited or "provincial" understanding of the meaning of local. Even the movement of his paragraph—from his "patch of riverbank" to the "Arctic" and "the tropics," to the "Appalachians" and the "Gulf of Mexico," and at last to "the world," and "the universe" moves outward from the relatively local and small to the cosmic and large. A homestead, and a household can be, all things considered, pretty big concerns. He comprehends that in the great mixes and churnings of geology and weather, in the movements of animals and water and air, any local place is, in important ways, related to a much vaster neighborhood.

Reading this on a warm January day when spring seems not too distant, when a huge mass of air has swept up from that very Gulf to temper this southern Ohio morning, I am reminded of the great event that happened in 1816. That was "The Year With No Summer," and all over the northeastern United States, killing frosts struck in every month of the year, destroying crops and darkening the land. What caused them? A series of volcanic eruptions tremendously distant from New Hampshire and New York and Vermont, eruptions in the Philippines, in Indonesia. The ash they injected into the atmosphere dispersed, blocking enough of the sun's heat to lower temperatures world-wide.

And here's the point: the dusts of those eruptions, and of the famous 1883 explosion of Krakatoa, and of the more recent eruptions of Mt. St. Helen's and El Chichón—the dusts of all these have settled, as others are continuing to settle, on the very land that has become our lawns and gardens here in Madisonville. Particles from meteorites are settling too, day in and day out. Cosmic events, distant terrestrial events—they are all a part of the very soil our tomatoes and bluegrass spring from.

As I write, trains roar through with their loads of goods from all over. Little Duck Creek, just down the street, performs its relentless southward drainage of our alleys and woods and yards. Air masses alternately roar down from the Arctic or up from the tropics. My neighbors hail from Kentucky and Florida, Kansas and Alabama. Variety, reach, and range—it is in the light of all these that I comprehend the meaning of local.

In the beginning was the Big Bang, the most intensely local of all localities, and the most concentrated of all Heres and Nows ever—the origin of both space and time. All that has happened since then, all the coalescing of atoms, molecules and movement into crickets, kremlins, moons, thrushes, earthworms, grocery stores and me—is a set of stories. Some are called science, some history, some theology. This book is one tiny set of local essays and narratives, reflective knottings and embroiderings of that common energy and power, focused through a single consciousness. They intertwine, unfolding and enfolding. They are not separate stories, ultimately, but layers, so to speak, of the same whole. They constitute a set of notes on this local Creation I live in, this house and household that I hold and that holds me, and in which I pursue many of my earnest occupations and play out many of my joys. They are accounts of what it means to be at home for a stretch of time at the same regional address in America, in the dawning decades of the new millennium.

DIRT RICH

Under normal conditions, a house stays put, a relatively permanent thing when measured against the sweetsour brevity of human generations. I remember as a child seeing a photograph of a great frame house, barn-square, jacked up onto timbers atop huge trucks of wheels, being navigated through a neighborhood somewhere. Trees had been trimmed back, telephone lines temporarily removed. There was something startlingly wrong about it all to me, as if St. Peter's Church, that huge pile of sandstone in the shape of a basilica which I attended every Sunday, were suddenly to rise from the ground and fly across the Ohio River.

I think my misgivings were appropriate. Part of the connotative meaning of "house" is a place that stays where it is. It may not stay the same, what with termites and storm-downed branches and heaves of frost and warps of summer heat, but it stays in the same place. It is this aspect of permanence in the notion of "house" that makes "mobile home" the oxymoron it always will be. There ought to be nothing temporary about the purposes and uses of a house, though I will admit here a deep and abiding sense of householding in a couple of trailers I have shared with blacksnakes and field mice, off and on, for substantial periods during my life.

In fact there are houses in the world that have been inhabited for millennia; certain cave dwellings, if you will allow the loosening of the definition of house to include them, may have been inhabited for even longer. Whatever their shapes or forms—bungalows, huts, geodesic domes, shanties, shacks, rock shelters, mansions, scalpeens, palaces, Queen Annes—houses are close allies of the earth. How about that marvelous city, carved into the side of mountain, and known as Petra, which St. Paul may have visited? Here in Madisonville, one of the oldest houses was built in 1807 by Benjamin Stites. My ancestors were still in Poland and Ireland; the list of things that had not yet been invented in 1807 would be laughably long to the contemporary cell-phoned nomads who make deals at eighty miles an hour on the interstates. 1807: Ohio had been a state for only four years; Thomas Jefferson, namesake of my native Ohio county, was President of the United States.

But houses hold permanence, at least on the human scale. And more: in temperate climes such as ours, houses are almost always built upon the land, unlike the floating abodes of some South American Indians or Southeast Asians, or the icy igloos of the people of the American North. Certainly the very basement of our house here in Madisonville, its fundamental fundament, if you will, is the dirt.

Outside, that base earth has been hidden now and then during December through February beneath the snow, but now it comes back to mind as our first winter thaws occur, and the garden beds we turned in the last sharp days of fall slump and settle. The song sparrow has recalled its tune after the dark amnesias of winter. Under leaf-litter and old mulch, the crocuses and daffodils have broken into light again. On warm days like this one, the earth releases the odors of readiness that urge us to think once again of seed and compost and green. Our affairs with soil are renewed.

What is this thing, this dirt upon which we raise our houses and our households and our children, and to which we commend our squash and tomato seedlings, our bush beans and cucumbers, and occasionally, our dead pets? Surprisingly various over the whole of Ohio, here in Madisonville it is most commonly a layer of topsoil five or six inches deep, underneath which a heavy yellow clay resides, dense and moist in spring, hard as concrete in the height of dry summer. A portion of the topsoil, I like to think, must certainly be the remnants of the original forest, the climax eastern hardwood community that built humus at the rate of an inch per century, and whose canopy made frontier Ohio a daunting realm of shadows and giants, relatively unchanged for twice the length of recorded history. Our peppers and carrots feed on the same elements that once were spruces and jack pines and then beeches and maples several thousand years before the pyramids were begun.

But also intermixed with this postglacial forest humus are the silts and gravels deposited by streams and by the wind after the last ice retreated from just a few miles north of here ten or twelve thousand years ago. A load of topsoil I purchased locally three years ago brought what might have been a part of Canada or the scoured bed of Lake Erie to the side of my driveway, where season after season plants that, before human intervention were never found in this hemisphere — peonies, for example, which originated in China — now thrive. The past is undeniably a living part of our present here, and it is not a merely human past, but a grand geological one, stretching back and even further back to a time when there were no humans yet on the continent.

In 1872, for example, as near to Madisonville as the mouth of the Little Miami River (about a half-hour walk from here, if I could go aground as the crow flies) a spring flood revealed the distant past that lies so surprisingly close to the surface of the present. A section of the river's bank washed out, exposing to the air "rafts of tree trunks" from an ancient forest bed. This was not all. The historian Henry Howe reports that in the "carbonaceous clay" common in our area, there were also found the "minutest roots of trees — some of the latter still in place — twigs and branches, layers of leaves, ripened fruits, grapes and sedges...all clearly distinguishable. Several of the species of trees could be determined, some by their wood, others by their leaves and fruits. Among them were the sycamore, the beech, the shellbark hickory, the buckeye, and the red cedar...the wild balsam apple was also shown to have been abundant by its seeds...preserved in the clay."

In addition to these remains, the bones and teeth of mammoths and mastodons were occasionally found, as well as "chips" and "axe-marked stumps" which later were recognized to be the work of beavers — though not of the giant once native to this area, a beast the size of a small bear. The giant beaver, it turns out, was an eater of rushes and cattails, and felled no trees. And then there was Jefferson's ground sloth, an animal that has to be seen to be believed — and a reconstruction can be viewed, in a replica of its natural habitat, at the ice age exhibit in Cincinnati's Natural History Museum. It was an animal that seems a cross, in general build at least, of the mountain silverback gorilla and the grizzly bear, though I would guess with little of the belligerence of either. Its size was daunting, though, and its long sickle-like claws must have been dangerous if one ever got riled. It is named after Jefferson because as president he was patron of the frontier naturalists who discovered its bones, along with many other Pleistocene animals, in places like Big Bone Lick, Kentucky, where Cincinnati's ice age exhibit, in its artful compression of space, terminates. It has not escaped my notice that I am a man from Jefferson County; there is a kind of connection here that may in part account for my enthusiasm over Jefferson's ground sloth, and which makes me rank it my second favorite Pleistocene animal, next to the woolly mammoth.

There are human remains as well; in the late 1880's, just before our house was built, Madisonville was the largest archaeological site in the United States. Dr. Charles Metz, head of the Madisonville Literary and Scientific Society, was gathering artifacts; among many other items, a cache of 50,000 freshwater pearls was hauled away to the Peabody Museum at Harvard. On a recent visit, I tried to view them and saw only a dusty card with a description, the originals swept away by some unknowable bureaucratic convulsion.

Beneath our streets and lawns, then, these riches and prodigies lay at rest, though so deeply now that even the hardiest roots of trees, or the deepest-plunging cicada larvae, rarely encounter them. They are a part of the earthhold's cargo, part of its treasury of meaning, beauty, and remembrance. And since our house is built upon that same rich earth, and even dips its basement into it to the height of a man and more, it not only is held by the earth, but holds something of the earth in itself. The damp breath of any basement is, in part, the life of the past, inhaling and exhaling more hugely and more slowly than even the advance and retreat of the ice.

But the topsoil, kindled by sun and drilled by worm and cicada nymph and churned by wind and rain and freeze, is our most immediate neighbor, inhabiting as it does that same thin layer of earth and air that we do, and it is constantly tapped by the plants in our gardens—and thus, indirectly, by ourselves. As we sift it through our fingers at seed-time, testing its tilth, we sift not only the glacial and forest remains of millennia past, but a living and vividly present community astounding in its diversity and numbers. In *Pilgrim at Tinker Creek*, Annie Dillard reports one researcher's discovery—in only the top inch of an eastern forest's soil—of "an average of 1,356 living creatures present in each square foot, including 865 mites, 265 springtails, 22 millipedes, 19 adult beetles and various members of twelve other forms. Had an estimate also been made of the microscopic population, it might have ranged up to two billion bacteria and many millions of fungi, protozoa and algae—in a mere *teaspoonful* of soil."

These incredible populations, of course, are perhaps not the same for our garden soil, but the microscopic life of it, too, must be high and varied for it to be productive. The importance of compost, for example, is not merely in the nutritive elements it contains, but even more essentially in the fungal and bacterial community it supports: a sterile soil, however rich in carbon and potassium and nitrogen, will not produce without the enzyme actions of living things which make that food available to plants. Good dirt is a living, breathing, metabolizing thing.

So, as spring approaches (coming steadily, wonderfully north at the rate of sixteen miles a day), and as we wait to plant our backyard beds and the Community Garden, I think of soil again, the past that it is, the future that it promises. "Whirl is king," the ancient Greeks cried, seeing the mutability of all things. But the whirl is not always a random flailing, a chaos of waste and destruction. In the great recyclings of time and place, our garden soils remain, at once remembering the ice age and the weight of mammoths and great beavers and ground sloths that compacted them. Yet they are thawing, right now, thawing and ripening again, to loose the rivers of bloom and fruit that will flow from them for the next seven or eight amazing months, thus helping to feed this very household in which I rise and have breakfast morning after morning, and in which I sit down now in quiet to write.

BACK DOORS

I hardly ever used the front doors of neighbors' houses when I was a kid. My best friend Roger Swartz's entrance was on the second floor; I had to go up ten steps to get to it, and the porch was so small that I could not occupy it and open the door at the same time.

So I almost always went around back and battered with my dirty fist at the wooden screen door at ground level. Almost instantly, I could hear the footsteps on the narrow stairs, and the turning of the inside latch, if it was locked at all. Then Roger's or his mom's face would appear and the screen door swing open into the basement, by far the most interesting part of the house. It was the real living and playing quarters for us boys. Roger's aquariums were down there, green, funky smelling, with crawdads and minnows and goldfish and one huge tiger barb that had a whole tank to itself. Even more exotically, the basement served as sleeping lair for Roger's dad Mike, a crane operator who worked shifts in the steel mill and who shaved—without soap or shaving cream—at the big double sink while glowering into a wallet-sized mirror that he'd nailed to an exposed stud. We could hear the scrape of the razor across his unslickened stubble and watch the edges of his eyelids flutter. He never flinched. He slept on a metal cot behind the furnace, a short thick man with fingers carved from dowels of some dark, knotted wood; if he had not been so good to us as boys I would be tempted to describe him as a troll, but that characterization would be completely counter to his presence and his helpfulness as we learned to be young men, in part, under his supervision. He was a good facilitator, if not a warm man. He took us to interesting places—to the river, and to Third Bridge, and to Mingo Junction, where his brother lived in a tiny house jammed between other houses and filled with the roar of the mill just across the street and the stink of the steaming coke plant across the Ohio.

Roger's mom was an upstairs person mostly, a neat thin English lady named Ada who had a kind manner and who brought curious

English customs to their household: tea and buttered toast at breakfast, and the boiling of any and all game meats that Mike might bring home — raccoon, squirrel, rabbit. I can say that I tasted each of them, once.

In the backyard of their house, just beyond the basement door, stood a tiny shed, its rear half jutting out over the steep hillside and shored up with timbers. Mike kept all sorts of things in there, though I can't say for certain that I was ever allowed in it. It had a small troll-sized door, too, and a window, forever blanketed by a permanently drawn sun-bleached shade. Over the hill from it, along the deep gully cut into the clay by a wet-weather run, Mike kept his coonhounds, mottled blueticks and ravenous, sad-looking redbones. In the woods beyond, mayapples flourished.

I might not have known much of this if I had been a front-door visitor only; back doors and backyards provide more intimate, less public vantage points. They are where the repairman comes in, and the plumber, and the kids. They are the ones left open when the front is locked shut; around them the wildflowers and weeds flourish, as opposed to the manicured and mulched front door gardens by which we prettify the public entrance. Back doors provide slouching and loafing places; they're especially good to you if you're barefoot — though you have to watch for rusty nails. Back doors are those through which you carry the watermelon out into the yard to eat and to spit the seeds. Before everyone got an electric dryer, back doors were where moms exited to hang the wash, creating waving alleys of snapping sailcloth for boys to swashbuckle through.

In my teaching of the writing of poetry, I see now, I am often deliberately blocking the front door from my students but leaving the back open, inviting them to approach poetry more intimately, informally, barefoot, so to speak, with all the sense of casual pleasure with which I often stepped into Roger's house. Knocking on the absolute front door of poetry often leads us into a polished parlor, from which the stiff butlers and maids of criticism and craft have rubbed every evidence of travail and frustration and wildness away, leaving a gleaming perfection that we are uncomfortable in, looking down abashedly at our own muddy shoes, our clogged metaphors, our lackadaisical, drooping, loose-belted lines.

How much more inviting to toss a few oddments and games my students' way, and let them fiddle around and get dusty and down on all fours, the furnace humming familiarly nearby, the blue orange of its gas flame just visible if you're almost prone. You can't do that in the parlor, next to the front door. There you have to stand up straight, and act civilized. Poetry's origins are not there, however; when poetry becomes canonical, it gets invited to many such formal places: the halls of the Pulitzer, the Nobel with its tuxedos and royalty. In the rich innocence of its infancy, however, poetry is a back door art, more likely to be fascinated by and to study, intently, the dark eyes of the Italian electrician and the smell of his leather tool belt and the weird music of his tools' handles clanking together as he fixes the light above the washtub than it is to exchange polite greetings with the mayor or the bald pastor, smelling of talc, come for his annual family visit.

Don't write *poetry*, I counsel. Sneak around back, and just jot a list of ten impossibly tiny sounds—a list of microsounds that hardly anyone notices but which someone like you, lying like a kid on the floor, smelling whatever danknesses there are down on the basement concrete, can hear, loud as a high school band.

Don't write a poem. Write something that includes a zipper, a zebra, and a blimp—and make it something about love. Don't start with the front door idea, start with the back door stuff. See how far you can go without falling off the edge of sense. Don't stand still in your shoes and suit in the blaze of polished floors, expecting the princess to be announced as you finish your lines. Come in the back door; feel your way through the dim dustinesses and the piles of offcast amnesiac toasters and heaters that do not remember their salad days upstairs. Don't worry about looking good to anyone. See what happens. See what comes.

And fame will not come knocking at the front door, either, if fame is what you want. It's all right to want a little of it; fame is one way, though imperfect and easily cheapened, that this poor awkward world has of acknowledging the deep mystery, the alchemical magic, the divine gracefulness of poetry. Like poetry, fame will enter by the back door; when you least expect it, while you are working hard on a poem about your childhood, a poem that includes wasps and lard and zeppelins, and that makes you, in the making of it, weep—not sadly, not sentimentally, but reverentially, gratefully—then someone will drop a note through the hole in the screen in the back door. You won't notice it for a week or two, perhaps much longer, lugging your poem around like a papoose, or like your old father who has not yet died but who can no longer walk on his own. Finally, the note will stick to the bottom of your foot as you're headed to adjust once again the leaking water heater. You'll stop, lean against the damp wall with one hand, pull the note off with the other, and hold it to the light coming through the window smeared with rhyme. The note will say: "Thank you for your poem about fireflies. I never knew such things as your poem shows me. Forever I am changed by it. Forever I will walk now in summer evenings as on a new planet."

It won't even be signed. You'll fold it up slowly and put it in your jeans pocket, along with your house key, sixteen cents in change, the broken shell you picked up at the edge of Lake Michigan last March, the dried wishbone of the Thanksgiving turkey, the inch of yellow pencil you keep sharpened there, always ready.

Or one afternoon you'll feel something coalescing in the warm dark of your future. Some little thing with a voice will be coming together, secretly, someday to knock quietly but insistently at the back basement door when you least expect it. Reluctantly, you'll stop what you're doing for a moment, that line you've just taken a hard look at, but now leave hanging from the page like the sleeve of a shirt you're halfway finished ironing. You'll walk from it just long enough to open the door, smile somewhat quizzically, and invite fame in with no more fanfare, but no less practical and temporary pleasure, than the meter reader come to adjust the bill in your favor, or the plumber to fix, for free, a balky pipe.

You'll talk a little while, pleasantly. Fame will give you a few tokens of its appreciation, speak flattering words, generally make you feel competent and appreciated. It will not be long, however, before you feel a nagging at your back, and you will cut the conversation short. "Good-bye," you will whisper. "Come again, it's been so nice to see you."

But your work is calling you. The poem's arm is hanging over the edge of the ironing board, and its hand is reaching from the end of the shirt sleeve there, and the fingers of the poem are working avidly, beckoning you back, reaching out, signing some sort of insistent, crucial message to you across the basement air.

WILDING THE HOUSE

"When I found the beautiful white bones on the desert I picked them up and took them home."
— Georgia O'Keeffe

My wife and I, in the late 1970s, before we had kids, took pleasure in autumn drives into the country, or walks along the railroad in our previous Cincinnati neighborhood of Evanston to gather dried weeds and wildflowers. We'd spot a hillside of thistles, which tend to colonize unpromising spots like roadcuts and barren medians and played-out pastures, and we'd pull over and take out the heavy scissors or pruners that we'd brought along. Or we'd flush a scrawny city rabbit from a clump of Johnson grass between the eastbound and westbound railroad tracks near Dana Avenue, and clip a few handsful of dried grasses and wildflowers and carry them beside us like sheaves.

Once we got them home, we'd spend some time arranging them in great masses in vases that Pam had made or had traded for from other potters. We'd set them around in the house in various places, liking how their earthy colors and loosely intricate natural lines played against the geometrical tile of the fireplace or the unstinting verticals of the dining room woodwork.

There was something important those arrangements of wildness did for our household and for our psyches. Those thistle stems and dried blooms and tall brown mullein stalks and whatever else we grabbed up, once brought indoors, softened the unnaturalness of the house. They made us feel somehow less disconnected, by cityscape and architecture, from the land.

It is important, especially for urban people, to maintain a felt connection to the landscape around them. I cannot say that it is essential, because quite clearly we can survive in such prodigies of the unnatural as Dubai or Singapore. But the issue is not simply survival. We are created not merely to survive, but to thrive, and the fact that we are creatures who once lived in trees, near water, and whose ancestors evolved in grassland environments with lots of sky and air, suggests to me that without those things, we are somehow cramped, shunted into a sterile, machine-addled environment that fails to support our full development and our deepest connection with the natural world.

The primary effect of such a troubled relationship is a kind of nomadry, not just among the poor who suffer displacement and eviction and homelessness, but equally among the well-off, whose migrations from sterile suburb to sterile suburb contribute to the decay of the inner cities, and to the mallification and uninspired, greed-motivated housing development of valuable agricultural or forested ground. Can we really feel at home in center-less places like Oakland, California, about which Gertrude Stein exclaimed, "There is no *there* there"?

Just the other day I read in the local newspaper about a phenomenon of "cruising" that has seized suburban youth and caused a great deal of trouble for traffic officials and merchants. For a mile-long stretch of suburban strip outside Cincinnati that includes a video place, a restaurant, and some sort of entertainment arcade, high school students are driving their cars slowly back and forth, destinationless, breathing in heavy doses of polluted air, adding bits of rubber from their tires and the grease and oil from their cars to the poisons already trashing the landscape. They do it, they say, "because there's nothing to do out here." I have to admit, I did the same thing as a kid, magically thinking that my dad's Chevy wagon sported a built-in party-detector. All my friends and I had to do was start the car and go, and we would be led to the action. It never worked, of course, and we spent whole weekend evenings aimlessly traveling, going nowhere.

There is a similar bleak truth to what the suburban Cincinnati kids say. All their houses are much newer than many in the city, and so need little work. The land has been commercially landscaped to death, so there's little puttering to be had in that line. There are no interesting city centers on a human scale where you can leave your car at home and walk or bike safely to, and partake in that nice European habit of the afternoon or evening promenade, during which romance can thrive, neighborliness be practiced, a glass of wine taken at a little table on the sidewalk, and exercise obtained without the stupendous boredom of a treadmill or the shouting frenzy of an aerobics class. Lacking this sort of thing, no wonder the kids get in cars and just go — there's no center to their suburban neighborhoods, and so they begin to suffer the same aimlessness of people with no center to their lives.

There is a cure, however. I would hereby invite them into my neighborhood, or any of the older city neighborhoods that resemble mine. There's a lot to do here: litter needs cleaning up, houses need fixing, gardens need planning and building and maintaining, children need tutoring, teams need coaching, public works need accomplishing. It would improve the world a great deal if we could simply count on all the juniors at Lakota West or Sycamore or Fairfield High Schools to come on into East Walnut Hills, or Over-the-Rhine, or Lower Price Hill, and help repair and restore the inner city. Let's not waste our civic pride on football teams that extort huge palaces from us, leveraging their ways into our pocketbooks with the bogus prestige a professional team brings to a city, or with the promise of income and jobs. Let's engender some real hands-on pride by getting our children's hands on real-life work, and real-life goodness, and real-life justice. By far the most laudable aspect of the Cincinnati Bengals football team over the last thirty years was former coach Sam Wyche's visiting of the poor in Over-the-Rhine every Sunday morning before the game.

In his "In Other Words" column about suburban sprawl in the now-defunct *Cincinnati Post*, Sean Halloran wrote, "Has anyone noticed how much Mason [Ohio] looks like Florence [Kentucky]?" When our places, different from one another in culture, history, and geography, begin to appear as similar to one another as McDonald's restaurants, we are in some weird kind of trouble. Though well-housed and expensively landscaped (often with plants, by the way, no more native to our region than sequoias, or the cedars of Lebanon) we are nevertheless lost, homeless, and there is no place to go back to from which to reorient ourselves. The compass spins, but the suburbs of Reading, Pennsylvania look exactly like the suburbs of Columbus, Ohio, which look exactly like the suburbs of Denver or Indianapolis or Dubuque.

Though we lived in Evanston, in a well-integrated and stable urban neighborhood, it must have been some sense of threatening placelessness that drove my wife and I to try to seek out the native plants and landscapes, and to bring them indoors as tonics and reminders. That, and the innate beauty of many of their natural forms and textures. But of course, it's not enough. Though Georgia O'Keeffe brought the beautiful bones indoors, she did not merely lean them in some corner and let them gather dust. She looked at them, hard, every day, and then at last she painted them, which created a relationship more intense and intimate than mere idle gazes. John Moffett, in his poem "To Look At Anything," says that in order to really see something, "you must become that thing." And in order to become something other, we have to be willing, now and then, to give up what we are, to retire from ourselves for a time, to retreat into a quieter, slower place of the heart. Only by knowing who we are can we know where we are—or where we should be—and whether or not we just might be better off somewhere else.

I didn't say more comfortable—I said better off. As long as comfort is a major determiner of where we choose to live, lots of important business in this country that needs doing will not get done. Race issues will not be faced head-on if white flight and middle-class black flight continue from the inner cities in the quest for comfort. Every time an inner-city mother or father or aunt preaches to the children that the best thing they can do is "Get out of here, as fast as you can," my heart sinks. I understand the need to escape from an environment that is unhealthy, yet I also know that without native, educated, placed, savvy people staying in their neighborhoods, caring for their block as blocks need to be cared for, almost as certainly as children need to be cared for, our cities will continue to lose their souls.

The ancient Romans had their *lares* and *penates*—domestic gods, whose presence sanctified. We ought to have something equivalent in our households, so that we don't lose sight of the fact that everything we have is a gift, ultimately, and that we owe homage to the giver of those gifts, however we name the Provider and Creator. Wilding the house, reinhabiting it with the things of the field and the forest and shore, pays homage to, and resacralizes our domestic space. It mixes the merely human with the realms of air and light and season, and blends the wild world's spirit with ours, however momentarily. Every passing glance at the weeds in the vase reminds us of the larger world. Wilding the house strengthens and blesses us. It is one enactment of our spiritual obligation to what poet Gary Snyder, in his 1969 book by the same title, has called "The Earth House Hold."

Pencil to the Page

When I was young, around the fourth or fifth grade, I used to earn candy by drawing strips of pictures for my classmates. Tommy Schaefer or Eddie Jack or Robby Anglin would say, "Draw me some tanks and bombers having a battle," and I'd do a half-dozen or so, in sequence, as in a comic book. The patron would check it out, show it around, say "Wow," and give me the loot.

More often than not, the payment was a sheet of those tiny buttons of pastel sugar plopped onto a long strip of white waxed paper. (I recently ran across one of those inane lists that appear on the Internet entitled "Reasons Why You Might Be a Redneck" or something like that; this was a list of things that would characterize you as "Ghetto." It included, "If you've ever eaten candy off a strip of paper.") They sold for a nickel a strip, I think: a yard of sweet, available after lunch from the makeshift counter set up at the alley door of St. Peter's School. A person's style of eating them probably revealed deep things about him or her. There was one kid who picked them off one by one, row by row, in a continuous and orderly hand-to-mouth motion that reminds me now of the grooming behavior of monkeys. There was the same relaxed intensity, the same minute precision of picking, the same oral climax to the job. Others put the paper in their mouths, partly clenched their teeth, and then drew the paper out, harvesting a whole row or two of the beads at a time. Once the section of paper got soggy, they would tear it off neatly at the beginning of a new row, and start again.

I have no memory, however, of how I ate the candy—or if I ate it at all. Perhaps I kept those strips of punctuated sweetness as trophies of my artistic conquests, treasure-hoards in my top dresser drawer that must have drawn columns of hungry ants. Perhaps every month or two my mother would follow their trail, discover my stash, and dump it.

*   *   *

In those grade school days I was calmly aware of the fact that I would grow up to be an artist. No matter that I lived in a city whose major industry was steel, and whose major after-work and after-school avocation for roughly a third of each year (counting the first summer sessions in August and the last championship games in November) was football. No matter that I was not aware of a single role model for such a life as an artist might lead. No matter that the only formal art instruction I remember receiving in grade school was Sister Mary Hubert's demonstration, with colored chalk on the board, of some principle of balance or other: if you have something red in one part of your drawing, put something red somewhere else. Later I dabbled in watercolors. One rudimentary work that has survived was done on a college Christmas break and depicts an old stone bridge in Steubenville's Union Cemetery. Also during my college years at Cincinnati's Xavier University I secured a commission to paint a mural of the Pied Piper of Hamelin on the basement wall of the campus coffeehouse. But even before high school was over, I had pretty much lost any serious intention of becoming anything more than a dilettante. I never took an art course in either high school or college.

The strange part of this — to me at least — is that I cannot remember how or exactly when the desire to be a visual artist died in me. What happened? Did I suddenly become aware of the possibility that I was no good? Was my early ability nothing more than some sort of hyperactive tiny organ which gradually lost its function in me? Did someone confront me with a great painting or drawing, making me realize in a thunderclap that I'd never be able to do anything like that? Did my working class environment stifle and at last smother altogether the small ember of art within me? I do remember that my mother, up until the day she died, was afraid that I might throw over my steady and respectable employment as a teacher and put my family at risk by trying "to be a writer."

I have noticed this fear — of making the practice of art a life's career — in parents other than my own. Many years ago I had a student who was an astonishingly accomplished jazz trumpet player. Certainly, at high school age, he lacked the life experience and technical expertise that deepens and enriches any performance of music; but it was clear, as they say now in sports, that he "had game."

His parents were highly educated and working in art-related jobs themselves. But they made it perfectly clear to this child that the life of a jazz trumpeter was not going to be acceptable. "Think of the people you would be working with. Think of the long stints in smoke-filled bars. Think of coming home night after night at two or three o'clock in the morning. Would that be any way to bring up a family?"

I don't know, but it seems to me that slowly, relentlessly — and fearfully, they must have talked the boy out of his gift, out of the pursuit of his talent. I am afraid that this happens frequently in our American way in which making a living seems so often to exclude the more important work of making a life. Our culture grows more and more unwilling to support the arts in institutional ways, and has become, especially on the political right, nearly paranoid about the tiny fringe element that so often seizes attention from the vast majority of fully accomplished musicians and painters and sculptors and poets whose works heighten and make worthy of contemplation and appreciation the details of our lives and culture. The immoderate and misplaced outrage vented against those few artists whose work threatens the status quo or offends the insecure only proves how shallow the experience of all the arts is on the part of the protesters. If they knew the hundreds of good works produced by artists in this country, in every sense of the phrase *good works*, they would have no doubt that almost all is well, and worthy of popular support. The few outrageous outriders and self-promoting provocateurs are necessary to the health of the arts; they provide the possibility of new directions of evolution, or are simply a part of experiments gone wrong, like the millions of species of animals and plants gone extinct since the beginnings of life. Art, like the cockroach, will find its way, (or, like the dinosaurs, not).

But the public's reaction to things like the notorious "Piss Christ" — a photograph of a crucifix allegedly submerged in the artist Andres Surrano's urine, exhibited in a show partially sponsored by the National Endowment for the Arts in 1987 — reminds me of my mother's response to F. Scott Fitzgerald, when my English class was reading *The Great Gatsby* in high school. She did not care about his art; she rejected him on moral grounds, based on her perception of his life as little more than unsuccessful marriage, wild drinking, and related misadventures. "He was a bad man," she concluded, "and I don't see how anything good could come of imitating him. I certainly don't want you doing that." It was as if she equated all writer's lives with the mess of Fitzgerald's; no wonder she couldn't find it in herself to affirm any kind of artistic life for her own dear son.

So was there really a conscious, constant, low-grade resistance to the life of the artist in my family and school culture when I was boy? I really can't say for certain. Whenever we look back over the shapes of our lives, we are confronted with a fractal dilemma. There are digressions, dead-ends, sudden bifurcations, complex divergences, new zones of influence opening and old ones closing almost every day that we can remember, making of our pasts, in retrospect, a fretful paisley of possibilities, a tangle often resistant to, and sometimes outrightly impervious to, interpretation.

*   *   *

I was hunting beetles in the neighborhood. At the time I considered a career of such work, and put together a collection of about a hundred species from the woods and ponds and fields around my home. I learned how to key them out in my *Field Guide to the Insects*; I learned how to mount and label them professionally; I learned where to send for good Riker mounts, solid boxes with glass covers, tight-fitting lids, and composition bottoms that held an entomologist's pin tightly. I learned the names of the parts of a beetle, and half a dozen ways of collecting them, including burying coffee or soup cans in the woods to trap ground beetles, or hanging a white sheet funneling down into a bucket from a clothesline at night, with a bright lantern behind it, then sorting among the insects that wound up scrabbling around in the bottom of the bucket. I put together a science project from all that, and took it to the regional science fair at Muskingum College, in the hometown of astronaut and later senator John Glenn, and it won a State Superior rating. In the Steubenville *Herald-Star* article covering local students there, the reporter got the title of it wrong: rather than "Coleoptera" — the scientific name for the order of beetles — I had conducted a "Study of the Cleopatra of Ohio." Whoever that "Cleopatra" was, I think I might have been interested in meeting her. My life might certainly have taken an interesting turn at that point.

I see now that I might have been practicing, unconsciously, a kind of "living art" in my gathering, arranging, and naming of those marvelously varied, colorful, intricately patterned insects. I did not comprehend that there might have been some connection, some synthesis that I might have made between art's habitation in me and that more scientific urge. Common to both was the desire to be in the vicinity of beauty. Sometimes we are not only discouraged, as my student had been, but in the absence of sufficient knowledge of self and possibility, hapless castaways.

Had you watched me then, in those days of beetle collecting and high school science labs, those days of keying out in the field guides then printing, with intensely colored pens, the intricate Latin names of my beetles on tiny labels that spread beneath them on the insect pin like patens under the chins of communicants, you might have bet that I would become some sort of scientist or naturalist.

I did not.

So what has come of all that instinct to collect, all that effort to classify and name, all that love of solitude in the woods or in my closet lab, beholding the complexly varied anatomy and coloring of beetles? Was it all practice for some life that might have been, but was not, for some chance turn of fate of luck? Are there really dead ends in our experience, back from which we cannot find our ways, whole seasons and years of interest and activity that have no relevance at all to our present lives?

I think not. There is a conservation of energy at work here. Though I did not become an entomologist, I have continued some of the same habits and activities I pursued in the fields and woods. I am still a lover of solitude, in doses of the right amount. I still retire to a small room to do my work. I still collect things; rather than seeking out the intricate jointed brilliances of beetles, I wander far and disparate places, gathering the verbal constructions of others, quotations from works that in their iterations of detail, in their various styles and diction and voices, are as diverse and thought-provoking and aesthetically pleasing as my beetles were.

"It is well, at certain hours of the day and night," the poet Pablo Neruda reminds me, "to look closely at the world of objects at rest. Wheels that have crossed long, dirty distances with their mineral and vegetable gardens, sacks from coal bins, barrels and baskets...from them flow the contacts of the man with the earth."

"We can ally ourselves," Wendell Berry suggests in "God and Country," using as strong a word as "ally" to suggest combined desirability and necessity, "with these things that are worthy: light, air, water, earth; plants and animals; human families and communities; the traditions of decent life, good work, and responsible thought; the religious traditions; the essential stories and songs." I can spend the rest of my life learning how to do each of these scrupulously. Energy applied well is energy brought alive, not wasted.

In another vein, connected to the alliance with "good work" Berry speaks of, I collect from Donald Murray's *The Craft of Revision* the following: "Do not minimize this gift. The joy—yes the joy—of crafting a text under my hand and with my ear is a daily satisfaction to me. I am so involved in the task that I achieve concentration and this is the reason we do these activities that give us the most pleasure. Casting for trout, painting a picture or a house, building a shelf, creating a great soup, conducting an experiment in the lab, constructing an arterial bypass of the heart or of downtown, we are lost in the making. Our life achieves, for the moment, a healing concentration of craft." I think each of these things is an "earnest occupation," a flow-inducing trance-like state perhaps comparable to any alcohol or drug-induced high. Or in William James' terms, akin to a "variety of religious experience."

Rambling on through my works and days, and acting once again on my lifelong fascination with names, I notice and collect this from *A Treasury of Railroad Folklore*, edited by B.A. Botkin and Alvin F. Harlow:

It is noticeable that Indian names predominated in the early deeper naming, even more so than in locomotive names, though more musical and attractive one were usually chosen. John Buchan, Lord Tweedsmuir, found 'names like symphonies' among our American Indian place names. An old-timer remembers that in the 1880's, fully four-fifths of the sleepers patrolling the Louisville & Nashville between Cincinnati, Louisville, Memphis and New Orleans bore Southern Indian names...Tullahoma, Tallapoora, Tallahassee, Tuscumbia, Tuscaloosa, Tuskegee, Etowah, Moscogere, Watauga, Wetempka, Pontooc, Oconess, Altamaha, Congaree, Aucilla.

From Emerson, I collect and consider this, looking into my own habits, and nodding at the end to see affirmed my hunch of the connectedness of things : "A man is known by the books he reads, by the company he keeps, by the praise he gives, by his dress, by his tastes, by his distastes, by the stories he tells, by his gait, by the motion of his eyes, by the look of his house, of his chamber, for nothing on earth is solitary, but everything hath affinities infinite."

Artists are in quest of what essayist Brian Doyle calls "the detail which catches the heart." In civilian life, it is details like these that we tend to overlook in our hurrying oversimplification of the universe. "Don't get caught up in detail" — then what *should* we get caught up in? Grand Abstractions? General Truths? The Big Picture? Is life nothing more than a generic free-fall through commerce, TV, and politics, a headlong relentlessly accelerating plunge into the crammed sinkhole of Time? A sometimes rapt attention to detail is a habit that can extend, rather than contract, our lives. It can offer, as Frost said poetry can offer, a "momentary stay against the confusion." I am thankful to Brian Doyle — and to all those detailed, particularizing, cataloging writers — who trust in the sacredness of the daily enough to pause before it and to name and enumerate its many facets with the wonder of children, saying, "Marvelous! Look at this!" and who turn it over and over in their simple attentiveness as if seeing it for the first time. Their wonder helps me see it freshly as well.

And if it is not these provocative passages, these crucial quotes that I gather, then it is my own poems I try to herd into the loose enclosures of books, accumulating, compulsively classifying and reordering them. For me at least, this making and understanding of my poems sometimes approaches that earlier work with beetles in terms of intricacy, attention, detail. I know I pore over the lines and shapes of my poems with something of the same intensity as I did over my living and preserved specimens years ago.

And I also know now that I may not have eaten sweetnesses off those long papers as a boy. But I have nevertheless continued to savor the blots, spots, patches, and patterns unfolding as my life takes its shape to this moment. When not putting pencil to the page, I sometimes write on a computer which prints out a continuous length of paper. It is possible for me to scroll back on the screen and see what I wrote ten paragraphs ago, ten developments ago, and then to scroll forward once more, to recover the present, to consider the temporary unity that has emerged, and to be reminded once more that the past is never gone. Though there may be gaps in the text, lacunae caused by burnt-out cells in the brain, or fires in the library of memory that have scorched the edges of the ancient text—or maybe nothing more than bad tear-offs from the printer—even then I know that gaps can only occur when something was there to begin with. Gaps cannot happen to nothing.

Our lives as teacher-writers are attempts to go back and fill in those gaps, to restore to unity and completion as far as is humanly possible the manuscripts of our lives. Much of this restoration is guesswork, hunch, instinct, what "feels right." Some is the accumulation and interpreting of facts. We roam the Renaissance in a mindscape compounded of rich and long association with the texts, knowledge of the scholarship, and a feeling of kinship with Raleigh, Marlowe, and madrigals. We attempt to put it all together with our students, to catalyze the grand synthesis that will make of all that disparate detail a coherent picture. We insist on bringing to our students some understanding and enthusiasm for Chaucer's multitudinous knowledge of people, fashion, food, animals, Christian doctrine, scandal, scatology, dialect, and fine manners, so that our students may dwell in Chaucer's world for a time, and come back from it enriched. We have faith in the past; we trust it will coalesce for us and for our students and readers; we trust that it can, and will, come alive.

But the result of such teaching, and the result of the work of such writing, no matter how orderly and convincing, no matter how elegant and rich, is always a version. Writing is, after all, a human endeavor by its very nature. It would not, nor could not, ever claim absolute truth.

Did I eat that candy years ago? Yes, if I can still taste its sweetness on my tongue. If I can still taste its savors of success and pride. If I can still reconstruct rainy Appalachian Ohio mornings in the 1950s, smelling of the steel mills and the paper plant a few blocks away, and if I can recall the textures of the girls' coats wet with drizzle, and the feel of the rolled-up rubber-banded newspaper we used as a football in our morning scrimmages.

No, if its taste is gone, like a fragmented file in a corrupted computer disk, or like a lost appendage, evolved at last out of the organism in which it no longer serves a useful purpose.

But here is something: it *was* sweetness—of that much I am sure. And that much has made it to now.

BREAKING IN

While there are millions of dollars to be made out there in the US of A, the Sunday supplement tells me, I'm sitting in a shabby little temporary school room, really no more than a glorified double-wide mobile home, jacked up onto concrete blocks in the middle of an urban high school's parking lot. Out the front windows (there are three windowless walls, paneled in fake pine) I can see the gray concrete block of the back of the gymnasium, and the blue trash barrel that holds the odd pop can or loose-leaf sheet or dead cat. The means of accumulating huge sums of money or fame seem very distant from this vantage point. Still, adventure knocks.

A couple of weeks ago, I arrived in the pre-dawn darkness to find a concrete block thrown through the glass window of the door. There was a dent in the floor but it nicely matched another one just a foot to its left, and the block was still in one piece, so I was able to carry it back outside with a minimum of mess. The floor where the shattered glass lay got thoroughly swept by Charley Ulrich, class of '74 and now our maintenance man, who also repaired the window with his usual alacrity and skill. So all in all, counting the new door light and the gleamingly clean floor, I came out a bit ahead on the whole deal.

Nothing important was missing. In fact, nothing at all was missing. If it had been a writer who had broken into my place, I could have been wiped out. Thousands if not hundreds of thousands of words of essays and stories were stored on the computer; my entire output of ten years might have disappeared more quickly than in a house fire. A few years ago, my friend Jim Webb lost everything in an act of arson that leveled his place on Pine Mountain in Eastern Kentucky. He lost his collection of over 3,000 records. He lost his stock of magazines and books and t-shirts, the sale of which occupied his time and helped fill his belly. He lost the manuscripts for an entire issue of *Pine Mountain*

Sand & Gravel, an anthology of writing edited by him and few others of our compatriots and published by the Southern Appalachian Writers Cooperative. His friends rallied and we had little fund-raisers all over the region, selling a bunch of donated chapbooks here, doing a benefit reading there, chipping in some money out of our own wallets. My students at Purcell Marian bought twenty or thirty chapbooks, and we sent a decent check; Jim got pretty much back on his feet—and his poem about meeting his own clothes, worn by the imagined varlet who rifled his stuff then set his place on fire, is a hoot. But then, less than two years later, it happened again. Someone burned him out of his new place, too.

So a brick through the window was a relatively minor hassle. Luckily for me, the window-smasher saw no use in an old computer, nor for that matter any of the tools of my trade—textbooks, pencils, paper, blackboard, erasers, chalk, desks, tables, piles of drafts, nor that hard-drive packed to the gills with a couple of full-length book manuscripts.

That place was where I worked as a writer for a time, in between stints as Coordinator of Writing Across the Curriculum, a job which every school needs to subsidize so as to avoid students knowing too many facts while having too little understanding of their meanings. It provides for regular writing in all classes—math, history, science—based on the assumption that writing is a way to learn; that making sentences and paragraphs work well aligns, sharpens, and clarifies one's thinking and learning. But that's another story. Previously, I wrote only at home, in a beautiful second-floor room looking out into the Japanese maple in my side yard in Madisonville. Almost completely lined with books, it is a room upon whose few remaining open expanses of wall are hung framed prints of Pre-Raphaelite women with auburn or golden hair and bee-stung lips. The less I have done my writing in that room, the more beautiful it has become.

If all you had to go on was the appearance of the places in which I really do work, you would think writing was a terrible, wracking disease. My writing haunts look like the scenes of violent burglaries, or the country trailers that tornadoes have sucked up, dismembered, then spit out. The room where I wrote at school was a dive. But it was a genuine dive. There was nothing crafty or phony or pretentious about it; it was a dive, straightforwardly, and thus charming in its own way, as a roadside beer joint can be comfortable and inviting, or a particularly experienced sofa left out to weather on a country porch. For years the place stank of my chain-smoked cigarettes and the mold in the carpet which increased in the rainy days of November and December, when the occasional downpour would rush under the floor as the

Deluge must have churned beneath the Ark. The four short cafeteria tables I'd pushed together in a square for the students to sit at were covered with my various projects' piles. I liked to think of them as compost heaps, those piles, in which a bunch of things I'd mixed together might come to some critical transformative heat or mass, and turn into a wise richness that I could shovel out into the plots of my writings and from which ultimately harvest prodigies and marvels.

In reality, though, the piles were a kind of papery and verbal pollution, more a testament to the weakness of my will to order my life and throw the garbage out than to any realized artistic gain.

If the doofus who trashed the door would have gotten in and lifted all my work, maybe he would have done me a favor. He might have, as Paul Valery once put it, "cleared up the verbal situation" for me; he might have performed the artful surgery necessary to reclaim something of sense from the disorder piled up that I was too clogged, too paralyzed, to deal with.

For a while after the smash-in, I considered leaving the door unlocked, hoping for the burglar's return. "Here's all my stuff," an invitingly designed sign in red magic-marker would say on the top of the stack of writing. "Take it, please."

But to tell you the truth, I think anyone complaining about his or her job in public, especially an artist or teacher, is a bit gauche. These are two of the most rewarding, if potentially punishing vocations that I know of — more head-achingly vicious sometimes than boxing, and more unpredictable than daredeviling. That some of us have managed to combine teaching and making art in our professional life, as my potter wife and I have done, and to regularly take health and renewal from them, is a gift we hardly deserve, an outright blessing. It is certainly "to mix your joys with your earnest occupation." It's as if the biology teacher actually gets to practice science, working on original research in the lab at the same time she is teaching students about meiosis. For me, it's the very definition of an integrated life: I get to teach what I do; I get to do what I teach.

I remember sitting in Arnold's Bar and Grill, many years ago, overhearing a conversation between a couple of fellows. One was a painter (not the house variety) and all he could do was complain about how poorly his work was selling, and how stupid and bourgeois the public was. As he became shriller, I became less and less convinced that he knew the slightest thing about art, or the history of artists, or about work and commitment and grace. He was reinventing the flog, and using it on himself. Those of us in the arts have heard this badmouthing of art all too often, and we begin quickly to suspect those who are most vocal about it of wasting valuable artistic time and energy complaining. It's the psychic equivalent of an infinite loop on a computer. *You're going nowhere. Stop already.*

The bottom line about writing, as about all the arts, is this: you do it because you love it, and because you are driven, and you would continue to do it even if you never sold a thing. That's it. You do it because it is you; it is what you do in the act of being you.

Teaching is a similar situation. As a literature and writing teacher, my job involves working sometimes hellaciously hard at things that the majority of human beings never spend two minutes thinking of, ever. The proper use of the semicolon, for example. The notice of, then avoidance of, sentence fragments, one of which I just committed in the previous pseudo-sentence. You either have to be nuts, or you have to believe, deeply and profoundly, that these sorts of things matter. You have to believe that much misfortune and discord in the world can be traced back to, as the warden in *Cool Hand Luke* famously drawled, "a failure to communicate."

But communication is, of course, more than just being grammatically correct or clear. It's also about being elegant, clever, memorable, graceful, flippant, stylish, novel, irascible—in short, it's about being individual; it's about becoming and continuing to be, a self.

I've heard that when Napoleon wanted to appoint a new general, he told his officers to bring him a sample of the candidate's writing: "Let me see his style." Effective communication is not only a matter of mechanical dexterity. Muhammad Ali was not primarily a boxer; he was primarily a stylist. He was something unique in the pugilistic world. Gifted though he was as an athlete, he was even more gifted at creating for himself, or out of himself, a presence that was his own, and new in the world (though the connections between this young black man, brought up on the Ohio River, and the frontier tradition of the tall tale and braggers and Ohio River screamers like Mike Fink are worth remarking.)

That individual style, that uniqueness of character, is in part what's at stake in a classroom. I'm dealing with people who, in high school, are in the very midst of forming a self. It's exciting to be in a place where that is happening. In some of the most magnificent Hubble space telescope photographs we can see the stunning turbulence and glow of stars being born. Huge horns of dust and light and scatterings of vividly colored obscurity as arresting as any ceiling of Michelangelo's spread across distances so vast we cannot imagine them. Inside these enormous structures, gravity concentrates diffuse matter into the incredible fusions that light stars; spurts of radiation glory forth from them in all directions.

There are in the human soul such great making places; they are where spirit and character are born. High school, despite the recurrent armed horrors, often is such a place as well. I have met there some of the finest people I will ever meet in my life, and I am speaking of the students as much as I am of my colleagues.

Forming a self is one of the the central occupations of adolescence, and the earnestness with which it is supported by the school and pursued by its students is an important gauge of the school's health and wealth. Schools are not warehouses. They are, or ought to be, "sane asylums," where people can gather in peace to do the important external and internal work of coming into their fullest being. Not just the athletic or physical being. Not just the intellectual being. Not just the spiritual and emotional being. Their fullest and most whole and most integrated being.

Wendell Berry reminds us of all this: "Like a good farmer, a good teacher is the trustee of a vital and delicate organism: the life of the mind in his community. The standard of his discipline is his community's health and intelligence and coherence and endurance. This is a high calling, deserving of a life's work."

When I look at my classroom and my students, I am looking, then, at something like a garden, at something like topsoil, and at a kind of work in which knowledge and skill are required, and in which awareness and responsibility to local conditions should govern. I am looking at a situation in which I must participate both as steward and cultivator, but in which I also must know when *not* to do anything. One skill of the gardener — and teacher — is to know when to leave well enough alone. At the Community Garden here in Madisonville, over-enthusiastic beginners often make the mistake of cultivating when the ground is wet. This results, of course, in a baked-clay mess when the clods dry in the sun, and defeats part of the purpose of the cultivation, which is to keep the ground open and breathing and ready to absorb moisture. As a teacher, I must sometimes stand back and not spoil the soil; I must let the growth occur, and not hobble or disfigure it, imposing too many of my own notions (or, increasingly, the notions of persons far away and completely ignorant of the local conditions that prevail in my classroom) upon the original and unpredictable growth of the student's mind and skills.

This is not a widely held notion of teaching practice. Our culture, generally, has expected the teacher to perform as knower and teller of information, to function as a kind of gatekeeper who asks, in the forms of paper and pencil examinations mostly, for the secret passwords. If you know them, you get to enter the realm of success in that discipline; you get an "A." Never mind that studies with college physics majors, for example, have shown that even high achievers in the class-room often cannot solve a physics problem when it is presented in a context different than the classroom or textbook. About a decade ago, when I asked a group of bright and articulate juniors in high school to write a paper about chemistry, which they were all taking and doing well in at the time, one of the brightest said, "I know a lot of chemistry. But I don't understand it, not in a way that I could write about for just anyone." It was then that I began to shape a program of Writing Across the Curriculum, to try to cure this malaise of undigested and unmastered knowledge. It was then that my teaching began to diversify, my paradigm of teaching to shift. I was breaking in to new realms of instruction and learning. I saw that the old information-delivery-system model was no longer adequate to the complexity of the job. I began to change what I invited students to read, and slowly to give up some of the control I had always thought I needed to keep—control over the books assigned, control over the sequence of readings, control over how students were to show what they had learned or had failed to learn. One of my students at this crucial time, Anne Endress, wrote a poem after reading *Zorba The Greek* which directly addressed the dilemma, and which expressed an accurate metaphorical solution. It's good and fitting that she, not I, gets the last word:

Teaching the Risqué

I mean,
how do you go about explaining
that Everything they know is false
and ought to be thrown out like
old baby diapers.

They'll just laugh at you like agnostics,
or just silently stone you, if you're lucky!

Few will understand that simply getting there
gets you nowhere
if you don't move in a
dancing way.

THE ELEGANT REDNECK

. With no fanfare and no fuss, my pickup turned 100,000 miles last week. Fittingly, I was on the way to work; to have hoped that the magic moment would come when I was bound for pleasure was too much, given the ratio of pleasure to work in my life. So, at the foot of Erie Hill, the zeros rolled around, and that was that. But now I have to think seriously about saying goodbye to this piece of machinery that has served me so well.

I make fun of people who lavish attention on their vehicles. I see them in their driveways, weekends, bent over Corvettes and vintage Cutlasses like lovers, buffing with expensive chamois until the sweat rolls down their faces and they squint in the glare with delight. It's possibly the height of the pathetic, this mesmerized fascination with the lifeless mechanical, the fancy and expensive gizmo; it bodes ill for the nation. Yet, I am not without a kind of earnest tenderness toward some machines, machines which, like famous swords or rifles, acquire a legendary, almost anthropomorphic grandeur.

The first great pickup I became familiar with belonged to Mr. Swartz, the father of my best friend. Mike, as he allowed us boys to call him, was a coon hunter, hellgrammite gatherer and general runner of the ridges in the country outside of Steubenville. In his garage — where, by the way, his truck rarely reposed, it being a sturdy Chevy, unafraid of the weather, and fitted with its own tent, a canvas cap that always smelled like camping — Mike had installed an old Bulova watch display case. He'd shagged it from somewhere down in Mingo Junction, and in it he dried his ginseng. Roger and I would sneak looks at those roots, little dried up men, some even sporting tiny, brittle phalluses that made us giggle. Later, when Roger and I became interested in collecting insects, wasps and beetles took their places next to the roots: intricate jewels athwart dun and twisted shrivels.

Many of our best insect-collecting trips were made in the back of Mike's pickup. He'd installed wooden seats over the wheel-wells, where Roger and I sat facing each other, hanging on to the pipes that supported the canvas. We were both skinny, hard-butted boys, and a good thing, for the roads Mike traveled were pickup roads, not your wimpy blacktop; after a summer foray we ached like soldiers and could not sit for long.

Mike liked to take us out the creek past Goulds, Ohio, to a place known locally as Third Bridge. The riffles there ran swift and cold: perfect hellgrammite water. While Mike waded, turning over stones, Roger and I climbed the bank toward the pier of the bridge, a slab of concrete set against the hillside. There, we'd been told, a wild man lived; Mike honked each time we passed, and portentously slowed down. Roger and I would lean gaping over the tailgate, horrified and excited. All we ever saw up there, though, were the scattered bones of small animals, which, we knew, spelled out secret messages in the wild man's crazy language.

Strangely enough, the most intense memory I have of that pickup in which I spent so many fine days is of cutting myself one afternoon. We were near Costonia, Ohio, fishing in the river below the dike stretching between the Ohio shore and the bank of Brown's Island. A thunderstorm blew up; Roger and I clambered into the back and broke out our lunches. I was slicing an orange, and the blade went too deep, nearly to the bone of my middle finger. I still carry that scar today, a milky crescent of moon, thin and vivid as the edge of an embedded fish's scale.

I do not know exactly when, many years later, that pickup made its last run. It must have been after I'd gone away to college, and Roger had enlisted in the Air Force. While I was studying in Cincinnati, and Roger was serving somewhere in Libya and later in Vietnam, Mike cranked up the old truck one final morning and came home without it. I think I'm beginning to know how he must have felt.

For, though it only distantly approaches the venerable dignity and absolute trustworthiness of Mike's, my own pickup has earned a brand of greatness. Soon after buying it—off the lot in Steubenville, after angrily abandoning a foundered Pinto on the interstate 250 miles away and hitching home in a rage—I took it on the first of what came to be an endless, wonderful confusion of journeys. My dog named Dog was still alive then, an aging border collie I adopted at the pound, and together we broke the truck in. We camped in the mountains of Pennsylvania, wandered idly and easterly across New York State, rushed through the madnesses of Connecticut expressways, and wound up aboard a ferry headed for Martha's Vineyard. The number of stripped-down shortbeds that have gone marine, piloted by adult runaways and their dogs, must certainly be small. But through it all, the dog and I and the pickup thrived.

A hundred subsequent adventures ensued. They are all now pleasantly and richly confused in my memory, bound together only by the frayed twines of place names, people, moments. I remember Fly, Ohio, and a certain pool table there, and a silent man in a red hat who, sitting at the bar at the stroke of midnight, commenced to grin, and had not ceased even when I staggered out two hours later. I remember the road from Hazard to Hindman, Kentucky, and a turnaround there, just inside the Knott County line, where for three consecutive visits I stopped to drink a bootleg beer and listen to the frogs. I remember hanging up in a ditch, alone, after dark, outside Graysville, Ohio, and the miraculous appearance of a man on a tractor with a log chain and time on his hands. I remember riding out Hurricane Belle at Cape Hatteras, my wife and I huddled in the camper, the truck awash nearly to its axles. I even remember specific loads of mulch and topsoil, hauled as many as five years ago, whose tinders and dusts still stain the corners of the bed. And I remember my dog's last ride, her stiff and voiceless decline on an old blanket beside me in the cab and the sad weight of her as I lifted her off the seat and carried her into the vet.

Things will, if they last long enough and are rooted in memory and meaning, become parts of our lives. They will become a part of the household we build for ourselves out of the timbers and shingles and salvage of our years. I used to believe that if I put two pieces of wood together and didn't move them for a couple of months, they would somehow blend with each other, become one. This was when my knowledge of the nature of things was a blessed mixture of fact and fantasy. It seemed reasonable to me that if atoms were always in motion, then anything placed on anything else would, indeed, move. And part of that movement would be together.

I know better now, sad to say. Rocks I have piled into dry walls do not magically fuse; each spring I pick some of them up, frost-heaved, and put them back again. Words I try to join fall ungrammatically asunder; old loves fall to the floor of memory like empty negligees, and forever disappear. But all movement and blending is not merely physical. My pickup and I have, in some way, grown together. It has been my sole transportation, my only means of getting from one place to another, through a decade of my life. And it's been a notable decade, spanning divorce, self-imposed exile, solitude, and remarriage. Certainly the changes of 100,000 miles have shown up on the truck; I only hope that I have worn so well, so mellowed in my scars and rust.

I imagine an old farmhouse, far down Brown's Run, below the place I lived in for a couple of seasons long ago when my pickup and

I were younger, still bachelors. I never drove there; greenbrier and sumac thicketed the hillside so intensely a half-crawl was the only way down. But that old house and my pickup have something in common—an ethos, a quality that expresses the complexity of a place, rather than a mere thing. Once I spent half a summer, each evening near twilight, sitting, in my mind, on the porch of that old house. Bindweed lashed the railings, thistles crowded the dooryard. I could look out over the creek to an outcropping where a family of foxes lived. Deer browsed at the edge of the former garden. Finches and buntings flashed in the last light up the hollow. Old crockery pots, filled with green water, leaned against the foundation of the barn. An antique harrow, weather-stricken and noble, disassembled slowly in a field. And in all of it—in the house's every board, in every wild rush of weed toward the door, in every bit of declining debris—there came to me a sense of the continuance of things; even, in the midst of gradual decay, a sense of their stubborn endurance.

So it is with my pickup. A few years ago, after blowing a head-gasket and suffering ill-repair, it ceased its usefulness as a full-powered vehicle, but assumed another, more important function. It became a kind of place in itself, a sort of mobile homestead, a moveable attic of treasures. Over the years, though mindless and inert, it has accumulated meaning. Behind its seat have been stored—or more poignantly, abandoned—a dozen heirlooms of adventures, a hundred rattling relics of good times. There's a Busch beer can, part of a mad pageant arranged for a departing editor and friend in the mountains of Kentucky; there's my old Zebco rod and reel, much the worse for wear among pipe wrenches, wrecking bars, and a copy of *Mandingo*. There's the rain gear I haven't worn since a long canoe trip down the river and whose mud-bronzed fossilized folds bring to mind some ancient Roman sculpture.

So it's going to be hard to say goodbye, goodbye to this elegant redneck of a thing, this burdened peasant in a city rank with the lithe Audi, the chic Mercedes. I am not looking forward to our parting; I'm not in any hurry. Its valves clatter (and so do mine); its skin is scabbed and scuffed. But, as they say on the cash-and-carry lots, it runs.

And with luck, so do I. Pulling its groaning door open every morning, I step gingerly over the hole in the floor below the clutch, and clamber again into a tentative continuance, surrounded by *memento mori*. I turn the key, listen to the engine falter, choke, clear its throat and rumble alive. "Hang in there, good buddy," I murmur. "Old ridge-runner, rust-house, beer hauler. Old back stoop of the cheapest motel. Hang in there."

WORKING BACK TO THE OLD PLACE

After his first visit to this 1890 beauty of a building that my wife and I purchased in Madisonville in 1981, my brother confided to my mother that he would never buy a "used" house. I smiled when I finally heard his phrase much later through the family grapevine. And I have had occasion to recall it, sometimes ruefully, over the years which my wife and I — and more recently our two sons — have lived here. For it certainly had been used, and used it certainly continues to be, this four-fireplaced, hardwood-floored, somewhat leaning old-timer of a house, this late Victorian, calmly vernacular carpenter's pride, this wonderful heat-leaking draft-catcher with its never-painted woodwork, its baroque and mysterious plumbing, its airy, high and haunted attic.

My brother's no fool. He built himself and his wife a new house in Mentor, and then in Twinsburg, Ohio, and then again in Reading, Pennsylvania. The walls of those houses are square; their steps go straight up and do not complain when trod upon. Their dusts are of a contemporary kind and not of archaeological interest, and their attics lack head room for even the most stunted of escapees from some dark Arabesque of Poe's.

Still, I think he's missing something. My wife and I have always been collectors of debris and suggestive junk; the house was simply the largest item in that line to come our way. Headed somewhere else one afternoon, we saw it and had to pull over. Trespassing excitedly, we climbed its sagging porch steps and pressed our faces to the windows. We squinted into the parlor and saw its grand varnished fireplace, the gorgeous gingerbread over the pocket doors, the gleaming woodwork, the dim promise of the rooms beyond. And stepping back, we saw the rotting posts of the porch, the rank barberries that crowded the front walk, and we noted the two rusted downspouts, hanging from broken gutters and bearded like villains with their dank overflow.

But we were caught; the house had us, and would hold us. Even the great dead maple in the front yard, so old a corpse that it had shed its bark and stood throwing its gray arms upward, as if in supplication or warning, did not daunt us. Within two weeks, we'd bought.

We moved in on the first day of autumn. The ash tree out back and the two maples in the sideyard — one of them a graceful Japanese beauty — had already begun to drop a few leaves; the recently mown year's growth of Johnson grass and poison ivy had commenced its slow rot, filling the air with carbonic exhalations and smothering the sparse bluegrass that struggled beneath the remains.

We were all ambition and excitement. We set up our kitchen, a hot plate on a card table, in the bay-windowed dining room. The actual kitchen looked as if it had been struck by a meteorite. There was a hole the size of a casket in the ceiling. An old refrigerator, which we had gingerly plugged in on our arrival, stood spattered with gore in a corner, its compressor muttering and gurgling. The original floor lay somewhere beneath successively more tragic layers of linoleum which peeled up here and there in painful strips like the flayed skin of a mutineer.

Blithely, we began to work. The entrance way, the parlor, and the dining room needed the least initial effort; a cosmetic coat of white paint, applied after soaking off an ancient wallpaper border printed with what appeared to be funeral wreaths, settled things down in the dining room. Its airiness became apparent; with the autumn sunlight slanting through the saffrons and scarlets of the maples outside, it glowed invitingly. Curious, we stripped the varnish from the top of the mantel: cherry. We smiled.

In the darkening days of that autumn, with the entrance, parlor, and dining room at least liveable, we attacked the kitchen. My father's reciprocating saw shrieked for ten minutes, and the old sink and cabinet — a mass of scratched enamel, loose rust, and floppy doors that reminded me of the wrecked Buick I'd once stumbled across at the bottom of gully outside Steubenville — was gone, hauled, appropriately, to the garage. A day's work by Mr. Hansen — a free-lance plasterer who had worked in the now-vanished house across the street forty years before — and the ceiling recovered nicely, only a few sags and uncertainties here and there hinting at its former decrepitude. My father took some cleanser and old rags to the refrigerator, and soon it looked spiffy, a rotund butler willing to stand in attendance, though still grumbling under its breath about some long-remembered outrage to its innards.

It was during those days, too, that we discovered one of the fundamental principles of interest to all amateurs who restore old houses.

After scouring the outside of the Kelvinator, my father attacked its interior with a mixture of household chemicals. In the course of his cleaning, it happened that now and then a few splashes of his elixir fell to the floor in a place where we'd peeled back the linoleum to preview what horrors awaited us. A quarter inch of black mastic, of the same consistency as the asphalt of LaBrea's tar pits, covered the flooring. And like the LaBrea goo, its was riddled with shards and remains: hairpins, slivers of glass, even a tarnished Mercury dime whose date revealed it had been minted just a few years after the Battle of the Bulge. But of most interest was the action of the refrigerator cleaner. Where it had fallen and soaked in, my father found that upon scraping with a putty knife, the mastic came up in a wet strip, leaving the resinous yellow pine beneath it remarkably well-preserved. A week before, dreading the job of getting the floor down to where we could restore it, my wife and I had called various businesses about the problem. All had warned us against using any but special liquids, liquids whose fumes were sure to turn our brains into calcified softballs and our lungs into sad bags resembling old pantyhose. But here we had something: not too offensive in the fume department, and cheap. If we worked fast, keeping it from soaking through to the wood and raising the grain, maybe it would do.

It did. We worked quickly, cleaning a two-by-two-foot space at a time, on our hands and knees, holding our breath just in case. And in a mere fifteen hours, we had a floor ready for sanding and finishing. One result of all this was our discovery of two important restorer's principles: first, there are probably more ways of doing any specific job in an old house than there are experts consulted, and second, the *right* way is the way you blunder on that works. Concomitant to these is the principle that the way you discover will always be the one that takes the most time.

They call it "sweat equity" in the old house game. We had improved the kitchen by one floor's worth; who was counting the hours spent and sweat produced, when the delight of *not* counting out dollars to some supercilious though efficient and knowledgeable stranger armed with years of experience and all the right tools for the job was the only alternative? As Thoreau inquires, "Shall we forever resign the pleasure of construction to the carpenter?" A sense of virtue settled on us; we began to drift into a mystical state compounded of blindness, exhaustion, and penury.

The blindness was the most interesting. We gradually noticed that living in daily familiarity with our house resulted in an increasing inability to see rather obvious problems. For example, the doorways at the bottom of the back staircase, which ends in a short passageway between kitchen and dining room, are three inches higher on one side than on the other. Rudimentary architectural speculation leads to a clear diagnosis: the post beneath this spot is settling considerably. I inspected it soon after, found it was so, though recently repaired. I made a note to myself to look into it later.

I still have that note, tacked to the cluttered message-board of my brain, and I am confident I will get to it before the turn of the millennium. (Note from September, 2014 — I didn't.) Meanwhile, I take what seems even to myself an almost masochistic interest in watching a rip in the wallpaper just above that door climb slowly ceilingward, growing a bit larger, a bit longer, each year. It holds a vague geologic or seismic fascination for me; it is the architectural equivalent of continental drift, or the slow creation of a new river in Nature. This house too, it says, is a living thing like the dirt it is built upon. And like any living thing, it will not stay the same.

ECLIPSE

It is one short of the last day of May; my first child, Patrick Cavanaugh, is exactly one month old. I sit among students in the school library and read their writing. Outside on Hackberry Street the light grows stranger and stranger; by half-past noon the sky is aquamarine, and the shadows thrown by the brush along the chain-link fence are darker than usual, dream-shadows under dream-sumacs.

In the old times, holy men prayed that the snake would not devour the sun. In fear and awe, their people stood at the edges of the village, watching the darkness deepen at midday in the woods. There were no guarantees, despite the power of the robed and chanting priests, that the sun would return. There were only the clean and tangibly edged sharpnesses of uncertainty, and the dancing, steadily darkening leaves.

At home, my son sleeps in a tunnel of blankets, hands at each side of his face, as it was with the victims in Pompeii. Forces are at work. I wonder if, and what, he dreams. Does the ancient bird in him, confused by this night-in-day, circle helplessly? Or is he as wise as he always looks asleep, tranquil, undulant, calm, riding like a gull the ebb and flow of his heartbeat?

For he is still a moon-child, a few short weeks away from the tidal existence of the womb. I believe he is still in touch with the original forces, closer than us adults to the tremendous and reverent silences of life's beginnings.

So it is, in this conjunction of things, that I pause in the midst of my daily work. I think of the intensity of moments, how much can be changed in the heavens and earth, in the mind and heart at once. I think of eclipse, and of the startling new light my own son casts, even as he sleeps, on the world we now share.

WALKING THE TRACKS

In the "scheme of things"—that great nebulosity of uncertainty we fall back on to explain the inexplicable—it was ordained that I should never live beyond earshot of a railroad. And so it has come to pass. Each place I've lived in over the years has, in its own ways, been different from every other, in architecture, tone of the neighborhood, proximity to bus lines and bistros. But each has had the railroad within hearing distance. For this I am thankful, strange to say, despite the cumulative damage worked upon the delicate inner ear and to the mortar of old foundations by ten mainline freights a day.

Socially, the passing of a train is a genuine event for visiting friends who live in the trainless suburbs, those underprivileged developments never excited by the roar of four units hauling a half-mile load of ball bearings. Folk who dwell in such pathetic asylums of quiet involuntarily jump up with their kids when the first thunders of a train trouble the distance. They race to the front yard, awed and agog, to watch eighty Chessie boxcars batter by after the horns of the diesels clear the eastward crossings. Then they return to the back porch, preceded by their offspring, and sheepishly try to convince us that they did it for the kids. But we know the adults loved it too: Such thrills are rare in a land long bereft of buffalo stampedes.

The noise, as my wife and I explain to all our visitors, is not unbearable. We grew used to it within forty-eight hours of moving here. The first night was rough, though. Our house is a ninety-year resident in good standing, and has learned how to react to a highballing freight a hundred feet away. It shakes.

That brought my wife and me, our first night in the house, up in bed right quickly. The horn first filled the room with a burst of orange noise, a kind of Doppler Effect blockbuster that seemed to explode from all directions. Then the shock wave hit. A picture we'd hung temporarily over the bedroom mantel beat a snappy tattoo against the cracked plaster; out in the hall, Bigfoot clumped down the front stairs, dropping what sounded like hickory nuts and roofing nails. Beneath us, the bed swayed to a New Madrid earthquake waltz; I had visions of the old eight-by-eight posts in the basement splitting down the middle and dropping to either side in cartoon slow-motion while the house collapsed upon us in a cloud of dust and lath and shingles.

Of course nothing of the kind happened. At last the caboose clattered by, and when it was all over, the only sounds to remain were the crickets fiddling under the backyard sidewalk and the muffled percussion of our hearts. The house still stood, the windows hadn't fallen out, the stairs still worked. The next night, we slept through, and we haven't been troubled since. Nor, a few years later, had our first son Patrick—even in his infancy—ever been awakened. He genuinely enjoyed trains, was an auditor of great discrimination, and hooted with glee when he heard one coming.

So it's not all clatter and boom. As a matter of fact, the din of the railroad in use only heightens the quiet that prevails along it for ninety-eight per cent of the time. The neighborhood sounds are a pleasant white noise then, against which the mockingbird's varied routine in the locust snag above the right-of-way sings out in brilliant counterpoint. And the apparent visual monotony of tie, rail and ballast affords a thousand delights for anyone who wishes to look a little closer.

Ever since my childhood, I've been a chronic collector of all sorts of offhanded, symbolic debris: wasp's nests and ladder rungs, turtle hooks and spent railroad fusees, carriage bolts and old marbles, bones and campaign buttons. And I have found that a railroad right-of-way is a trove of wonderful objects. An hour's careful walk might net a whole catalog of riches: pieces of blue and green glass, spilled corn, bucketloads of fine beige sand, abbreviated fragments of machinery as ancient-seeming as Tintagel shards or stele scratched with hieroglyphics. Mostly one finds old railroad spikes, though, each of whose funky heft is pleasant to the hand, and which leaves, in the summer, an inch-wide band of warm rust across the palm as confirmation of its being.

Such relics are suggestive. Now and then I like to think of them as the artifacts and remains which some future archaeologist might study. What kind of world, I wonder, might the student of such things construct from a day's gathered stuff? It's good exercise, I think, this speculating over railroad debris. At least it's a better way to spend a few moments than sitting through a thirty-second dog food commercial, say, or listening to a shrill spiel about hot tubs on the local rock station.

Actually, I have come to learn that there is an intensely contemplative side to walking the tracks. This arises from the physical layout of a railroad. Anyone who has walked the tracks knows that the ties are not set to coincide with the gait of the average man or woman. They are either too closely spaced or too far apart. One cannot get into a natural rhythm. One has to stutter-step or take giant strides. In a word, one has to *concentrate*. And after a hundred ties or so, if one is really paying attention, a kind of mantra arises within, a bipedal, repetitive *om* of the muscles and glands which, if repeated for a half hour or so, or better, a whole morning or afternoon, never fails to calm the vicious soul. Exclusively to use the railroad in this way, however, is an abuse, and not to be overdone. Lost in the railroad mantra, the walker is liable to rude and swift dismemberment by the 3:43 coming through to Cincinnati, and the therapy fails.

In the light of this, then the best walking tracks are the older, unimproved ones. Their ballasts have settled to gentle slopes, and the sharp creosote tang of the ties has been mellowed by sun and rain. Best of all, such aged tracks all have, along one side or another, paths worn smooth by local kids taking the short cut to school, by dandelion gatherers and berry-pickers and tatterdemalion itinerants mumbling scripture to the winds. Such paths afford the walker a more relaxed experience, and are the ornithologist's delight, the wildflower addict's garden path, the collector's free flea market.

There is a concept in ecology known as the "Edge Effect." Essentially it points out that wherever two habitats meet—for example a second-growth woods and a meadow—the greatest variety of wildlife will appear in the transition zone between them. In the city, a railroad right-of-way often provides such an edge. I know several birders who make the railroad a part of their daily round. Song sparrows and an occasional towhee or thrush chorus in the tangles closest to the tracks, among the berry canes and sweet pea thickets, in the stalks of Johnson grass and day lilies, in the wild roses and poison ivy. Further back, in the scrub that develops into what is often substantial second growth, vireos and bunting and goldfinches flash among the leaves. Mourning doves, too, are ubiquitous along the tracks; I think they like the dust baths dried-up puddles provide, and they get gravel from among the crushed rock of the roadbed.

The plant life by the tracks is surprisingly varied too, and presents the pedestrian with numerous studies in toughness and beauty. My favorites are the mulleins. They pioneer even the newest, most coarsely ballasted roadbeds, spreading their basal rosettes hardily in drought and heat. Their leaves are flannely and succulent, pelted with fine silver hairs, and can spread a foot or more in the first season. But the second year is the mullein's glory. Starting in early summer, each plant sends up a flower spike that may rise to seven feet. This spike is of the same pale green as the leaves, but knobbed and bossed with buds which at last burst, a few at a time, into a bishop's staff of dime-sized yellow flowers.

Incidentally, if one's feet begin to ache during the walk along the tracks, the mullein — of Flannelleaf, as one of its many folk names has it — offers a remedy. Its foliage was used for many years as comfortable linings for shoes, and Native Americans softened its leaves with a hot stone, then tied them to the soles of their painful feet.

Other vegetation — grasses especially — colonize not only the edges of the tracks, but the very wasteland between the rails. Growing two or three feet high, they are champions of resilience, and offer a lesson to us more stubborn creatures. When the coal train roars down upon them, they bend beneath its passing and then spring up again, scuffed a bit, shorn temporarily of their seed heads, but alive nonetheless. It seems to me that they are well-adapted to technology, able to coexist with it, and in the sunshine after the train's passing go on with their immortal transformations of primordial energies into life and flower and beauty.

Oddly enough, then, just such things — life and flower and beauty, the suggestiveness of the debris I find — draw me to walk the tracks. Perhaps it's an ironic commentary on our civilization that I have to resort to the paths of one of our culture's archetypal symbols of industrial capitalism and power for such rewards. But perhaps not. The challenge may be to discover significant anchor-holds of the natural world even in the midst of an increasingly technological one. A pessimist's attitude is reflected in the abiding fear of machines, as if trains, or computers, or TVs have a life of their own, and are engaged in a malevolent attack on our beings. It is reasonable, however, to remind ourselves that these devices are tools — not the users of tools. How we perceive them is fundamentally important. If we can continue to find the natural and the human amidst them — if we don't let them crowd out the living — then we can still count on a world that is healthy, animated with the spirit of life and its attendant mysteries and reminders of joy.

Bending down along the tracks to touch the wooly leaves of the mullein, I do not think of the strange and dangerous cargoes carried by the trains — the chemicals that can kill, the radioactive substances on their way to some temporary and futile burial. I know about them, and they worry me. But not now. Creation is polar, positive and negative, tensed and relaxed, happy and sad. We cannot worry too much; keeping the potential enemy constantly and naggingly in mind blinds us, enslaves us to fear. Suspending the tension, coming alive to the present good, is essential to health. Walking the tracks, skirting the edge between the technological and natural, using common sense to see and to hear and to touch, seems to me an opportunity to put ourselves exactly where we live these days, and to exercise the spiritual muscles of hope. Under the blithe June sky, the smells of wild rose and rust mingling richly, despair and dark thoughts are useless. The gay blue flowers of the chicory by the signal mast are not Persephone's dark gentians; the world they grow in, even one troubled by the tumult and iron of the railroad, is not necessarily a hell.

Sermon in the Stone

It's small enough to lay atop a quarter. Patrick found it when he was two, along the stretch of Little Duck Creek between Roe and Settle streets. We'd sat down at the foot of a sycamore to watch minnows and water striders. Idly, we'd picked up small stones to toss into the riffles.

Gravity, the laws of trajectory, the properties of waves, all evident in the tossing of a pebble into the water, were beyond him yet. I'd taken him there for simpler things—the grackle-dazzled air, the music of the stream over stones, the adventure of the little woods so close and yet so distant-seeming from home.

It was our first creek walk together, and it brought to mind a hundred such journeys I'd taken as a boy in the tow of my father and grandfather. Once Pap Pap and I had hiked all the way from Logan Street to downtown Steubenville, then across the Ohio River by way of the Market Street bridge into West Virginia. There, we'd crossed Route 2 and then clambered along an old haul road littered with slate and shale into a steep hollow. I saw ferns and mayapples, beetles and vireos. We didn't talk much; my grandfather knew better. He let the details of the landscape, its slopes and glens, its small waters trickling toward the river, its mixture of the wrecked and the surviving, speak for themselves.

"What's your project?" he'd already begun to ask me in those days. Gradually, I came to understand that my project, as far as he and my father were concerned, ought to have been *to see*, to grow aware. Even when fishing late at night from the river bank below Logan Street, I was expected to pay attention. They taught me how to hold the line lightly between my fingers, how to feel for the first tentative nibble of the catfish thirty yards offshore. By example they taught me, in the woods or along the creeks and runs, to sit still, to hold my tongue, to listen. They instructed me, in a word, to *observe*, and they gave me peace and quiet, and they took me places where I could practice. So I did not talk too much that day at the creek with Patrick. And in the quiet, the stillness and light, in the relaxed attentiveness which was the atmosphere of such lessons, we were rewarded. He picked up a dark, roundish pebble, then paused, studying it.

"Look at this one," he said. He held it out in his palm; I looked. All around us, limestones packed with fossils jutted from the silt of the creek banks, and the stream ran mumbling over the shapes of crinoids and brachiopods. The former are slender, stem-like fossils found everywhere in southwestern Ohio, in what is called the Ordovician Arch, an upthrusting of geology more ancient than the Pennsylvanian sandstones I grew up among in eastern Ohio. The latter, the brachiopods, are thumbnail-shaped fossils of shells common in the same stones. Most frequently, they're casts, concave impressions of the originals. But what Patrick held out was a one-in-a-hundred fossil, a brachiopod whole and entire, 3-D, top and bottom, positive and negative forms. Rather than merely study its echo in a stone, we could hold this in our hands, feel its heft, consider its wonderful curves with our fingers. Washed from its imprisoning limestone, it had, by common miracle, been spared the relentless erosion of water, the quick destruction of its details by crashing along the creekbed's rocks in high water. It had come to rest in a cup of sand, dried in the sunlight; after 250 million years, there it was: itself.

I smiled. Together we admired it. I put it in my shirt pocket, promising we'd study it again back at the house. We tossed a few more stones, watched the grackles, then climbed up and out of the hollow, past Dutchman's Breeches and Rue Anemones and beer cans, to flank the traffic on toward home.

How long will it be until Patrick looks again at the brachiopod, now resting on a glass shelf in my study next to a collection of shells, the Oaxaca pottery bird, the dried monarch butterfly folded like a summer prayer into a sparrow's nest? I have the notion that this small thing, discovered of an idle afternoon in the neighborhood, might be the test of his entire education.

Not for decades will I—nor any teacher or professor—know whether the world, his nation, his culture and community, or even us, his own family, have taught him well and fully. The examination will not be any administered by school or institution, for so many of them now are too big, too blind, too defensive or burdened or struggling, to take much notice of such small, unquantifiable recitals. It will come incidentally, unannounced, unprepared for in any official way—perhaps even Patrick himself will not understand when and if he has passed it.

And so, God willing and if the creek don't rise, I hope I do. If, in fifteen or twenty or twenty-five years from now, home from college or the Himalayas or with his own child in his arms, Patrick picks that brachiopod up and says, "I remember this. Let me tell you about it. Let me tell you about that day," and if his telling truly tells, counts back those millions of years, remembering, as in some epic chanted backwards, the great tale of life on earth, if he knows where that little brachiopod fits, not only in the grand scheme of Creation from as close to the beginning as we can know it, but as well in the modest, quotidian history of his own home place, and if he knows, too, the private and familiar meaning of that day we found it, and can tell that, too — then I'll be assured that he's been taught, and that he's learned. In small things live the proof of the largest; in the tiniest moments may be told the whole scope of a study and a life.

It's a long way, I know, and no sure thing. But it's something to look forward to, something to hold out for. I'll be watching.

SYCAMORE COUNTRY

It's less than a ten minute walk from here, not far away at all from the rap-hammering, traffic-conduiting, long-suffering heart of Madisonville. I walk down littered Erie Ave., go left past the dusty piles of the Stone Center, out onto Madison Road loud with traffic, past the Speedway gas station and the dudes gassing their hoopties in the lot, trunk-crowding woofers drumming and vibrating. I pass my wife's former studio which has stood these many years empty and ugly since her slumlord doubled the rent, saying, "I've got lots of people just waiting to take it," and then went on to trash the whole place. "It's only Madisonville," his attitude groused. "Who cares how shabby it looks? Who cares about its land?" He filled the side yard with vehicles, dumped a load of gravel over the lawn in the other side lot, and left piles of broken glass and debris on the sidewalk in front. When we saw it coming, my wife and I hurried up there and dug out a few of the vintage peony bushes that had grown in the back yard since the time of the Lammers family's habitation on the land. A week later, dump trucks were parked over the holes we had hastily filled in. What makes it all the worse is that those of us who have taken the time to learn a little local history and so try to align our minds as well as our senses to where we live, know that the building he is treating thusly is one of the oldest in Madisonville, the site of the first general hardware store here, built by the Lammers family with bricks made of clay dug on the site. It's a paragon of the local, even its materials arising literally out of its place. Generations of Lammers are buried in the Laurel Hill Cemetery, six blocks from here. To see this history obliterated by some arrogant parvenu is doubly offensive. He even nagged the city until they removed the Urban Forestry trees they had planted on Madison Road. I pass all that, cursing him, then turn left, check out the oncoming traffic, and make my move to cross over to Camargo Road. A couple of hundred paces north, past tiny hillside-hugging houses leashed to barking dogs, I walk beyond where the sidewalk ends. I step onto the weedy shoulder, turn a gentle curve, and am out of sight of the city. And at that moment, I realize how bitter my thoughts have been, how destructive. I resolve to open myself to what is good, to re-focus, reconsider.

For nearly a mile, the road could be anywhere in a thousand places in Appalachia. I have to crane my neck and look deliberately up to see any sky; the road skirts the creek, which crosses beneath the pavement through a concrete culvert the size of a railroad tunnel, and which my younger son Brendan discovered as a boy and adventured in with his friends. The hillsides of the winding hollow through which the creek runs are steep and densely wooded, and along the rocky banks, huge sycamores glow white this time of the year against brown tree trunks and the umbers and sienas of the forest duff. One is espe-cially elegant, rising thirty feet before its first branching, and the pat-tern its pale limbs make against the background of the hillside, I sud-denly realize, is the pattern for the stylized trees I have drawn all my life. Their branches always start out from the trunk almost perfectly horizontal, then suddenly rush up, creating squarish frames of white in which segments of blue sky gleam like lenses. There is something hypnotic to me about this pattern. I repeat it and repeat it and repeat it; early on, the sycamore entered my consciousness with a kind of visual fury, and its architecture was burned indelibly into me, becom-ing the archetype of all trees.

My late friend Joe Enzweiler, who grew up in the village this road leads to, used to take me on sycamore hunts. In his drives through the countryside looking for "bullrock" with which to build the beauti-ful walls at his brother's homestead in Campbell County, Kentucky, he'd discover huge sycamores, invariably along a creek, down in a hollow, each tree larger or more ponderous than the last. He'd make a note of the location, and then some winter Saturday, he'd take me there, and we'd stand near its trunk and snap a photo or two, while casually admiring its size and its wild beauty. Men and great trees have always stood next to one another thus; there exist hundreds of photos taken everywhere from Eastern Kentucky's virgin white oak slopes in the 19th century to the stiffly posed lumberjacks and pil-grims in the Pacific Northwest's redwood groves. If, as Melville says, "water and meditation are wedded forever," there is also some kin-dred union between humans and trees, though too often involving the destruction by the former of the latter.

I imagine that sycamores were tourist attractions even back in pioneer days, before the first Brambles and Whetsels and Muchmores and Stiteses settled in this neck of the woods and who, upon dying, gave their names to the streets of my village. A big sycamore is a land-scape event. It is so visible in its place that it can be used to give direc-tions — "Walk up the creek until the third big sycamore on your left — the one with the hollow trunk — then climb the hill directly to the ridge-top. Look west and you'll see my house." When I summered in east-ern Ohio during my premature mid-life crisis forty years ago, I visited now and then a little town called Sycamore Corners, where there was a General Store, a gas pump, and a creek. The sycamores edged the stream like a procession of white-robed deacons. Sitting there, I felt more than the usual need to keep in line. And, of course, a tree with the size some sycamores achieve can even, if one is pressed hard enough, provide a dwelling for a season.

A huge old sycamore rises in Lindner Park, off Indian Mound Avenue in Norwood, a few miles from here. Visiting it once, I felt like a pilgrim; I lingered around its sprawling base as one would linger in the precincts of a European cathedral, trying to imagine the past, wondering what creatures may have overnighted or overwintered in its dim enclosure.

As I walked Camargo Road in the presence of these sycamores, I was also in the presence of the creek itself, with its variable voice, its multiple songs. A four-foot cataract exits a culvert, and as is usually the case, below it stretches a deep long pool. The water cascades into it with a musical rush, a kind of aural shrine.

We in the city who need these moments and these relatively un-domesticated vistas have to practice what the poet John Keats called "negative capability," which involves living patiently with contradic-tion. Instead of wrestling with ourselves over the mess and ugliness of the city as set against the natural countryside, wishing we could have more of the one and less of the other, we have to be able to simply close our spirits' eyes as we pass through the ugly, and open them on the beautiful. Little beyond a kind of short-lived catharsis can come of railing against the litter, the Mad Dog bottles in the gutter, the sloth and greed of slumlords, the stink and honk of traffic. We are given what we are given, and though I am not advocating passivity in the face of that which attacks our spirit and our sensibilities, neither am I advocating constant dissatisfaction. This enervates us, and renders us unfit for our necessary battles against meanness and ignorance and hostility. We still have to endure the Community Council meeting, crammed with the frequently inconsequential but nevertheless unignorable crises of neighborhood democracy; we still have to make the irate phone call to the proper city agencies or to the police; we still have to take time out to draft the letter to the housing inspector or the county engineer. But we cannot allow ourselves to be nagged to death by these things; we have to enjoy what we can, while remianing loyal to the local.

So I hike Camargo Road, or whatever region of solitude and beauty I can find within walking distance of my home. The Laurel Cemetery nearby on Roe Street affords a pleasant quiet, a few large trees, though nothing near as admirable as the Camargo sycamores, and to the middle-aged saunterer and reader of headstones, a quiet reminder, as if he needed it, of mortality.

And if I were to live where there are no such places, I think I would feel a bit diminished. I would have to ask myself such questions as, "Is it acceptable that the only place I can go for leaves and shadows and the sound of water is a place I might have to drive to, adding pollution to the very thing I want to preserve?" Or, "Remembering Thoreau's observation that the cost of a thing is how much life I must give up in order to obtain it, how much is my peace costing me? How much is it costing the environment? Is there some way to live more gently and more lightly on the land, so that I do not cost it its peace and wholeness?" Or, "Am I content with the fact that my children interact with video games more intently than they study the intricate and varied world of nature around us? Is it appropriate that they know better how to blast an enemy on *Grand Theft Auto* than they know how to attract a hummingbird to our yard? Do I have any neighbors who keep a record of the weather?"

One cold day last winter, a glaze of ice covering everything, I was walking toward the cemetery when I heard a loud pounding beyond and above me, as if someone were working on a roof. As I scanned the houses, I caught a sudden movement in the top of an old silver maple along a side street. It was an astounding sight to me — first, because I knew exactly what I was seeing, and second, because it was the last thing I expected to see in the city. It's called the pileated woodpecker, and I first saw one as a boy in the woods of Wayne National Forest, in the hills of Appalachian Ohio. Now I was looking at one less than two blocks from my house, in the middle of a neighborhood better known for its rappers and car-repair joints than for its wildlife.

What a treasure to see such a thing that day. I wanted to rush around to my neighbors, pounding on their doors and crying out the good bird news to them, or to hustle my own kids out of doors for a once-in-a-lifetime sighting, but I knew I'd likely embarrass them. Still, the presence of that animal in my neighborhood, like the presence of the sycamores and their quiet creekside so nearby, was news more important than is covered on most of TV. It revived something in me that otherwise might have continued to decline for the rest of the long darkness of winter. I have looked again for it each time I walk that way, but no luck. Though the bird's presence fades to dream and memory, it is already the central point of a story I will tell and tell, hallowing in words its epiphany in this unlikely place.

SKIRMISHES AND SALLIES

Like many common things in the world of nature, it goes by several names: gilly-over-the-ground, ground ivy, and its scientific one, *Glechoma hederacea*. Related to the mints, it is aromatic, tenacious, an inveterate spreader. It makes tiny bluish-purple flowers at this time of the year, especially after rain, and like rain, it seeps into every low spot and shaded nook of the yard, its puddling greenery almost literally flowing over the lawn.

I've been mildly at war with this plant ever since moving to Madisonville. I say that with regret; it's an admission of failure on my part. I have designs on the land around my house; I do not mean to let it be. I have notions about how this parcel of earth should look, and under normal circumstances — that is, the thoughtless sleepwalking I often substitute for living and acting deliberately — such notions are acceptable, even admirable. "You're really getting the place together," my neighbor says as I lean wearily against my fence, fatigued as a guerrilla. "It's really looking good."

But when I think about it, when I wake from the mindless fuss and fiddling I fall into when outdoors, I'm not so sure that "looking good" — in the sense that my neighbor means it — is the best thing to be desired of this land. For, among other things, making this place look good requires me to uproot the ground ivy that swamps the perennial bed and that sends its subtle stolons spreading wildly across the lawn.

Two summers ago, I decided not to mow my side yard. I'd been reading Thoreau again. That always gets me into trouble, with myself mostly, for his work invariably jerks me suddenly, and uncomfortably, awake. His ideas are hell on sleepwalkers. Anyway, the passage that struck me was this one, from "Walking": "I would not have every man nor every part of a man cultivated, any more than I would have every acre of the earth cultivated; part would be tillage, but the greater part will be meadow and forest, not only serving an immediate use, but preparing a mold against a distant future, by the decay of the vegetation it supports."

That notion of not cultivating every part spoke clearly to me; I knew, and took pains to preserve, the streak of wildness in myself; it only seemed right to preserve something of the wildness in the land here, too.

So I didn't mow. The patch of ground in question stretches between two maples, and is the western side of the lot. At best, only a few hours of filtered sunlight dapple it each day, and it doesn't make much in the way of grass, or anything else, for that matter. After four months of being left alone, only a few patches of some low, obscure and thinly-flowered plant struggled in its shade, dying off in the heat of late August. Even the ground ivy languished. My neighbor stopped one afternoon as I stood in the middle of this ambiguous vegetation, this scraggly outpost of the wild. He looked quizzical, but was too polite to say anything. Awkwardly, I explained to him that I wanted to see what would grow there, what was natural to it. His eyes wandered across the yard, and then he said, "Well, it don't look like much, does it?"

No, it didn't. But then who's to say that wilderness must always be spectacular? Distant as we are from unspoiled places, visiting them only occasionally after long and hectic drives, we have come to expect that any land substantially untouched by people ought to look like an Ansel Adams photograph. And if it doesn't, what the hell, let's land-scape with dozers and rollers, douse it with Chem-Lawn, and have at least a nice-looking postcard.

Sorry to say, I mowed. I restrained myself from full retaliation and kept the promise to myself and to the earth that I wouldn't use chemicals. But I mowed. I still do. I get down on my knees, a perverse posture to assume, given the nature of what I am doing, and scrape my knuckles bloody pulling that ground ivy out. Now and then, as today, I stop and imagine what I must look like. And I remember an anecdote reported by one of the associates of the Swiss psychologist Carl Jung. Traveling among the North American Indians, he reported to Jung an aged chief's thoughts about white men. "They're always wanting something," the old man said. "And when they work, they have such cruel, thin lips. We think they're all crazy."

At war with the ground ivy, I don't even know what I'm doing most of the time. And worse, even when I do know, I can't help myself; I have designs on this place; I do not mean to let it be. And so I debase myself—and something of it—in the name of making it "look good." I suspect, in moments of clear thinking, that the old chief was right. I have ideas, notions, visions—but in the end they may well be bad notions, bad ideas: bad medicine.

SKIRMISHES AND SALLIES RECONSIDERED

One of the attractions of gardening—and writing and teaching— is that there is always the opportunity, actually the *obligation*, of revision, rethinking. If a clump of divided peonies doesn't do well where I've planted it this year, I can, with care, dig it up next fall and start over in another section of the yard. I've moved the divisions we rescued from the old Lammers property here in Madisonville several times now, searching for the right microclimate and soil conditions for them in the yard. Likewise if a sentence, or paragraph, or even a whole essay founders, or if, in reconsidering it, I decide it's just no go as it is, I can revise it, cultivate and alter it so that it grows more successfully toward what I mean to say. If the elaborate lesson on *Hamlet* falters, I can go home, study on it, maybe write an exploratory reflection on it, and try to fix it for the next time.

In "Skirmishes and Sallies" I overdid it. The extravagant self-criticism of my "war" against the ivy, and the characterization of gardening as an attack on nature, was, I think, mistaken. So in the luxury of revision, I'll try again (taking comfort in the fact that the very word "essay" means just that—an *attempt*, not the final word on anything.) I do this in hope that this current clump of thoughts will more successfully root itself in the loam of good sense.

While still nagged by second thoughts, I just happened to run across an essay that brought me back to some straight thinking. It's by Thomas Werge, and appears in an old issue of *Notre Dame* magazine that I read at the home of my brother-in-law, Tom Preston. Werge takes as his subject two major contradictory images of nature that inform American writing, and tries to draw some conclusions. He quotes Faulkner's "The Bear," a story which deals powerfully with the tensions between human and non-human Creation; in particular, the story recounts Ike McCaslin's restatement of God's role in Genesis: "He made the earth first and peopled it with dumb creatures. Then he created man to be his overseer on earth and to hold suzerainty over the earth and the animals on it in his name, not to hold for himself and his descendants inviolable title forever, generation after generation, to the oblongs and squares of the earth, but to hold the earth mutual and intact in the communal anonymity of brotherhood."

"Mutual" and "intact." Key words, and they stand for notions that European Americans have had a difficult time reconciling their actions to in the history of our country. Virgin forests fall under the weight of fear (savage places full of wild creatures), greed, and capitalistic, even imperialsitic notions of progress and entitlement. Farms become suburban subdivisions, flood plains becomes cities, buffalo traces become Interstate highways, and instead of "woods," we're just as likely now to speak of "wildlife corridors," "green spaces," "parks."

Notwithstanding, Werge goes on to observe that "For many Americans this call to the cultivation of nature, to be its nurturer with God, became a form of worship and propelled our persistent agrarian spirit. 'What is a farm but a mute gospel?' Emerson claimed."

True and suggestive, especially that burst of Emersonian metaphor. I was pleased to recognize my own thought that gardeners are "accomplices in revelation." But to return to Werge's thesis: he immediately follows Emerson's remark with a statement that for me captures a fundamental problem in American culture. He writes, "...the margin between taming and conquering, ordering and ravaging, is not broad. And our guilt as a fallen people, our hatred of limits, our love of power and our fear of death all compel us to seek mastery over that which we cannot fully understand and to exploit that which overwhelms us. Unable to grasp its mystery, we reorder creation in man's image and likeness."

Indeed we do. And many of our reorderings imply an "image and likeness" that is full of secret self-hatred, projected onto nature, a hatred and fear of what is wild, untamed, or, in the modern euphemism, "undeveloped." Thus the vast sterile wastelands of mall parking lots (not to mention the burden they place on local drainages during heavy rain); the cruel slashes of roadcuts through the Appalachians; the barbarous temples of sport we've erected on the once lush and productive silts of our river banks; the moonscapes of strip mines and mountain-top removals; the commercial "corridors" we blithely plan for the edges of our neighborhoods; even the artless monocultures of perfectly manicured and chemical-drenched lawns.

So, as Werge observed, we must keep in mind that there is a difference between taming and conquering, between ordering and ravaging. And as I rethink my essay, and therefore my image of myself as gardener, I see that I labored in "Skirmishes and Sallies" in a too-narrow and unnecessarily literal notion of my relationship with the garden.

After all, my yard is not — nor is any yard here in Madisonville — actual wilderness. It hasn't been for at least a hundred years, and probably for even longer than that. True, the fencelines that I haven't mowed (and which I refuse to nuke with chemicals), preserve a certain undomesticated nature: every March, when the first warmth returns, I see the garter snakes there, out of their hibernaria in the stone dry wall along the garage. Deadly nightshade, the source of the drug belladonna, thrives in the wild growth along my west fence, and I am worried that I won't root it all out and that my curious and omnivorous sons may inadvertently eat its fruit and be poisoned. Jimson weed (the famed "locoweed" of Westerns) is a regular here — this year, it has shown up in my cold frame. Its exotic, deeply-notched and pointed leaves are the harbingers already of its trumpet-shaped white blossoms, and I know they play a dirge. But displacing these indigenous things must not, I now see, be perceived as a senseless ravaging. There are things in nature after all that are not conducive to human health: influenza, smallpox, brushfires, locoweed. In reacting to such threats, humans are simply doing what comes naturally — as naturally as the body's immune system defends us against infection.

So yes, I will continue to contend, but in good faith and clear spirit, with nature in my yard. And having rethought and revised my previous interpretation of the relationship, I think I see more clearly that what I can do in writing, I can do in living and in gardening. I can change my mind. As long as there is no recklessness, no dissembling to self and others, in such changes in thought and action, so there need not be wrong in my cultivation of the land. It's a thin margin, all right, between taming and conquering, between ordering and ravaging, between fictionalizing and remembering, but I have the time and opportunity — and, I firmly believe — the obligation, to be careful.

Maybe my yard, ground ivy and all, can discover some happy medium, some golden mean: maybe the balance I find between the wild and the domestic will strike some harmony the earth itself will sing to in the green duet of our labor. Nature and I can exist "mutual and intact," in a balance that is not only healthy for both of us, but which, as my neighbors and the city legislators in their wisdom seem to require, looks good, too.

Volcanoes, Gardens, and Resurrection Lilies

My friend Jim Quinlivan, who knows about such things, having grown up among the bountiful corn and hogs around Richmond, Indiana, called my attempt, the first two years here in Madisonville, the Atomic Garden. By late June, its twin 4' x 10' raised beds had relinquished their spring crops of Black-Seeded Simpson and Bibb lettuce and spinach and kohlrabi and were already busy transforming sunshine, smog, and tap water into an almost grotesque abundance of tomatoes, beans, peppers, squash, and cucumbers. Jim liked to stand behind the tomatoes when he came over for a beer; I guess the confusion of stakes and vines tickled the anarchist in him.

As for myself, I'd developed the proper humility mixed with pride that a certain class of gardener demonstrates. Every mini-lecture by the beds suggested, "Great stuff, but not all my own doing. Nature, you know..." I had cultivated an attitude as well as a garden, and the harvest was equally as ideological as agricultural. I had set out to prove that the funky ground I'd reclaimed from half a decade's accumulation of trash, burdock, wormy lumber and dog dung was capable of impressive things. For gardeners, whether conscious of it or not, are optimists, believers; they expect the best of the land and are willing to urge it on.

I did not then—nor do I now—apologize for what must appear to be so much foolishness. Two summers later, knowing full well that for all my pride I might get up tomorrow and find slugs the size of mud puppies on the eggplant, or a population of earwigs sufficient to call down the rapture on a convention of pesticide manufacturers, I say it again: There is nothing better than a garden, a fat and burgeoning garden, most especially, in the city.

Many of my neighbors in Madisonville have made the same discovery. Everywhere I look, I find gardens—long, narrow ones tucked in against the railroad right-of-way, bordered by day lilies and feral sweet peas; platted geometrical ones, sturdily fenced, brooded over by languid Dobermans basking near the cabbaged shores like furred sharks; intense and tiny ones, Eddie Arcaro gardens, producing winner after winner.

Mr. Nash, who lives up the street, grows beautiful beans on his fence. This is noble and wise. But more importantly, he is also the designated gardener for those on my block whose lives make it impossible for them to garden, but whose spirits make it impossible for them not to try, even if by proxy. Mr. Nash mows the lawn next door, straightens the bricks that edge the sagging peonies, trims the yews that front the porch. I think he wants badly to sneak in a few beans by the lamp post, tuck in a few Rutgers seedlings among the snapdragons that line the walk, but he holds off. Still, when we talk of gardening over the fence, he smiles and tells me, "It's good for the old arthuritis," meaning, "It's good for the soul, young man, and you and I both know it."

He's right. I've never been wholly convinced of the claim that gardening is good physical exercise. It might be if a person gardens in the old row-fashion, leaving great wide areas open to weeds and the compacting rains. But most people I know who garden in the city do it intensively; that is, they build good soil, plant closely, and let the crops themselves shade out the weeds and protect the ground. About the only unavoidable exercise I get (outside of the few hours' work preparing the soil in the spring) is leaning over to pick bush beans or to snip a recalcitrant pepper from the stalk. Now certainly I invent a lot of work; for example, I vie with earthworms in the soil-moving department. A contemporary of Darwin estimated that the worms in just an acre of soil process eighteen tons of earth and organic material a year. That sounds about right for me, too, counting all the times I dig in the garden just to be there, among the tendrils and vines. My point, though, is that all this travail is a purely gratis outlay, not a necessary expense.

So Mr. Nash's smile implies the deeper truth. Gardening is a state of mind, not just a state of physical activity. It is done as much for the spirit, as for the pulse rate. It is true, of course, that there are those who garden because they have to. They need the extra food, and they are the most important and archetypal gardeners. There is a special grace to their work, a marriage of elegance and necessity. But for the majority of us, gardening is done for other, less utilitarian reasons. As for me, the primary reason is my belief that there is something sick about a mere lawn, something barren and unrealized about a soil whose only fruit is bluegrass. If we want to gape at vast expanses of mowed green, let us go to the country club where, staining our nice white shoes, we can engage in golf—that curious penance Mark Twain once dismissed as "a good walk, ruined."

The most potent harvests of the city garden are not primarily physical. They are, if we wish to accomplish the full crop, aesthetic, even spiritual. One of the greatest delights, of my city garden at least, is the unexpectedness of it all. Last year, in the middle of one of my raised beds (a bed that had been double-dug two years in a row, mind you) a canna lily suddenly appeared among the beans. It erupted like a green Vesuvius overnight and within a month had created a cone of shade extending a yard in all directions. The beans gave up; they fell back from this prodigy like the trees knocked down by Mt. St. Helen's blast.

I am reminded of the Mexican volcano Paricutín, which erupted in a garden. The man who came to work his rows that day fled to the local priest, who, upon hearing him tell of it, was promptly astonished.

There's the truth of it. Especially in old neighborhoods like ours, in places with creeks down the street and old plantings that have languished for a year or two between changes of ownership, the earth renews surprises. Not yet completely numbed by the faxed, xeroxed, e-mailed helter-skelter existences of office, school, and factory, we humans hunger for wonder as much as for Beefsteak and Bibb. We get out there on our hands and knees, scratching and pushing dirt, and we garden with an almost religious fervor, as if expecting a miracle.

Sometimes we get just that. One of the highlights of my garden is the appearance, in mid-August, of the resurrection, or mystery, lilies. (I have since learned that they have yet another, more unlikely name: naked ladies.) Their foliage, so green and strapping in the spring, has long ago died back, until I've almost forgotten. Then, one morning, standing on the back steps, sipping coffee and looking beyond the Atomic Garden, I see their spare, leafless—all right, naked—whips leaflessly arising from the debris along the old garage. A week or so later, those same whips ignite with bloom, pink, immense and glowing, and like the Mexican priest, for a moment I am astonished. It's among the best of the whole season's harvests: a festival for the eyes, a salve for the oppressive heat, a tonic for the soul's old arthritis.

LEARNING THE TONGUE, TEACHING THE EAR

Around the seventh grade — after my boy-soprano voice cracked and I was dumped from the choir, and the first pimples began to erupt on my chin and forehead, and girls had ceased being irritating rivals and had become maddeningly interesting problems, Sister Mary Ursula demanded I become an altar boy. Calling me brusquely into her office, she commanded, "Report to Sister Isidore tomorrow morning at seven sharp, young man. Don't be late." A sliver of smile, thinner and more dangerous than the blade of a shiv, slashed the bottom of her face.

"Yes, S'ter," I mumbled, chewing down part of the word as we all did when in a hurry to obey.

Next morning, I was handed a thin gray hard-backed book. "Learn pages 22 to 25 by Wednesday." Sister Isidore was a tiny intense woman brimming with Hail Marys and bristling with curt ejaculations: "Jesus, Mary and Joseph!" The black of her Dominican's veil contrasted with the stark white of her habit, out of which her tiny, narrow-fingered hands sallied threateningly forth like the claws of a velociraptor. "22 to 25, mind you. Then I'll hear you recite." I knew I had no choice in the matter; the nuns were divine in their authority, and had secret daily correspondence with my parents. The slightest disorderliness or laxity on my part meant hell to pay at home.

Spurred by fear and duty, I returned to my classroom and sat down while the other kids talked before the bell rang. On the cover of the book which Sister gave me is a color drawing of a priest, fully robed for Mass in the sacristy, baretta in place, holding his chalice covered by the paten and the cloth. He's wearing a red chasuble — it might have been Pentecost. I congratulated myself on already knowing the meanings of liturgical colors — although if I hadn't, it was there to be found on page 21. To the red-robed priest's right stands a boy in cassock and surplice, pointing at the clock behind him and laughing. To the priest's left, just entering the picture, is another boy, and I am struck by how much like myself he looks. He is in the very act of ripping off his jacket and glancing up sheepishly at Father. Obviously late, that boy — and the message, obviously, is, *Don't resemble him too closely, son, or you're in deep trouble.*

My father must have been handed a book exactly like that one twenty-five or thirty years before, because we were never late for Mass, not even once, ever in my entire life at home. My father was incurably premature for every appointment; it was as if he did not trust clocks, believing that they all lied — and that they all lied the same way, getting the time wrong by being terribly slow. So if Mass were at 8 am, we'd get there by 7:30. We'd sit silently in the car in the empty parking lot until the congregation slowly made their ways up the side church stairs, gazing amusedly into the windows of our car and waving.

The front cover of this book carried the title, appearing above the picture I've just described, *Memories of My Altar Boy Days*. In the same yellow type, below the picture appeared the date: *1961*. Inside the front cover, lined in pink paper, was the motto *Ora et Labora* — "prayer and work." The first page said "Thanks" at the top of it, and contained a printed message: "There are many who are appreciative of your devotion to this duty — not only the priests, the nuns, your family, your friends, but all members of our parish." And the message ended with "When the year ends, place this book among your keepsakes as it will be treasured in the years to come." And after that it is signed, "H.J. Grigsby." Monsignor Grigsby was a kind and florid man with a great voice full of power and, as I remember now, a sort of roisterousness to it. He always appeared to be glad. He inspired love and respect in all of us, and I was pleased to have such a message from him, and believed it very much.

The first seven pages consist of testimony by Cadet John L. Carroll (US Air Force Academy) concerning his privilege of serving Mass at the Academy chapel. (A color picture of a Mass being served by two young men in uniform appears on the back cover of this book, over the caption "Immaculate Lady of the Air Chapel, U. S. Air Force Academy, Colorado Springs, Col. Cadets, members of the Acolyte Guild serve regularly, in uniform. Story on pages 3-6".) Following Cadet Carroll's account are the photographs and brief biographies of college athletes, including Dave De Busschere from Notre Dame, and other players from Marquette, Detroit, St. Bonaventure, Creighton, Boston College — all Catholic institutions, of course, and heavily weighted toward the Jesuit schools — which makes the one public school kid, Dennis Fitzgerald, of the University of Michigan's football team, seem like an also-ran.

But again, I got the message — these boys are fine upstanding fellows who have maintained their devotion to the Catholic faith. You, too, sonny, could be one of them. Learn your Latin, kneel up straight on the altar, and maybe someday you will swoop exhiliratedly in the arms of our Immaculate Lady of the Air.

The real stuff began on page twenty-two (the pages were not numbered with numerals; the whole word, "twenty-three," for example, was printed at the bottom of each in italics. I was impressed by the elegance of this, and touched the leaves lightly, careful not to bend them or fold their corners.)

"Prayers and Deportment for Serving at Mass" it read in bold red letters across the top. A brief description of how to get started, following the priest's lead, followed, then the first response. In regular type, the priest's part:

In nomine Patris, at Filii et Spiritus Sancti Amen. Introibo ad altare Dei.

Then, in bold, my response, the part I was to memorize and get the pronunciation of right:

Ad deum qui laetificat, juventutem meam.

And then, underneath that, in red caps, for those unfortunates completely in the dark about how to pronounce Latin:

AD DAY-OOM QUE LAY-**TEE**-FEE KAT YOO VANE **TOO** TAME MAE-AM

I could feel my lips and tongue forming the Latin words. The ecclesiastical pronunciation was familiar to me from years in the choir, but I still felt a thrill to be again in the presence of this strange and beautiful language. I spoke the words inwardly, at first, to rehearse their rhythm and movement, getting the accents on the syllables in bold print right. Then I tried it out loud, low, murmuring to myself:

Ad deum qui laetificat juventutem meam.

About a decade ago, I asked a student to read aloud, the first time she'd ever seen them, the wonderful opening lines of Coleridge's "Kubla Khan."

> In Xanadu did Kubla Khan
> A stately pleasure dome decree:
> Where Alph, the sacred river, ran
> Through caverns measureless to man
> Down to a sunless sea.
> So twice five miles of fertile ground
> With walls and towers were girdled round:
> And here were gardens bright with sinuous rills
> Where blossomed many an incense-bearing tree...

On Liz Allensworth went, making her way through "Five miles meandering with a mazy motion,/Through wood and dale the sacred river ran" and then on...

> And all should cry, Beware! Beware!
> His flashing eyes, his floating hair!
> Weave a circle round him thrice,
> And close your eyes with holy dread.
> For he on honey-dew hath fed,
> And drunk the milk of Paradise.

When she had finished—silence. Liz lingered over the words on the page, her long honey hair hanging in the shapes of wings at either side of her face. I finally asked her, "What do you think?" She looked up, a kind of guarded rapture on her face. "I have no idea," she said, looking down at the page again and marveling, "but those words *taste good* to say."

It was the same way with me and my altar boy Latin. I loved the feel of the words in my mouth, on my tongue and lips, and since there was no translation, they could live as aural entities without any distracting meaning getting in the way of their song. *Ad deum qui laetificat juventutem meam* — what James Agee, speaking of this very same church Latin, called "thrilling brooks of music."

There's a story told about the poet Milton, voracious reader and author of *Paradise Lost*. As his eyesight grew worse, ending in blindness, Milton taught his daughters to pronounce Greek. I said *pronounce*. He did not teach them to understand it; he did not teach them the language. He taught them only the proper pronunciation. For years thereafter, we must imagine the plight of Milton's daughters: they read daily to their distinguished father, droningly, at length, agonizingly and exhaustingly. Aristotle. Thucydides. Aristophanes. And they did not comprehend one word, not one iota of it. It was all Greek to them.

So it was with me and Latin, in the seventh grade, at least. And I consider this strange, singularly aural relationship with a language — and its environment of ritual and antiquity, sanctity and mystery — as the beginning of myself as a poet and writer. Latin was sacred; it was the conveyor of power and holiness — and it sounded beautiful to me. What a thing to be able to accomplish with words.

Many years later, during what were perhaps my most crucially formative years as a poet, I was so enamored of the very sound of language (and so very oddly callous to the sense of it) that I earned in my college writing fraternity the nickname "Vague Hague." And yet

I am sure that this "Milton's daughter" period in my development was necessary and valuable; to hear the language, as it were, unlanguaged—to play it primarily as sound and rhythm and texture, separate from meaning, to fly it as the Immaculate Lady of the Air might have flied it—was all. It helped me develop an ear, and to form useful habits of listening.

It's no wonder that the poets I read most avidly and with greatest delight were Dylan Thomas, e.e. cummings, Shakespeare at his wildest, and most of all, Hopkins:

> I caught this morning morning's minion, king-
> dom of daylight's dauphin, dapple-dawn-drawn
> Falcon, in his riding
> Of the rolling level underneath him steady air, and striding
> High there, how he rung upon the rein of a wimpling wing
> In his ecstacy!

What a fabulous beginning. I wish I could remember the first time I heard those lines, the initial thrill I must have felt as they burst open the doors of my spirit. The movement of them is so remarkable, as are their assonances and alliterations, that I like to think Hopkins must have absorbed them from the Welsh culture he lived in (and that I like to think I, too, have inherited in some part through Maude Mae Davis, my Welsh-American maternal grandmother). It is a performance of language likened by another Welsh poet to "red hot waves of ecstasy."

Yes, a fabulous beginning, matching in its movement initial wing-flapping then subsequent gliding of the falcon, followed by that long, unparalleled string of adjectives, which might be clearer if you read all the words as one long hyphenated compound adjective: "the rolling-level-underneath-him-steady air." Astonishing.

But this is no less fine than the ending, in its almost groaning, grief-filled awe:

> No wonder of it: sheer plod makes plow down sillion
> Shine, and blue-bleak embers, ah my dear,
> Fall, gall themselves, and gash gold-vermilion.

If you listen to those last two lines, and all their "ahs" — "ah", "fall," "gall" "gash" — it is as if you have joined the universal choir of woe, chanting some brilliantly awful doomsday.

And then there is this, in "Pied Beauty," in which the speaker catalogues the fresh loveliness and sparkling detail of the world, an emanation of God's glory:

All things counter, original, spare, strange;
   whatever is fickle, freckled (who knows how?)
     With swift, slow, sweet, sour; adazzle; dim;
He fathers-forth whose beauty is past change:
        Praise Him.

These words, also, would have made Liz Allensworth exclaim how good they tasted to say. As would have these lines, from Dylan Thomas:

All the sun long it was running, it was lovely, the hay
Fields high as the house, the tunes from the chimneys, it was
    air
      And playing, lovely and watery
      And fire green as grass.

And for unbridled force, how about Kent's verbal reduction to tatters of the simpering Oswald in *King Lear*:

...knave, rascal...eater of broken meats...base, proud, shallow, beggarly, three-suited, hundred-pound, filthy, worsted-stocking knave...lily-livered, action-taking, whoreson, glass-gazing, superserviceable, finical rogue...

But for me the problems of sense remained. Some of my poems, as I look back on those that have survived from college, were as strange as could be, music-pieces mostly, with no connection to the intellect or heart, those important seats of poetry. In them, I was engaging in the poetic equivalent of what Wordsworth described as his "glad animal movements" in "Tintern Abbey" — movements through a world solely physical, a world that, though it was literally sensational, lacked the depth of sympathy and understanding that would "chasten and subdue," or that would connect him with the "still, sad music of humanity."

It's a matter of maturity. I see that I may have been at the same time working to master one aspect of poetry while inadvertently ignoring others. Too many balls to juggle for an inexperienced writer. Still, I remember the first time I heard William Butler Yeats. He was recorded late in his life when, the liner notes report, he was "almost tone deaf." The voice comes high, riding a high uncertain register, but it is confident and steady. "I will arise and go now, and go to Innisfree." There is hardly any modulation; I can picture the aged Yeats, white-haired, his eyes closed as he chants this poem from his youth, and as he remembers reading *Walden*, which inspired it. The accent is purely Irish, and it sets off native archetypal resonances in me. St. Peter's (originally called St. Pius) was the first Catholic church in Steubenville, and was solemnly blessed by Bishop John Baptist Purcell, the namesake of the school, far downriver, in which I have worked all of my teaching life. Purcell was an Irish immigrant whose pronunciation of English may well have been much like Yeats's. My great-grandmother Annie's maiden name was Butler; I imagine, as I listen, that I am hearing an ancestral voice. I am mesmerized, transfixed. I want to make language like that; I want to chant myself and my life as if language were incomprehensibly immortal.

Not long ago, a colleague celebrated his marriage in a local church. It happened to be Trinity Sunday, and one musical selection was the old Latin hymn, *"Pange Lingua."* Both its melody and its words brought back many memories of old St. Peter's, and the ceremonial grandeur of Latin. To a boy steeped in Catholic ritual in the pre-Vatican II days, it was a moving and detailed remembrance, perhaps not quite as extensive but certainly as powerful, as the moment when Proust brought that madeleine to his lips, and *Remembrance of Things Past* began. As a boy at St. Peter's in Steubenville, pursuing the Immaculate Lady of the Air, I became an acolyte of the language, and throughout the terrors and beauties and upsets and triumphs of my life, I have remained a servant and server of words.

The Atmosphere of Names

1: To Have Knowledge of Things

"If one does not know the names, one's knowledge of things is useless." This is attributed to Isidorus, and I do not know if this is the Greek Isidorus or the other Isidorus, the Bishop of Seville; but now put it another way: to have knowledge of things, one must first give them a name.

— Jamaica Kincaid, "In History"

My hometown, which irritating rubes sometimes deliberately mispronounce as "Stupidville," was named after Baron Friedrick Von Steuben, the Prussian general who trained Washington's troops at Valley Forge. The fort built on the site of the town in 1797 housed soldiers of the First American Regiment, the original army of the United States following the Revolution. The structure stood a few hundred yards from what was later to be dubbed "The Patch," the riverside neighborhood where my ancestors — including my great-great grandmother and my great-grandfather and namesake Richard — lived for over a century and a half, beginning only about forty years after the establishment of the fort. The names of the streets in their little neighborhood remember the past. At the foot of Dock Street, for example, a ramshackle shantyboat was still moored when I was a small boy, and Virginia Avenue memorializes the fact that before West Virginia's secession from the Confederacy in the time of the Civil War, right there, across the river, stretched the state of Virginia, where there were slaves, and whose easternmost border was the Atlantic Ocean. I remind myself, too, that the state's name remembers Elizabeth I, the Virgin Queen, a person who though admirable and astounding in many ways, and for whom I have had a long and complicated intellectual crush, remains nevertheless *persona non grata* to my family and people, for she was one of the most ruthless oppressors of the Irish — and thus, of some of my own ancestors—in the troubled history of that troubled nation.

Of course, the name of the river and my native state is interesting too. Some say it comes from the Shawnee word "oyo," meaning "beautiful river." Because of the topography and scenery, one of the several hilltop neighborhoods in Steubenville from whose edges you can see the river, is called "LaBelle" (in Steubenville it is pronounced *Lay Bell*), recalling the French explorers of Ohio, who called it the same thing as the Shawnees, though in their own language, "*La Belle Riviere*," the Beautiful River. And in a nod to another Romance tongue, there is a Steubenville neighborhood, also having a river view, called "Buena Vista," (*Byoona vista*) "good view." Just for good measure, there is also a hilltop neighborhood called "Pleasant Heights"—where, appropriately, my maternal grandmother, the lovable and pleasant Maude Mae Davis Heights lived.

My home county is named after the third president of the United States, another intellectual paragon, and, in terms of that ongoing tension in American life, The Ideal vs. The Real, a contradiction: a champion of freedom who kept slaves. There are many Jefferson Counties around, (Louisville, Kentucky is in Jefferson County, as is Birmingham, Alabama) and their number attests to the influence of the builder of Monticello, founder of the University of Virginia and the Library of Congress, sponsor of the Lewis and Clark expedition, and patron of the first explorers of Big Bone Lick, down the river from where I now live, the site of a wonderful cache of mastodon and other Pleistocene animals' bones. Jefferson's ground sloth (*Megalonyx jeffersonii*) wandered the landscape all around here; perhaps one fed where my house now stands.

When I moved permanently to Cincinnati, after graduating from Xavier University here in 1969, I had to live my way into a whole new set of names. Before it became Cincinnati, the pioneer settlement was called Losantiville, certainly one of the most curious namings of American places ever. Instead of the settlers adopting the local name, they invented, as if by imperial decree, an elaborate and unwieldy acronym: Losantiville. The *L* is for the Licking River (that itself a translation of the Indian name); *os* being the Latin for "mouth;" *anti* being the Latin again for "across from" and *ville* from the French and ultimately Latin for "city or town:" *Losantiville: town across from the mouth of the Licking River*. This awkward mouthful, though dropped quickly, as you shall see, still lingers in a Losantiville Road not far from where I live now, and which, in typical American disregard for apt place-naming, is miles from the mouth and utterly out of sight of the Licking River. Not to worry, for the whim of another powerful white man, Arthur St. Clair, the first governor of the

Northwest Territory, soon changed that. On January 4, 1790, St. Clair visited the village, declared its name unsuitable, and replaced it with Cincinnati, after the Society of the Cincinnati, a club of Revolutionary War generals to which he (and the namesake of Steubenville) belonged. Cincinnatus, alas, was no Ohio Valley native, steeped in the geography and ecology and climate of the place, with prehistoric family roots in the land and creeks and river, but rather an ancient Roman general, as far removed from wilderness Ohio as could be. But that's the name that stuck. Power and naming have a long and intertwined history—one that the mere mention of the name Malcolm X, or Muhammad Ali (formerly Cassius Clay) opens up in complicated and telling ways. Ralph Ellison, author of *Invisible Man*, writes about the effect of his father naming him after a white 19th century philosopher, and about America as a place of names, and about the earnest occupation of each of us in coming to realize—to literally make real—the meaning of our names.

My current neighborhood, incorporated as the village of Madison in 1809 and later renamed Madisonville, memorializes another American president, James Madison—an associate of Jefferson's who lived in the shadow of his mentor. Madison's history and the history of my neighborhood intersect and diverge in interesting ways. James Madison, like Jefferson, kept slaves; Madisonville was settled, in part, by escaped and freed slaves, who crossed the Ohio near the mouth of the Little Miami River and homesteaded in the bottoms extending all the way to within a brisk twenty-minutes' walk from my front door. I can saunter in the Laurel Cemetery, established just after the Civil War, and read the names of my neighborhood's streets off the monuments covered with lichen below the few remaining oaks: Clephane, Bramble, Roe, Whetsel. (I do not think any of the streets are named for black people.) The fact is, there is hardly an unnamed place in our country anymore; we humans assign places names almost as mindlessly and automatically as a dog pees on a fire hydrant. We are setting the boundaries, making our mark.

For all our nominative fecundity, though, we often miss the mark. When I look at the names of streets in recently created suburbs, I see Indian names in ersatz subdivisions two thousand miles from the actual ranges of such tribes. A very quick look at the Cincinnati phone directory gives me Pawnee, Pawtucket, Osceola; not only a Mohawk Street but a Mohawk Place, too, and finally, perhaps most ridiculously, a Navajo Place, named after a Southwest desert tribe—this in a city that sometimes gets as much rainfall in a single spring as Navajo country does in a decade.

Figures no less formidable than Edgar Allan Poe, Washington Irving, and Walt Whitman have addressed this misnaming. Occupying a little-known nook of history, a story lurks like an unheeded warning, a lost opportunity. In the early 19th century, following up on a suggestion by Washington Irving, Poe complained: "It is a thousand pities that the puny witticisms of a few professional objectors should have power to prevent, even for a year, the adoption of a name for our country. At present we have clearly none." Well, of course we did, but Poe and his fellows objected, as Whitman would later, that the name was not indigenous, that it was, in fact, "fetched on" as they say in Eastern Kentucky for anything that has been brought in from outside.

And so Poe suggests a better alternative than "America": "There should be no hesitation about 'Appalachia,' " he says. "In the first place, it is distinctive. 'America' is not and can never be made so."

This has probably shocked you, dear reader, because you have seen, in a flash, the ramifications of Poe's bold suggestion. Not only the Hatfields and McCoys, but, for example, William F. Buckley, Malcolm X, Queen Latifah, Bruce Lee, Snoop Doggy Dog, Walter Cronkite and Jackie Onassis—all would have been Appalachians, *hillbillies*. American history, and the history of American bigotry, would have taken such a swerving turn that it is difficult to imagine the outcome. Though the old argument that "a rose by any other name..." might be invoked here, so equally might this be: "With the telling of every name there is the fullness of story." If America had changed its name to Appalachia—a name Poe admired because it is indigenous, because it pays something of our debt to the natives, "whom we have despoiled, assassinated and dishonoured" and because it is beautiful—"nothing could be more sonorous, more liquid, or of fuller volume, while its length is sufficient for dignity" —had the change occurred, the very history of our nation may have been altered. The natives, the owners of the word "Appalachia," would have been the face our country put to the world, not the European transplant's, and places like Eastern Kentucky and West Virginia and East Tennessee then, (two of the three bearing native names still) may have been able to resist their imperialistic industrial-capitalist extractive exploiters and hunkered down to some serious self-realization; "Appalachia" could have been the most prestigious address on the continent.

"Nonsense," Thomas Aquinas would say. "Appalachia" might be no better than the "America" it could have replaced. In an essay entitled "What Is My Real Name?" Josef Pieper goes on to paraphrase the great Doctor of the Church: "The names by which we call things do not penetrate to their core."

Maybe. Try telling that to someone who has been stabbed with "nigger" or "kike" or "greaser" or "bohunk" or "hillbilly."

2: Elt, Ironhead, Dickie, and R.W.B.

"For a person's name is not like a coat which is merely draped around him and which no one can do more than tug at and tear a little, but instead is a perfectly fitting garment which, like his skin itself, clings to him from head to foot, and no one can scratch or flay it without wounding the man himself."

—Goethe

My full-dress, wedding-and-funeral, meet-your-long-lost-cousin, ceremonial name is James Richard Aloysius Cavanaugh Prosser MacGillicuddy Christopher Thomas Heywood "Heywood" Hague, Jr. The majority of this loollapalooza of a handle was laid upon me mostly by my grandmother Helen, whom my grandfather James Cavanaugh "Ironhead" Hague mysteriously called "Elt" around the house. The name was drilled into me by Elt and her sisters Nonie, Lamb, Dorothy, and Miriam Madigan. Though at times such an elaborate nomenclature seemed an unfair burden to a child, I see now quite clearly what the elders were up to. My name was a way of reminding me of my history and my heritage; it was also the presentation to me of a gentle but insistent obligation to explore all the stories of who I am and where I have come from. So, many years later, when we baptized our first-born, he too carried Cavanaugh as his middle name, by way of passing along to him something of that same obligation of self-knowledge and heritage.

The entire atmosphere of my childhood and boyhood was filled with names—Logan Street, St. Peter's, Lincoln Boulevard, Paddy Mudd Road—and the wonderfully diverse names of kids I went to school with—two Mary Anns, Vernarsky and Orsini, Candace Babella, Carol Stasiulewicz, Donna De Mayo, Anne Ignac, Myra Gotch, Joey and Danny Abramowicz, Tommy McGough, Cecelia McDevitt, Linda Kirkpatrick. From my grandfather's porch, I loved to watch trains go by with their boxcars flashing the names of their lines: Burlington (the Route of the Zephyrs), PRR, Nickel Plate, Norfolk and Southern. I developed a habit of collecting names that has been not only pleasurable but quite useful to me.

In Ohio's Monroe County, (yes, named for another slave-holding President), where I keep a sort of dilapidated camp on fifteen acres in the middle of Wayne National Forest, I have made several name-collecting trips. One summer in the Seventies, I was in the old library in the basement of the Court House, and noticed the *Monroe County Atlas*. Paging through it, I discovered, among others equally delicious,

Levin Oakey, Zepheniah Gaw, Jephtha Duvall, and Roseberry Cline–
the last of which, in a memorable coincidence, I found written on a
Greenbrier Grocery receipt, dated in the early 20th century, just a few
hundred yards down Greenbrier Ridge from where my trailer sits. (In
a triumph of localness, Charles Cline and his brother still live within a
few moments of the place.)

What a great list, that Monroe County one, suggestive of frontier
lives filled with bears and woods and maybe even a stray elk or two in
those wild southeastern Ohio hills. Equally suggestive is another list,
this one of some members of the Ohio Company, the band of New
Englanders who in 1788 settled the beautifully named Marietta, which
vies with my hometown of Steubenville for the honor of being Ohio's
first city. These newcomers bore names like Peregrine Foster,
Theophilus Larned, Return Jonathon Meigs. As a character called
Mister Billy says in a story I've been tinkering with ever since collecting these,

> Names ain't just words, you understand. If they was,
> why a person could go up to Forrest and read the phone
> book, and be satisfied. But here's what happens when I do
> that. I'll see eight Sweets, say – Arthur Sweet, Carol A. Sweet,
> Eben Sweet, you see, and I'll drift off, right there, wondering
> about the folks that holds them names. Oh, it gives me plea-
> sure – ain't nothing finer. I'll see Carol A. Sweet in my mind.
> Now Carol's a woman forty, never been married. Carol
> sounds like a young person's name, it sounds like a song, you
> see. But no, Carol Sweet's forty for me, and she ain't never
> had a man, and she lives upstairs in a big white house on
> Marietta Street, and teaches school. None of her pupils knows
> her first name. They call her "Mrs. Sweet." Kids think all
> women is married, especially school teachers. But Carol Sweet,
> she ain't. Once, years ago, she took a shine to a fella. He was
> a railroader on the narrow-gauge that used to run through
> here, name of Hubert Cline. Folks thought he was the best
> looking young man in the whole county. But he had one big
> fault, and he was always falling over it. He was a liar.

My earnest occupation with names consists in part in taking the
images and associations I make with a person's name, or a place's
name, and running with them, seeing where the associations will go
and what surprising turns the images may take, and what unexpected
places in imagination and memory they might touch. For example,
what exactly might happen to a person called Emelda Junkin in a

town called Mouthcard? (There's an actual Mouthcard in eastern Kentucky.) Or to Pardon Starks in the village of Vest, or Solomon Hooper in Mousie, or Wiley Wilcox in Dwarf (to name another set of actual Kentucky places). In Ohio there are some doozies, too: how about Donna Redbird in Newcomerstown, or Mrs. Whiteyes in Dille's Bottom, or Christian Hartline in Mingo Junction? I'm indebted to the late Evan S. Lodge, of Kent State University and the Ohio Poetry Day Association, for his gift to me many years ago of a book of his entitled *A Garland for Ohio*. The title poem is built of colorful and curious place-names in Ohio:

> Roundhead, Buckeye, Yellowbud,
> Redhaw, Burgoon, Brokensword,
> Redbirds, Robins and Wren,
> Philo and Shiloh,
> Chilo, Crabapple,
> Alpha, Delta, and Omega.

And in the spirit of Poe, he remembers the native places:

> Oneida, Ottowa, Mingo,
> Huron, Wyandot—
> Kanauga, Tontogany, Tymotchee,
> Okalana, Wapakoneta, Kinnickinnick,
> Wakatomika, Moxahala, Tuscarawas...

If nothing more, Lodge's lists are holy chants, remembrances, charged with the associations and meanings stirred in their hearers. "A name should be a magical invocation to the muse," Erica Jong says. And so the poet writes down the names and places that pop up in the midst of her days; she returns to them later, after they have simmered in the underground workshop, and discovers they have assumed rich lives, like one of those computer games programmed to build, completely unsupervised, an elaborate simulated city over a period of hours or days.

Even more a part of my earnest occupation with names is this fact, in the same Pieper essay referred to a little earlier: even as he accepts the Aquinian assertion, he writes, "Nevertheless there do appear to be differences to the degree to which names may capture an essence...certain names possess, in our minds, a more essential, more profound, less easily dissoluble relationship to the things they designate."

In the matter of my family names, this is certainly true.

James was my father's name, and his father's (it's Seamus in Irish). I never answered to it, though; my relatives were acute enough to foresee that a household with too many Jimmies in it might get a bit out of hand. Instead, I was always Dickie, the diminutive of Richard, my middle name. I wonder if the earlier Richard Hague, who hauled through life the heavy moniker Richard W. B. Hague—the W. B. from William Bigelow, an early pastor of the Irish Catholic church our family belonged to—I wonder if he, too was a "Dickie." I can't imagine it, for his namesake, the Reverend William Bigelow, was a man larger than life, who perished of smallpox as a result of tending to the sick— "many of them Protestants," my St. Peter's church history records— during an epidemic in 1872. He was just 29 years old. I think his presence in the name of R. W. B. Hague would have disallowed the diminutive "Dickie"—too cute for the man whose funeral was "the largest that Steubenville had ever seen at that time."

Aloysius, I discovered, may come from the next famous pastor of St. Peter's, Martin Michael Aloysius Hartnedy. The Dean (as he was called after being appointed a sort of head-priest over eight Appalachian Ohio counties) had a flamboyant and, in the end, unfortunate tenure in Steubenville. Thinking to erect a new St. Peter's Church as a one-quarter replica of St. Peter's in Rome, he raised some money, tore the old church down, a fine and solid edifice itself, then submitted his grand plans to the bishop in Columbus—only to have them rejected as too big and too expensive. He scrambled to finish off the job, and did—his is the church I attended as a boy. He also built The Deanery, a fine stone Victorian stone building, used for years as the convent for the nuns who taught at the school, until it was at last torn down.

So being named after such a man—was it as a warning against too much ambition? Was it a subtle reminder of our working-class, compliant, obedient station in life? On the other hand, to a bunch of Irish Americans, some of whom became the mighty and recalcitrant Molly Maguires of the eastern Pennsylvania coal fields, the requirements of "compliance" and "obedience" applied in very specific contexts only and could be otherwise swiftly and violently suspended. One deigned to be compliant to the good Monsignor, and the Sisters, and one's parents, of course, but beyond that, it was not certain that the crooked chief of police would get your full compliance, or the fat-cat owners of the steel mill in which you worked, or the stingy mine operator whose coal you dug, or the Pinkerton thug brought in to bust your union. There was a reason my grandfather's nickname was "Ironhead."

Ironhead's middle name and one of the contributions to mine, was Cavanaugh. As I have explained elsewhere, Cavanaugh was my great-grandmother's maiden name. Her family sailed from Ireland in 1837 and eventually married into the Hagues, though I cannot find the original Hague ancestor. My Uncle Paul Hague and I, discussing our fragmentary and unclear pedigree, speculate that the Irish poverty and hardship the original Hague or Hagues escaped may have been so severe that it was relentlessly expunged from family memory. Nevertheless, Cavanaugh is a fine name, from the Gaelic O'Coamhanaigh, meaning "descendant of the handsome, gentle one" and, according to *What's In A Name?*, our ancestor was an 11th century king of Leinster. (There was a Cavanaugh at St. Peter's school when I was there, but I know of no connection between our families.)

When I asked about the Prosser connection (was it my mother I asked, the year after my father died? Why had I waited so long?) there was no reply but shrugged shoulders. As is always the case in such blank spaces, I began some nearly unconscious inventions to bridge the gap. It came to a head one hot Cincinnati evening on the back deck of Hap's Irish Pub, not far from where I live. There was an Irish band playing, and I spied, leaning against the pub's wall, the then-coach of Xavier University's basketball team, "Skip" Prosser. I had learned through the alumni magazine that he had been born in Carnegie, Pennsylvania, a working-class suburb of Pittsburgh that my Aunt Annie and Uncle Adam had lived in when I was a boy. I remember well our annual pilgrimage to their sooty brick house high on a hill there. Whenever I saw Skip Prosser on TV, I would say out loud: that man looks like a Hague. He most resembles several of my Hague cousins, Tim and Kevin and Mark—a red-headed amalgamation of the three sons of my red-headed Uncle Jack. Was there a connection between the Prossers of Carnegie and my family?

I sauntered up to Coach, and introduced myself by my full handle, and said I thought we might be related. He laughed. He was an easy, friendly, talkative man who had once taught at two high schools near where my sister went to school at Mt. deChantal Academy, in Wheeling, West Virginia and who was interested in one of the athletes at my school, whom he later recruited. We made no headway on finding family connections, though. With better questions from me, based on better knowledge from my family, would it have gone differently?

Because I did not take care of that business when it was possible, interviewing my parents and grandparents when they were still alive, now I have to scramble, ransacking history and probability and guesses for some sort of truth—a sort whose name I do not know. It is not "history," nor "autobiography" nor "fact" —it is something else, something soft, though tangible, like an old scar in the lip. I know it is there, I can feel it, but I cannot remember the occasion upon which I re-

ceived it. I collect and respond to what facts I can gather; I sift and
weigh the possibilities; I write, and hope that the writing holds up. In
the meantime, I know that my name means something; I know that I
have grown into it; I know that, as Freeman Dyson suggests is true of
the universe, my name knew I was coming.

THE POEM TEACHES HIM HIS NAME

Hague: Eng. or Irish, "one who lives in a fenced
enclosure, one who argues over fences" related to
Haig and Haggler
—*What's In A Name?*

I hear tell you hung over fences
in the old time, got a name
for arguing and haggling
over the hedges
that enclosed your camp:
so it's a fence,
two-posted,
one stringy rail across,
you start with,
followed by a pumpkin
with a little stem.
But in the middle
lives a root,
circling underground.
I think that's where you
come from, Irish scalpeen,
Ohio coal mine—
heading down, deepening,
entering earth:

    Hague

But out you come again,
risen as two pickets,
adventuring toward your
ending—
you strike out,
then turn back,
rise up and around;
you almost circle,

as if relishing once more
the lay of land
in this place you call your life,

and then go on,
as all things must,
only suddenly
to disappear.

There is a hint of mortality in a name—we receive it at birth, the beginning of the journey towards death; at baptism and at funeral our name is spoken over and over, in the company of the saints. No earnest occupation with names can evade forever these lists of the dead which are carved not only in the marble that is inevitably, as Shakespeare complains, "besmeared by sluttish Time" but in the softer stuff of our hearts.

As I suggested, there is a prophetic element in my family name: every place I have lived in, starting with my parents' house in Steubenville, through Mrs. Paul Slack's House For Unwed Fathers (so we boastingly—but hyperbolically—named our bachelor's quarters for the two middle years of college just off the Xavier campus), to our apartment on Ledgewood Drive, to our home now for the past nearly thirty years—every place has been either fenced, or in part or whole, surrounded by a hedge. And I am not known for easy compliance; I am argumentative, a haggler, and have been all my life. It's as if I grew into my family name over the years.

As for MacGillicuddy—I always thought it was a joke, that there could be no such name in the real world, that it was a kind of Irish jest. But one day, perusing the large map of Ireland I'd just bought for my students who were studying Irish literature, I saw the name *Macgillicuddy Reeks* printed over a region in County Kerry. *Wikipedia* tells me that "Macgilllicuddy Reeks (*Na Cruacha Dubha,* meaning 'The Black Tops') are a range of mountains in County Kerry, Ireland. Stretching slightly over 19 km (12 mi.) they include Carrantuohill, which at 1041 m (3414 ft.) is the highest mountain in Ireland."

Thus I am free to assume that some distant ancestor was from that place, or that he gave his name to the roughest and highest country, geographically speaking, in my peoples' land. I'm always climbing to the top of things, or at least I was when I was younger. Once, on an outing to Buzzard's Roost in Adams County, I found a crack in that lofty slab of dolomite, and chimney-stacked my way to its top. Chimney-stacking involves getting your back and feet involved, literally wedging your way up by alternately pressing your back up, then pushing with your feet against the opposing side of the crack. What motivated me to do that without ever trying it before still eludes me. My friends Jim Webb and Jerry Tolliver live in the second and first-highest dwellings in the state of Kentucky, atop Pine Mountain. I've just recently returned from a visit there. What seemed mere comedy may contain a serious note of significance that I must attend to.

Or not. I also find in my researches that MacGillicuddy was the maiden name of Lucy—the zany wife of Ricky Ricardo in *I Love Lucy*. If the show hadn't begun in 1951, four years after I was born, I might have believed that the name got laid on me as part of the habit of nicknaming that ran in my family. But I really do remember having to say most of those names at a very early age, perhaps even before the show appeared.

So now, if life presents me the chance, I'll have to return to Ireland and explore all this. When I get there, at the foot of Carrantuohill, and cry out my name, "James Richard Aloysius Cavanaugh Prosser MacGillicuddy Christopher Thomas Heywood Hague"—will I be home? Or will I hear echoed back the banshee cry of Lucille Ball: "Ricky! Ricky! Ricky!"

My wife says that the name MacGillicuddy was spoken in her house. Her father's mother's maiden name was Mehan, so there's a lot of Irish there, with its attendant folklore, wit, and tradition. My hunch is that McGillicuddy or MacGillicuddy or Macgillicuddy is a kind of generic Irish surname, like Paddy or Bridget as first names. I probably am being too serious about it all. I should lighten up and just take my name for granted, showing it off at parties and on the back decks of bars as a curiosity of some kind, and little else, Goethe be damned.

Along those same lines, if I trekked to Macgillicuddy City, North Dakota, hoping to discover some roots, I'd be sorry again. Macgillicuddy City was, up until a few years ago, Granville, North Dakota, not far from Minot. The Sazerac Company of New Orleans, Louisiana, manufacturers of two varieties of schnapps, offered a $100,000 prize to any town that would change its name to remember what to all appearances is a fictional Dr. McGillicuddy, 19th century owner of an emporium called "The Shady Eye Saloon" and whose name furnishes their product with its brand name, thus making it, like Johnnie Walker or I.W. Harper or Evan Williams, or Bulleit bourbon, an eponymous liquor. The town's web page slyly reports, "Residents like Danny Seright (See right? Shady Eye? Is there some hoodwinking going on here?) welcome the additional economic boost brought in... 'We really didn't have anything going on here before,' said Seright, a rancher and board member of the city's development corporation. 'Now, this weekend event (McGillicuddy City Days) is good for business. It brings a lot of money into the town. This whole name change thing has put us on the map.'"

"This whole name change thing." It's perilous in the world of nomenclature; the amateur onomatologist (or is the word, as " E.J.M." names it in an editorial in *America*, "onomastician"?) like myself had better be careful, and have a thick skin, especially if he hails, as I do, from a diocesan seat whose principal church is The Holy Name Cathedral. The sacredness of names is no longer sacred. The respect for the power and significance of the name is expressed, for example, in Inuit traditions of referring to themselves to strangers not by their names but as "someone," as in, when approaching the Hudson River Company's agent's cabin, replying to the question from inside— "Who's there?"—the native answers, "Someone's got some skins to trade." It would be foolish to reveal something as important as one's name to a stranger. A related Inuit belief is that the human being is made up of three parts, body, soul, and name, and that the reason for a newborn's cries is that it wants its name; this, combined with the attitude toward names expressed in the divine commandment "Thou shalt not take the name of the Lord thy God in vain"—all of this, then, simply shows to what height people have held the holy power of the name, which now has been sold out to crass economic expediency. Are you broke, Bunky? Sell your name. Can't pay for your new sports palace? Let Cracker Jack or Rustoleum paint its name all over it, for a fee. I just read that if you'd like your name attached to a collection of antique instruments, among them several Stradivarius violins, donated to the New Jersey Symphony orchestra, you can—for a cool million and a half. "The Renata and Joey 'The Eyeball' Massarelli Stradivarius String Collection." Yes, doesn't it roll trippingly off the tongue? And as for Granville, North Dakota? Who was that Granville—some Scottish lord? And what was his story? Who cares—throw it away. History is bunk. Names are cash.

In her memoir *The Creative Habit*, Twyla Tharp, the dancer and choreographer, has some interesting things to say about the changing of names.

I am not exaggerating the magic or power invested in names. Names are often a repository of one kind of genetic memory. Parents, who are the arbiters of all given names, certainly feel the power; that's why they name their children after ancestors (or themselves). They honor those who came before while connecting their child with his or her past. . .

The essayist Joseph Epstein has noted, "A radical change in one's name seems in most cases a betrayal—of one's own birthright, of one's group, of one's identity." I don't agree. In a sense, it's a commitment to a higher personal calling. And it's not uncommon among creative souls.

Similarly, Francine Prose writes in a "Bookends" column in the *New York Times Magazine*,

> Over a lifetime that lasted from 1760 to 1849, the great Japanese painter Hokusai changed his name roughly 30 times. The final name he chose meant "the old man mad about art." I remember reading about this long before I imagined being a writer whose name would be known to anyone outside my family. And I remember thinking, Way to go!

Meanwhile, the overnight trumping of Granville, North Dakota by McGillicuddy City has nothing on what happens with the last save one in my own litany of names. James Richard Aloysius Cavanaugh Prosser MacGillicuddy—and now, poor Christopher.

Of them all, this was the only name I chose for myself. In Catholic ritual, there is a sacrament called Confirmation; it is administered at around the age of puberty, and is indeed a confirmation of the near-adult Christian into the grownup practice, profession, and, if necessary, the defense of his faith. One of the details of the ritual used to be a symbolic blow to the cheek by the bishop, which I always thought was a great concrete sign of being able "to take it." It also provided the occasion for inane macho adolescent blasphemies like, "That guy hits me, I'm going to stand up and let him have it." We all took it, of course, and there were no cops called, nor bishop's mitres knocked wopperjawed. But there's another detail of the ritual which is even more symbolic—the taking of a saint's name. You are free to choose any you desire, and the nuns encouraged us in school to take care with the process. I chose Christopher— Chistophoros, St. Kitt— and again, as I look back, it seems that name—and some important details of my life—knew I was coming. Christopher, of course, is the patron saint of travelers, and I've put in a few miles over the years— not only in The United States, but in many overseas places as well. Especially in a recent nerve-wracking sprint to Dublin, the presence of some guiding power may well have been at work. I certainly would not have dreamed, as a kid, that I would travel to Rome, or Heidelberg, or Lyme Regis, or Reykjavik, or Fairbanks, or Orvieto, or Salzburg, but it has come to pass. Christopher was legendary for carrying the

Christ child across a torrent; there I was, a river kid, a clamberer of bridges in downtown Steubenville, as riparian as a muskrat, and as tiny as Christopher was large (in some versions he's a giant, the bearer of the weight of the world in the form of the young Jesus, and statues of him were, fittingly, often erected near bridges). He's also a patron of gardeners and archers, among other arts and occupations—and of bookbinders. For the me I have become since picking the name when I was thirteen, it has been in all details a perfect fit.

But in 1970, at the famous Second Vatican Council, something strange happened. St. Christopher was more or less expunged from the roll of saints. To make a long story short, it seems that Christopher's feast entered the Roman Calendar relatively recently—in 1550—and the date of celebration, July 25, was already the feast of St. James (James!) the Apostle, a saint of more "universally important significance" to the Church. This, coupled with the results of a "critical study of the history of the lives of the saints in the Church calendar of 1960," revised history, in a sense, leaving Christopher a bit out of it. Still, devotion to him continues locally, and a letter explaining the Church's position on the matter by Monsignor William B. Smith, of St. Joseph's Seminary, meliorates: "Although the Acts of the life of Christopher are legendary, the existence of his cult is very old." The fact that there are dozens of parishes named after him in places as far-ranging as Bahrain and New Zealand and the United States makes it hard to throw him comfortably out, so local devotion is still acceptable.

For me, all this hagiographical and historical haziness seem exactly right. My namesake Christopher is no more or less real than my own as-yet anonymous and invisible ancestors; old Kitt dwells in the same limbo of possibility as them all. I am free to believe of him what I like, to imagine what I can. (Of course, now even "limbo" is on the block—if theologically the concept of limbo is expunged from Catholic doctrine, as Pope Benedict XVI decreed, it will take down with it a name and a word that really serves a useful and I think indispensible place in our language and thought.)

There is one more moniker I have carried. In college, I was invited to join Mermaid Tavern, the writing fraternity at Xavier University in Cincinnati. It had been founded by an Irish-American Jesuit named Sweeney, and existed to provide support and a meeting place for creative writers on campus. Each initiate was to take a patronymic—a "father name"—from some contemporary of Shakespeare. The Warder, or faculty moderator of the Tavern during my tenure was the Shakespeare and Chaucer scholar Karl "Will Davenant" Wentersdorf. I was assigned the patronymic Thomas Heywood, from a minor Elizabethan playwright whose most famous work was *A Woman Killed With*

Kindness. This name did not carry the same obligation as the ones my family gave me; for a couple of summers, home from college, the neighborhood guys would occasionally call me Heywood, but it never took root deeply, and now, except for the battler with *Thomas Heywood* inscribed on it that I still have in an attic crate somewhere, it has returned to obscurity once again, as is often the case.

WHAT OUR NAMES DO

At night, they climb out
of our bodies like maggots or ghosts,
eat cheese crackers in the dark kitchen,
make plans: they find a corner
in the basement, pull wood
around themselves like splintery cocoons,
and think *Fire!*

Names like trouble: it makes
them famous. They see
themselves bannering the front page,
for a day or a week
nominated to time's brief presidency.

For all our safekeeping of them,
our hoarding them against slander
and gossip and forgers,
they escape us from time to time
into a careless public, where they live
their visible lives: *Marilyn loves me*
scrawled on the wall of a restroom,
Vote Judge Mirlisena orphaned on a Hyde Park lawn
three months after the election,
David L. Jones staring up
from the lost driver's license
half-drowned by rain in the gutter.

Some survive the flesh they have grown to,
living like monks in memory's spare cells:
the name of the ancient general's horse,
while the general is forgotten;
the name of the pale, blond child
fallen somewhere in Nebraska,
her body retrieved from a well

and mourned on the national news.

But most go underground
with their owners,
the sweet strange songs
of their sounds breaking down
to leach back through grave
and unlettered depths
like measures of salt
dissolved in the moistures of silence.

3: THE NAME OF ANYTHING

"You can love a name," said Gertrude Stein, "and if you love a name, then saying that name any number of times can only make you love it more." "Poetry," she adds, is "really loving the name of anything."
— *A Book About Names*, Milton Melzer

When my older son Patrick was two and a half, I walked into the kitchen one evening to find him in the middle of the floor, surrounded by every pot and pan that had been stowed in the lower cabinets. He looked up and said, "Me want egg-machine go whirr." For a moment I stood stunned. What language was this? Had I completely misheard? Could a toddler have a mind-addling stroke? "Egg machine go *whirr*," he insisted, and he pointed toward something in the back of the corner cabinet.

Then I understood. Ah. The poet in him, Emerson's "the Namer." And I was reminded again of the delight of things, the power of metaphor, the joy of onomatopoeia. In *American Poetry from the Puritans to the Present,* Hyatt Waggoner writes about the brilliance and originality of Emily Dickinson, observing that in her poetry "She saw all things freshly, as though for the first, and the last, time. The 'genius' of Dickinson's poetry, that which gives it both its uniqueness and its value, rests finally on an unhabitual way of perceiving, an angle of vision that found both formal and thematic expression."

Something of the same synesthetic exactitude of Emily's description of a ruby-throated hummingbird as "A route of evanescence/ With a revolving wheel— A resonance of Emerald/ A rush of Cochineal" was being reenacted in Patrick's naming of what we would call, in our prosaic matter-of-factness, "the electric mixer."

The entire difference between poetry and all the rest of language is exemplified in his phrase. Which is more mysterious, strange, melodic, sensual, concrete, and just plain fun—"electric mixer" or "egg-machine go whirr"? (Now I have to pause here and say that the word "electric" is a fine one, and arresting in its own way, especially when we remember the story of its origin in the Greek "elektron," meaning amber, in which, according to the *Chambers Etymological Dictionary*, "electricity was first observed." And of course, amber, that ancient substance valued as a gem, is also the repository of the preserved bodies of ancient bees and flies and wasps; is an ancient metaphor embedded in that association with the vital powers of the small buzzing and humming things whose force made hair stand on end? The marvelous names of things lead on and on into stories that lead on and on—or rather back and back—into time.)

So there was Patrick, long before any schooling, pulling off a couple of fancy literary devices as easily as laughing. So it is with poetry: its nominative power and authority, its inevitable rightness, its surprising novelty, its perennial clarification of thought and vision. Poetry—naming—is one of the earnest occupations of my life. The making of it, the reading of it, the teaching and sharing of it—all occasions of joy.

On January 26, 1996, while I was putting my "Names & Naming" collection of articles, notes, and be-jotted napkins together in a folder, Kelly Schiller, a colleague of mine who had been off on maternity leave, was in the 7th bell class just across from my office. She had her new baby with her. I went over to greet them. One of the other gathered visitors asked, and she launched forth on a long story about his name, Matthew. It linked him with his father and grandfather, she said, and it was a great evangelist's name (Kelly Schiller is a religion teacher), and then she went on to talk about how Matthew's middle name, Joseph, linked him with St. Joseph, as Kelly put it, "a pretty nice guy." She also knew that the Hebrew meaning of Matthew means "gift from God"—she and her husband had had a great deal of difficulty getting pregnant—so Matthew's name was a kind of prayer of thanksgiving each time it was spoken. It's this way often with names—they become loaded with significance and meaning; they are more than mere labels or differentiators. That they ought to be is made clear when we think of George Foreman's unfortunate choice to name all his children George. At least, as Italians do, give them nicknames that indicate birth order: Primo, Secundo, and so on.

Names can help define us, too, and make statements all our lives. When she is eighty-eight, frail, and in a rest home somewhere, I wonder what Valley Girl Moon Unit Zappa will think of her name. In the course of my teaching, I have discovered some startling namings, some beautiful and strange, others just strange. I once gave a girl a ride home from school whose name was Crystal Lockett; in some sort of eerie symmetry, there is now in my school a girl named Mercedes Carr. Rashana Reynolds tells me of sisters named Wine and Vodka; Kassey Wagner reports sons named James I and James II, and sisters named Latricia A and Latricia B, Ingrid Langdon bemoans a girl-child called Chlamydia, Kelly Sheehan's dentist is Chalk Frey, and Kristen Guckenberger played as a child with Rosie Lipps. I taught a delightful and aptly named pacifist named Serenity for a couple of years recently. There have been Meeka and Kilolo and Othello, and Kirby Irby, who, in order to survive this certain naming disaster, simply appropriated the first name of Tatiana; there have been Nell and Rena, Rudy and Denesha, a hundred Johns, an overflow of Kims, Lisas, and Megans—and one Yashar. Yashar Yeshuron Israel told me the story of a stern schoolteacher she had in an early grade who complained to her mother, "This child's name is a burden upon her. It should be changed."

But in a democracy like ours, where freedoms of all kinds are taken for granted, especially when reflected in the act of naming, such proscription is not possible. Consider how this situation, reported by the Associated Press, would fly in Yashar Yeshuron Israel's's family:

NORWAY AND PARENTS TUSSLE ON BABY'S NAME

OSLO, NORWAY— Gesher's parents have been ordered to give their 10-month old son a more acceptable name. Something normal, like Odd. Or Bent. Or Roar.

Norway has an official government list of acceptable names, and Gesher is not on it. His parents face a $420 fine unless they rename him.

Gesher's mother, Krisi Larsen, is willing to fight in court for the right to name the youngest of her 13 children. She said the name came to her in a dream, as the word *bridge*, which she translated to the Hebrew *Gesher*.

"If we accept the fine, it's like we're admitting some kind of guilt," Larsen, 42, said yesterday. They were fined for failing to submit a legal name to the local population registry.

Even if they lose in court, "we're still calling Gesher Gesher," Gesher's mother said.

Norway's strict names law dates from the 1800's, and is intended to protect children from names that sound or look strange. Other acceptable names are Dits, Fridvall, Gilsur, Glasius, Wrold, Anond, Raabi and Skagj.

That final list, meant to be funny, lessens somewhat the serious import of the article. Naming and power—inseparable parts of the human condition. To see another spin on the power game, look at this, by L. A. Johnson of the *Pittsburgh Post-Gazette*:

STUDY: NAME MAY BE KEY TO GETTING JOB

They expect her to grow into an intelligent woman who fearlessly faces life's challenges and perseveres, and they selected her name to reflect those characteristics.

Assata Akili Flannigan.

Assata means warlike or she who struggles, and Akili, which is Tanzanian, means bright and smart. "It's like willing it to be true," says Anika Flannigan, 24, of Wilkinsburg, Pa.

The name is meant to define her—not diminish her in others' eyes or expose her to undue discrimination. However, a report from the National Bureau of Economic Research indicates that some employers discriminate against applicants based on the Afrocentric or black-sounding names on their job resumes, regardless of education, job experience or qualifications.

Of course they do. This form of racism is insidious and difficult to root out. But if there were equal sensitivity to the etymologies of African names, or to the family history, or plain creativity of many, it would be a different matter.

"It's *Hemingway*, I tell my students, not *Hemenway*"; getting names right, then, is one of the crafts of living well. It's also a matter of political care, as well. People actually get in fights over the relationships gathered up in names, in their connotations and designations.

It seems a long time ago now, but Jim Joyce, who was "County Beat" columnist for my hometown newspaper, *The Steubenville Herald-Star*, wrote about the controversy stirred up by the naming, in 1966, of a new school district near Steubenville. Mingo Junction, Cross Creek, and Wayne school districts were to be consolidated. "Feelings ran high," he reports, "particularly among the Mingo Junction people who lost a long court battle against the merger." The board came up with the name Indian Creek School District, "Indian" remembering the Mingo Junction athletic teams, the Indians, and "Creek" remembering Cross Creek School District. "Wayne came up on the short end in the name contest," Joyce observes. And since there is no place by the name of Indian Creek on any eastern Ohio map, Joyce suggested, as did Poe and Washington Irving more than a century before, that the district be given an indigenous name, for example the name the original inhabitants of the country had given Cross Creek, which was She-nan-je.

He goes on to tell an important story connected to the place called She-nan-je. It's the saga of Mary Jemison, whose parents and home were destroyed by Indians in 1755. She had been taken away by the Senecas to Mingo Town, just downriver from what was to become Steubenville, where her captors stripped her of her white-girl clothes, decked her out as a Seneca sister, and adopted her into their family as a replacement for a brother who had been killed the year before in George Washington's 1754 campaign. She went completely native, became known as De-He-Wamis, "pretty girl," and lived her life with her three children among the Senecas back in their original homeland in what was to become New York's Genesee County.

A remarkable story, attached to the place name—it would have made sense to adopt it, and by its means convey some history and an interesting story along with it to anyone who bothered to ask. But it didn't happen. The school board adopted the synthetic "Indian Creek," and in the kind of despair that often results from such poor naming in our culture, Joyce ends his column with the half-hearted wish that "maybe someday someone will tack [the name She-nan-je} onto a new subdivision or something."

Probable—but no improvement. The story of Indian Creek school district is another example in the long line of naming failures (which are often, when examined closely, seizures of power) in our country. As Weller Embler observes in "Language and the Truth," "If the using of names with precision...is of a higher order of mind than the mere information as to the names for things, the making up of names, the giving of names to things requires real creative ability." Perhaps the Mingo Junction School Board should have turned to, say, their own Larry Smith, then a recent valedictorian of Mingo Junction High School, and an aspiring poet, for suggestions. I'll bet he'd have gotten it right.

4: Who Are You? Where Have You Been?
What Have You Done? What Have You Seen?

What do we have for animal magic
but names, our mumbled spells and charms,
baskets of epithets spilled down the page?
— David Young, "The Names of a Hare in English"

I suppose it's no surprise that my late friend Joe Enzweiler, the poet, seemed cannily compulsive about naming and noting everything. He had a dandy traveling diary that he kept in his pickup; in it he recorded every tank of gas he has bought since moving to Alaska in the mid 70s, how much it cost per gallon, and, if there was a rider with him, a note and perhaps the rider's own signature, there on the pale green page. When we embarked on a series of pool games back in the 80s, when Joe began to come back down to visit his family and to build beautiful dry-stacked stone walls around his brother's homestead in northern Kentucky, he insisted we name each of the sessions. Looking back over them, I see now that they constitute an "abstract and brief chronicle of the times," as Hamlet says of the plays his actor chums bring to Elsinore.

The titles range from the obvious—The Yule Invitational, played on December, 24, 1986 and then the Second Yule Invitational, played on December, 23, 1987—to the quite topical—The Spreadable Latex Sudden Death Tournament, which took place after Joe did some painting for us, to the Mr. Panic: Black Tuesday Dow-Jones Memorial Tournament, which occurred during October of 1989 and whose winner was dubbed "Mr. Panic" and the loser, "Mr. Freefall." Another one commemorating a topical subject was just after some serious winter weather in December of 1987, The Gale-Force Open, in which the winner was "Mr. Windstorm" and the loser "Mr. Blowhard."

Since moving to Alaska, Joe had become an accomplished figure skater, and—always from a distance—had lusted after the alpha females of the sport. Thus the Katarina Witt Epithalamium Tourneys, in which, sadly enough, I earned the title "Mr. Cold Shower" for losing to Joe, "Mr. Sexual Frenzy." Falsely inflated, or perhaps dangerously preoccupied with his success, however, Joe lost the next two to me: Special One Game: For the Hun (his politically incorrect term of endearment for the former West German Katarina) and even more piercingly, Second Special One Game: For Tai Babilonia. Even more sadly, in 1992, Joe was down for another visit and a three-way tournament with Joe, myself, and my neighbor Roger Miller, the results of The Katarina Witt Leap Day Safe Sex Round Robin Invitational were as follows: Mr. Safe Sex with the Hun—Roger; Mr. Drives Limo to Hotel—Joe, and Mr. Gaps Plugs in Limo—Dick.

Other events were memorialized as well: The Mapplethorpe Exhibition Tourney, celebrated after Sheriff Simon Leis ("Simple Simon" to rabid liberals in this town known for his battles with pornographer Larry Flynt and the alarming arrest of David Barrie, the Contemporary Art Center's director, after he mounted a show of Mapplethorpe's photos entitled "The Perfect Moment" which included a few explicit photographs of gay sexual behavior.) Joe's titles for our tournament that day were: "Mr. Perfect Moment" and for the loser, "Mr. Anal Retentive."

There were the Probable Debris Flotsam and Jetsam Tournament, celebrating the publication of my collection of poems entitled *Possible*

Debris, and the Hail Brittania Invitational, just before I left for six weeks' study in England, and the Hail Columbia Homecoming Tournament, when I returned. During a particularly sticky time for the Cincinnati Reds, there was The Marge Schott Late Season Recall Referendum Invitational, (this named by Roger) and in 1991 The Desert Sheath Open and the Mother of All Invitationals, in which the winner was "Mr. Scud Stud" and the loser, "Mr. Shiite On A Shingle."

Enough. As it is with all inventions of the human mind, sometimes things can go terribly awry.

But I am so addicted to lists and names to go at it one final time, this based on a pottery road trip my wife and her friend Louise Jenks took a couple of years back. Struck by the kitsch in the Wisconsin Dells, an otherwise beautiful region, they made this list of the names of roadside attractions, which, taken simply by itself with no comment, opens many avenues of speculation about America, about the state of education here, and about the genius (or insanity) of free enterprise:

>Cruisin Chubby's Gentleman's Club
Moosejaw Pizza and Brew Pub (dog décor)
Noah's Ark and Noah's Incredible Adventure
Native American Dancing at Subway
Ghost Outpost Haunted House
Top Secret Highly Classified Adventure House
Poseidon Underwater Experience and Go-Cart Track
Castle of Terror
Trojan Horse Go Cart Track
Medusa's Café
Wisconsin Ducks (former landing craft)
Alligator Alley (for feeding)
Brother's In Law Nightclub
Carousel Inn and Suites With Pink Mountain (Barbie's Motel)
Camelot (motel in castle shape with moat and waterfall)
American UFO and Sci Fi Museum
Wisconsin OPRY
Ho Chunk House of Wellness
Mobil gas station (and walk-in clinic and pharmacy)
Mountain Faith Church (and auto parts store)
Paul Bunyan's Famous Cook Shanty
Robot Land
Dell's Ducks Main Duckdock
Neptune's Econo King
Goody Goody Gum Drops Candy Kitchen
Wax World of the Stars

What's left to be said after such a list of names?
Dear reader,
                    Bon voyage, fare thee well.

5: To Name a God or Spirit (Or Child Or Poem)

Interviewed by the friskily-named Tenaya Darlington shortly after the publication of her award-winning collection of poems *Why The
Ships Are She*, my friend Terri Ford responded to Darlington's characterization of her as "The Queen of Titles" by saying, "Actually, in
most workshops I've ever been in, I am the self-proclaimed Title Bitch."
Her point is that the name of the poem, even if read in the table of
contents, must itself be somehow arresting and attractive, otherwise,
she will not read on. Titling a poem—its naming, in other words—is
indeed a crucial part of the creative act, and ought to involve some
effective inspired work. I look with chagrin over many of my own
titles, for I know Terri Ford is right. In class, I try to impress my students with the importance of titles, and try to make it visceral by pointing out that a poem without a title is like a baby without a head and
that it will spill blood all over your lap until it has one.

But one of the unexamined notions about poetry that manifests
itself in the spate of "Untitled" poems in creative writing classes is
that a poem ought to be an "open" event. The misteaching of poetry
by elementary and secondary teachers with faulty understanding of
the nature of poetry (and of close reading) causes aspiring writers to
think that a poem "can mean anything the reader gets out of it." In
such a line of reasoning, a specific title over a poem would somehow
limit the possibilities for the reader. With a particularly nifty writer,
once, I came to the end of my patience (though in playfulness as much
as in censure) with such truck:

"I Don't Do Titles," She Said
for Colleen Glenn

Neither did God,
self-invented physicist,
swashbuckling buckaroo
breaking the bronco Chaos,
tied to the pommel as tightly as His tongue
was tied inside His mouth (nothing else around, no need for
        talk)
then left-handing this into creation, that into being,

upchucking forms and shapes by the tens of thousands
and all wordlessly, obscurely
nimbused and swooping here and there,
lassoing His strings into and out of Creation,
dragging nothingness down into form like a calf in the dust,
but always, (according to old Nicholas of Cusa)
nowhere,
and always (though gospelled as the Word at the Beginning)
saying nothing,
He sowed everything in silence,
grim planter.

But later, coming to,
Adam saw the mess He'd left
and so, mumbling, started in, sorting and arranging:
grampus, weevil, sneezeweed,
dik-dik, bongo, oryx,
earwig, chafer, pillbug,

and then some others
followed, Adam's grandsons,
(O yes he named them, and named them good:
Hamphat and Shadrack and
Spitnshine) and they, to
get revenge, continued, always naming,
always poking words
at things until they stuck:

hellbender, platypus,
ichneumon,
Coleoptera, Coelenterata,
coelocanth and ouzel,
Betelgeuse, Arcturus,
Wiwaxia, Opabinia,
Hallucigenia,

until all had a lettered address,
a handle, sobriquet,
most carefully binomially nomenclatured,
and would, if rightly called,

answer to a name: hadrosaurus,
smilodon, paramecium,

Popilla japonica, Rana pipiens,

spadefoot, hornbill, horntoad,
rufous-sided towhee:
and so to all (and you, my title-less dear,
and your dear name-hungry reader)
to all a title says:
I have a name,
I live in this world:

hello, hello.

Colleen took this breathless nominative explosion in good spirit, and changed her ways—not so difficult a thing as she had expected it to be, I think. There is a delight in the naming of a poem; Wallace Stevens played marvelously with titles: "Disillusionment of Ten O'Clock", "The Idea of Order at Key West", "Floral Directions for Bananas", "Peter Quince at the Clavier". James Wright also named some of his poems with a kind of downbeat vigor: "Depressed by a Bad Book of Poetry, I Walk Toward an Unused Pasture and Invite the Insects to Join Me". "In Response to a Rumor that the Oldest Whore-house in Wheeling, West Virginia has been Condemned". "A Message Hidden in an Empty Wine Bottle that I Threw into a Gully of Maple Trees One Night at an Indecent Hour". My favorite, perhaps, is "In Memory of the Horse David, Who Ate One of My Poems". The rest of the page beneath the title is blank.

Recently, I gave one of my creative writing students, Alexis Henry, a special bonus for the exceptional titles of the poems in her portfolio; I think from now on I will take inspiration from Terri Ford and declare a Title King or Queen each time portfolios come in.

6: Serendipity, or Finding Some Way Toward an End

I've just re-shelved the *Oxford Guide to English Literature* after reading the entries on "Asolando" and "Pippa Passes" in reference to the poetry of Robert Browning. Decades ago, during the first serious creative writing workshop I'd ever attended, in Hindman, Kentucky, I found myself in nearby Pippa Passes, named after the poem, background for which I just revisited. It's because I'm working on an auto-biography-via-poetry, and in the one-thing-leading-to-another adventure that writing often is for me, I notice in the next bookcase back issues of *Poets & Writers Magazine*. I pull out the last one (July-August 2012) and open to the table of contents. I see that there is a section on literary agents — I don't have an agent, probably never will — and thumb through it. But in the Literary Life section I come across an article entitled "Practical Poetry: The Art of Brand Naming," by Margaret Wulfson. A brief skim confirms that I must read the whole thing.

For almost two decades I have been occasionally working on this essay on naming — it fills an ever-expanding file stuffed with clippings, hand-written notes, and the last few equally expanding drafts. For years, I have worried about how to end it. Maybe this is it, I tell myself. Maybe by sheer luck and brute force I can get out of this thing...

So: on to reading what she has to say.

Still, no matter how inventive or musical, names will never rival great poetry or literature. But as friend and Farrar, Strauss and Giroux publisher Jonathon Galassi pointed out one night over dinner, 'brand names are a kind of poetry — albeit practical poetry.' I couldn't agree more. While these two verbal arts have radically different purposes — one seeks to make sense of the elusive human experience, and the other, to drive goods and services into the hands of elusive customers — they share common features. Both use sonically charged language, lively description, and/or compelling metaphor to achieve their goals. And like poetry, brand names add linguistic pleasure to life.

Wulfson goes on to relate an anecdote about a recent paint-shopping trip she'd made. Admiring the names of the colors, she says, "It was so much...fun to ponder hues with names like Silk Pillow, Silvermint...Quixotic Plum and Tricycle Red."

This reminded me of a similar experience of mine years ago, while I was working on my shabby trailer in the woods of Appalachian Ohio. I had need of a gallon or two of paint. I drove to the hardware store in the county seat and surveyed the possibilities. I'd always painted the trailers. The first was an old sleek Airstream whose original luster had faded to dull gray, and the second a much larger but hulking model fully functional as a house: hot water, refrigerator, heater, electricity. One by one, though, each of the amenities wore out or malfunctioned until, afraid of being killed in a trailer fire, notorious for their quickness and intensity, I cut off the electricity. Eventually, the thing became little more than a storage shed, a place where my cot stayed dry, and where I could stow coolers full of food and beer safely away from the raccoons and possums.

At any rate, there were plenty of paint colors available in the hardware store. From the sample cards I settled on one called "Warm

RICHARD HAGUE

Uncertainty" — it was between a purplish tan and mauve — and decided on a pint of a muted orange-ish trim paint that people down there in the woods would have, after first frost, called "persimmon." When I requested the colors, which had to be custom-mixed, the clerk, a man in his early 50s, tall, tanned, wearing jeans and a flannel shirt, repeated the name with a crooked grin. "Warm Uncertainty, eh?" he said. "Sounds like me and my wife at bedtime."

The names of things, as Mr. Billy suggested, have the potential to beget stories. Some comic, some ludicrous, some penetrating to the heart of things, or complicating things, painfully. Marshall McCluhan, the media guru of the Sixties and Seventies, asserted rather dourly that "the name of a man is a numbing blow from which he never recovers." Though that seems a bit over the top, I can see what McCluhan is saying. When I was younger, I did not like my name. It sounded too much like "egg" I guess; a lot of people mispronounced it. "Hog" was the most embarrassing (and called up the most laughter from my elementary schoolmates). "Hog-way", though an attempt at a sophisticated, vaguely Frenchified pronunciation, was acutely irritating. To this day, when phone solicitors ask, "May I speak with Mr. Hog?" I flush with anger and shout, "He's in the barnyard with Mr. Chicken and Mr. Cow! Call for him there!"

In school, part of my problem with my surname was because "Hague" is so curt, monosyllabic, mean-sounding. Whenever I shared a class with the ethnically diverse kids from Steubenville, when roll was called, my name came out like a belch in the middle of a madrigal. Linda Kirkpatrick, Linda Ormsby, Lucille DiBenedetto, Rosemarie Zyrini, Roseann Sfarella — the Italian names, especially, sang, so that mine fell harsh and ugly amid them, a piece of coarse gravel in a sibilant streambed of gems.

And then there is the particular (and pardon the pun, more prickly) problem of my familiar nickname. There are male students who confess to calling me "Dick" behind my back, although often with an "a" before it. And the female students? There are dozens I have been friends or acquaintances with for decades who are still clearly uncomfortable calling me "Dick." In paroxysms of accommodation, I offer suggestions. "Please don't call me Mr. Hague" after all those years of crossing paths on the street or at reunions or weddings. "If you want to, call me 'Richard,' but please, no more 'Mr. Hague.' " This generally solves the problem. But there remains, nevertheless, a consciousness of the vulgar meaning of the word/name. It ripples the otherwise calm waters of relationship.

Not as much, I would guess as others from my archives of troublesome names. There is the infamous case, probably apocryphal, of

- 106 -

Shithead, for example, spelled exactly as I have done, but allegedly pronounced *Sha-Theed*. Or the names one of my informants encountered in Little League baseball: Unique Robinson, Princess Elena. Amy Schlegel reported a conversation in which the word "dynasty" appeared. "What dynasty?" one of the speakers asked. "My baby, it's my baby's name," the other replied.

"Oh. I see. How do you spell it?"

"D. Y. Nasty."

It would clearly be a challenge for a child thus named to, as Ralph Ellison says we all must in his essay "Hidden Name and Complex Fate," "establish the unity between herself and her name." But is it really any more difficult for her than it is for anyone, even those with the most currently popular mainstream names or older, even more traditional names? Can a Helen or a Thor or an Esther or an Isaiah or a Kim find self and wholeness, living their way in to their name in a way no one else has done before? Ellison's challenge remains:

> …we must wear our names within all the noise and confusion of the environment in which we find ourselves, make them the center of all our associations with the world, with man and nature. We must charge them with all our emotions, our hates, loves, aspirations. They must become our masks and our shields and the containers of all the values and traditions which we learn and/or imagine as being the meaning of our familiar past.

The Princes of Serendip, the former name of Sri Lanka — progressed though the world by "always making discoveries, by accidents and sagacity, of things they were not in quest of."

Likewise with the rest of us pilgrims, scrambling up "the mountain of names," as Alex Shoumatoff put it, seeking to discover who we are, what our names meant before, now, and what, over time, they might stand for. To discover the range and textures and deep resonances of what we call ourselves, one another, the multifarious creations of the natural world. We spend our days saying "What?" to names when they are called out. "Who?" "Yes?" This is why identity theft, that increasing form of cyber-larceny, is of so much concern in an age of increasingly cross-referenced, eternally-stored information.

What's in a name? Especially nowadays, almost everything.

NOT APPLES ENOUGH OR TIME

I had not written at my desk for a long time. Spring had been devoured by the new baby and work, by the baby and getting the garden planted, by the baby and sleepless nights. Weary and silent, I had grown nervous. Could I now recover something of myself and a few stolen hours of quiet to compose something that made sense? Could I seize the day so as to press from the fruit of life some juice worthy of distillation into the brandy of art?

Nope.

It was like what happened to my apples this season. In late May, the trees were so laden with fruit that already I'd had to haul two-by-fours from the garage to prop the branches clear of the driveway. I imagined preparing redolent gallons of Wolf River Red applesauce; I computed bushels and pecks and hundredweights of Roxbury Russets; every morning, backing past the trees, I chuckled to myself in anticipation of the green sour-sweetness of the Granny Smiths.

Then the bugs hit. Goodbye to all that. So long.

The apples' decline began innocently enough, tiny maculations pocking their glossy skins—the merest fly-specks, mini-zits. "No problem," I assured myself. "Just a little blemish, a blister of scab here and there." But as I watched, day by day, each tiny imperfection festered like a tragic flaw; soon open sores blighted fully half the crop. Once their skins had been breached, the apples were set upon by hordes of yellow-jackets, whose lopping jaws chewed deep nickel-sized holes in them, creating havens for clouds of fruit flies that took up where the hornets had left off. I watched, cringing, as apples perfect a week ago were transformed into pocked grotesques, the insects' ceaseless chomping reducing them to grimacing shrunken heads, demon knobs, mummies: bad dreams.

And then, in the otherwise pleasant days of early June, the cicadas launched their blitzkrieg, and all of what remained was lost. No one in the region escaped suffering this year's emergence of those gaudy, red-eyed maniacs whose obsessive, synchronized drones pushed us to the brink of madness, whose decibel levels rose to just shy of pain, whose cast-off nymphal skins clung like varnished ghosts to our porch furniture, window frames, chimneys, rose arbors, downspouts, even the odd pair of corduroys hung foolishly over a chair to dry in the yard. Nor do we need reminding of their millions of dead insect bodies, which, as a warrant of Nature's capacity for extravagantly bad taste, rotted on our lawns for weeks after, the scavenger possums and house cats glutted, the mice fat and bored as Medicis. Intelligent Design, indeed.

Before their mass generational extinction, the cicadas added their bit of damage to the apple trees. It was more subtle than the frontal attack of the flies and hornets, but it would last longer. The bottom of every branch of every apple tree had been lacerated in the characteristic bark-splitting zigzag of the female cicada who laid her eggs there. Not long after, hundreds of larvae dropped to the ground beneath the trees, dug in, and began the cycle anew. Next year the trees will bear only lightly, if at all; the removal of up to a third of their damaged branches will put the kibosh on any sauce next Fall.

And as it is with the apples and cicadas, so it is with the essayist. Lean season follows the full, and a brooding, even sullen silence overtakes the garrulous voice. Catastrophe or unexpected complication occurs, cutting short his exuberance. Then slowly but surely, an emptiness arises in him, as if a well were somehow to go dry from the bottom up. At last he is left looking over his shoulder as the talkative crowd of his thoughts, a crowd that has now long passed by him, that grows unclear and finally fades in the distance, leaves him in a company of one, struck mute and blind.

In such a state, the essayist wanders in a world shuttered and closed to him, locked solitarily in the Alcatraz of self. He wonders if he will ever write again. He wonders if the harvest of his words and days will ever come in. He wonders if the apple of his writer's eye will remain only a phantom delight, never real and tangible, tart and crisp, there on the page before him.

SEVEN TIMES SEVEN SONS

1

For several years, since passing the age of fifty, I have been making a serious effort to accomplish the clearing of my desk. In actuality, what I am trying to do is to pull together more than seventy years of life, sixty years of experience with school, four decades of serious writing, and all the paper which that work has generated, in files, boxes, garage attic-stashes, basement hideaways, manuscript hoards, forgotten drafts, and unfinished books. I tell myself that I am attempting to live up to Hemingway's chillingly simple dictum that a writer is someone who finishes what he starts.

The problem is, I know it's not about what Hemingway said, all this attempted ordering of things. It's about mortality. It's about death and dying—my own. Lurking deeply under all my busyness and virtuous filing of things and even my daily hammering away at projects almost finished, is the indisputable sense that I am much closer to death than I was when I was thirty: I don't have much time. I lost both my parents in the space of two years. A couple of friends of mine roughly my age have already undergone bouts with prostate cancer; several college chums and early colleagues from teaching are continuing or recovering alcoholics; another has died of pancreatic cancer; another has been struck down by brain cancer; I have for more than a decade now been teaching the children of former students. All of this adds up to an imperative that drives me powerfully. *I have offspring to create; I must be about my work's business.*

But around every unfinished story and poem, a kind of universe of difficultly hovers. Can I go back to this story I started twelve years ago and re-enter its secret pulse and carry it to its finish? Can I recapture the smell of it, the gist of its curves, the timbre of its voice? Or is it too far gone from me, completely unfinishable? And these poems—

could I really have been the one to set these words down? Wasn't that someone else entirely, someone who still could run in the afternoon after two hours of writing and whose knees would still bend the next morning and whose heart did not stammer for days on end, and whose life was not yet mostly over?

What kind of problem am I facing at this juncture in my writing and teaching life? Do I give up on the past, all those unfinished stories and poems; do I sacrifice the hours I spent hunched over them, attending them like a dresser of sycamores tending the roots of his trees, or a midwife the births she assists? Do I turn my back to them and pull off that classic American magic trick, that trick Jay Gatsby and Huck Finn and a hundred others mastered in the hands of their makers: the New Beginning, Starting All Over, Inventing A New Life?

The present is the very tippest of the tips of the iceberg; the past is monstrously huge, heavy and unwieldy, grave as all the universe, as all time, as all who have loved and lived and now do not. It is packed densely with detail—with conversations, dreams, lies, exclamations, vows, prayers, pyramids, cries of despair, addresses, shouts of defiance, telephone numbers, revolutions, the scents of a hundred perfumes, the tones of ten thousand songs, and each set of words and images and impressions drags along with it all the stories that lead up to it, or that are tangled into it. "Heard melodies are sweet, but those unheard are sweeter." In this context, the honeyed thought of Keats takes on a bitter aftertaste. The largeness and complexity of the actual universe of past and present is incomprehensible; even more oppressively and smotheringly so, the largeness of the universe that can be imagined.

Thus the great trouble I find myself in: I am trying to organize that immensity, as all writers do, and I am trying to do it, as in my late-life gathering up I must, without losing anything important. And at the same time I have come to that state of awareness in my life, sharpened by impending mortality, that there is nothing that is *not* important.

So no matter what I do, I keep running into the problem. In the very act of "clearing my desk," I am actually digging up the past, literally, from piles that are several years deep. And I know that each of the items may very well be important to the writer I am, important as a potential poem, essay, story, or God help me, book. I have to go back, not forward, and try to discover the meaning of each of these things in order to understand the present that so harries me, and to which, ironically, I am most of the time hardly present.

2

So it is that I have before me on my desk an obituary from the *Monroe County Beacon*, a weekly from eastern Ohio, where lies my occasionally-occupied chunk of the unglaciated, reforested, wild-turkeyed and most recently, black-beared Appalachian countryside. Its subject is Edna L. Daugherty, who died October 29, 1992, at the age of 69. From the time of my boyhood – that's more than fifty years ago, now – my father and I had been part-time neighbors of Edna Daugherty and her family. She was, the obituary reads, the daughter of the "late Edgar and Cecilia Hooth Gibbons." Great names those. "Edgar Gibbons" – a fine British one, firm and strong as its alliteration. "Cecilia Hooth" – the patron saint of music married to the call of the Great Horned Owl in "some dark holler where the sun refused to shine." Stories and ballads and complex ethnic histories hang on both of the these names as numerously as apples on a homestead tree – or as buzzingly troubled as hornets in their huge humming nest. And though I am drawn to digress here and explore some of the remote territories of the ancestry and life of Edna L. Daugherty, I am compelled by the plain force of the obituary facts to press on.

Edna L. Daugherty "was a member of the Graysville Church of Christ." Yes, I know the place (there's a story there, but not for now) and the countryside around it (another story – actually a suite, or country atlas of stories – again, for later) and I know where Edna lived of course (I can't go into it here), and where I visited with her from the time I was a boy until years after I became a father with boys of my own (many, many stories there, too.) Interestingly, my father, dead like Edna now, always considered Edna and her family among our closest, kindest, and most loyal neighbors, though in a part-time way. For most of the time we technically shared a Greenbrier Ridge address, we actually lived from 90 (my father in Steubenville) to more than 200 miles (me and my family in Cincinnati) apart. (That's a set of stories to unfold, too, though impossible to embark upon here.)

"Experience is multiple," Melville reminds us constantly in his death-haunted, dark, Nature's cathedral of a book, *Moby-Dick.* "I look, you look, he looks," and what each of us sees is a different story, another cosmic cascade of detail, another gestalt of what human experience smells and tastes and feels like. For me, there is both wonder and despair in this. Wonder over how rich and textured and unpredictable and suddenly beautiful life can be; despair over how impossible-seeming the job that writers take upon themselves – to somehow sift this avalanche of the actual, to create some pattern or meaning out of its shimmering flux, its relentless protean fluidity, its overwhelming implacable abundance. There is never any bottom of things to get to.

As I resume reading the obituary, what comes next startles me. For after telling us that her husband Ralph has survived her, it continues the list of her survivors: "seven sons, Heber, Ronald E. and Reginald K,. all of Woodsfield, Lloyd of Minerva, James E. of Lower Salem, Gary D. of Graysville and Charles E. of Canton..."

Now some of these sons, I don't know which or how many, were the children of Ralph's former wife, long ago deceased. But I don't believe that any of them was very old when Ralph and Edna married, so in effect she raised them all.

Seven sons. Seven boyhoods enjoyed and endured. Seven teeth-cutting, bandaged boyhoods; seven puberties. Seven sets of injuries, infections, stitches, broken bones; seven times seven, perhaps, sets of girlfriends—taken together the entire female population in any given year of Graysville Skyvue High School—an entire generation of Perry Township girls, all brought into the cluttered front room of the Daugherty homestead, all dipped up, perhaps, a ladle of murky water from the well, all spoken with and listened to at length (their own lives beginning to weave like threads in and out among the chairs and car parts and boxes and dogs on the Daugherty porch, adding to the incredible tonnage of narrative gathering there.)

Seven drivers to train on the steep, switchbacking, narrow roads of this ancient Appalachian Ohio—the very roads on which I learned to drive, and on which I have nearly sideswiped death myself two or three times. Seven marriages, maybe more. Divorces, stillbirths, miscarriages, kidney infections, dead wives (dead daughters-in-law), blood poisonings, firings, quittings, layoffs, sets of agonies and runs of bad lucks, multiple dissolutions and conjoinings.

Seven sets of holiday and birthday and funeral and wedding visitors with their children and later their children's children, and later again their children's children's children. Seven sets of worries, seven sets of exaltations. Seven sons: seven new lives, each in event and adventure and hardship and sorrow and triumph as uncountable and unaccountable as any medieval prince's or king's story might be. The difference in the case of the Daugherty boys is that each of their lives will remain unrecorded. Day by day as it happens, each will be pretty much finished, gone from the memories of all but a few relatives.

But the story of Edna L. Daugherty, the great accomplishment of her womanly and matronly life—as worker, gardener, butcher, cook, counselor, conciliator, wife, daughter, and so on and so on, stories as deep and far-ranging as the deepest Appalachian coal seam, and as full of antiquity and fire as her seven sons—this clearly should be a saga, a novel. Only such spacious forms might comprehend the scope of even a handful of the most dramatic events of she and her seven sons' lives. But I know I will not live to write such a work, even if I survive another couple of decades. There is too much else to do, too many other tasks upon which I have embarked, and which are more realistically achievable. In my late years, I must go on, weigh and consider, choose and reject. When I was younger, I let the winds of whim steer me where they would; I had time (or at least I thought I did) to play and mess around and wander and walk away. Now, time is a-flying, and I had better get on with the things I've begun. I'm not immortal, as I may have thought decades ago, and though I may not have world enough and time to do Edna justice, neither can I let her memory slip into the ocean of the forgotten, unspoken or unremembered by anyone but her family and a few friends and rural neighbors. I do not have the time for amplitude and scope, so I must work small. I want to create at least a little eddy of words, a slight murmuring verbal complication to slow the steady draining of her memory into silence.

She was not pretty — I first met her when she was in her mid-30s, I estimate, when she was three decades younger than my own wife is now. But in my memory Edna was never young — her hair is steel gray, her teeth sparse, her skin cracked and wrinkled like leather long exposed to rain and sun, her eyes the bluest blue — bluer and bluer as she aged, as if gems in an increasingly darker setting, and so seeming the brighter. Talking about pretty and Edna is like talking about nice and a glacier — they're not related in any way that's meaningful. Edna's life was an elemental one, bereft of material luxury though rich in family life and dwelling in place. Her shaping of what she was given and her populating of the world with decent people is what's pretty, if we need something pretty here to hang onto.

On the other hand, her face had great character. It was a handsome, wise, tested, historical, tragic face. It was a complex text, and the more you studied it, the more it expressed. It spoke to our history as a species, our durability, our knack for survival. It spoke to the history of Appalachia, the Scots-Irish immigration into Pennsylvania in the 1700s and the continuation of that migration into the highlands and mountains to the south and west. It spoke to the knowledge of childbirth and death and planting potatoes and seasons of wrens and blacksnakes. It spoke of winter and cold midnights. It spoke of the taken-for-granted quality of many women's heroism in the adventure and hardship of their days. But whatever difficult stories her face told, when she talked to you, her eyes smiled. Her presence radiated plain welcome, the hospitality of the survivor. Even physically, she maintained her tough clear-eyed resilience up to the last time I talked with her.

The same sentence in the obituary that tells us she is survived by seven sons, "Heber, Ronald E,. and Reginald K, all of Woodsfield,

Lloyd of Minerva, James E. of Lower Salem, Gary D. of Graysville and Charles E. of Canton," just to speak it again, continues, after a semi-colon, with this: "and five daughters, Doris Francis of Nankin, Reba Nailey and Evelyn Daugherty, both of Woodsfield, Donna Kindle and Mary Scott, both of Graysville."

I pause once more here, letting the fact settle into my conscious-ness that Edna L. Daugherty was mother not only to seven sons, but to five daughters, too. Something deep begins to turn inside me. I be-gin to see the shadow of some rare and even slightly fearsome thing closing in. This is not a big family. It is a huge one, even by the stan-dards of one who has married into a family of ten children. The feed-ing and raising and educating and training and socializing and disci-plining of Edna's family was accomplished on a series of part-time jobs, seasonal work, and hardscrabble gardening. It was accomplished over four or five decades without ever once—this is a guess, but I think accurate—having a new car. It was accomplished in a house with no city water and until recently, no trash pickup. It was accom-plished despite one and two-hour bus rides to and from school for many of the children. It was accomplished with dignity and pride by people who were, probably most of their lives, living below poverty level in one of the poorest counties of Ohio, but never in squalor, physi-cal or spiritual. This is the darkness I spoke of—the thing most of us have never experienced, and do not want to acknowledge: the dark-ness of the truth that in the richest nation on the planet, lives such as these unfold unnoticed, unacknowledged, or, if made briefly public by some usually unfortunate accident—a mine explosion, say, or a flood—are often caricatured as backward and mean.

I know most of the girls; have since I was a boy. Evelyn's nick-name, the one she goes by to everyone except the mailman, is Chub. She's about my age, maybe a little younger, friendly, rotund, almost always smiling. Often when I lived there in the summers, she would walk up the road, smoking a cigarette, carrying a squash or some cucumbers from their garden for me, and we'd talk away a half hour or so. Once, years later, when my sons were along with me, she took them up to Woodsfield, the county seat, to watch her son Bubba play in a softball game. My father was fond of Chub, and when he died she wrote a note remembering him to me. Donna I know also, though not as well as Chub. The youngest is Mary. Once, when I had brought a group of school children down to the woods for an Easter Break out-ing, the Daughertys invited us all over for a game of cold weather horseshoes. Under the gray, early Spring skies, among the shouts of eight or nine city kids out in Appalachia for the first time, Mary hov-ered at the edge of us all, shy, pretty, curious.

Donna and all the rest of these girls have become mothers themselves by now. When Edna died, there were, according to the next paragraph of her obituary, 27 grandchildren, 21 great-grandchildren, and a great-great-grandson.

That's forty-nine additional births, seven times seven christenings, raisings-up, family dinners, scraped knees, busted lips, broken arms, school dance dates, driver's licenses (although I heard that Edna herself never applied for nor held a driver's license in all the long years of her driving into the county seat for work). That's forty-nine more sets of football games, high school diplomas, marriages, divorces, crashed cars, failing healths, poverties, strokes of good fortune, short employments, long bouts of necessary gardening, odd jobs, scrapings by, and miscellanies of travail, struggle, and joy too numerous to mention. Forty-nine more sets of stories, forty-nine more romances and tragedies, comedies and pastoral narratives, sagas of the intersection between human life and the countryside, between hunger and satisfaction, between nomadry and staying put—all such stories now vanishing tales in the reign of King Interstate and his addled consort, Suburbia.

And having begun all this great work, having given birth to the chapters which beget more chapters which beget even further chapters, each annotated and footnoted and full of digressions and subplots and climaxes and long stretches of drudgery and routine, filling the world she created with lives and conflicts and talk and resolutions and speechifying and vowing and proposing and reverent, brooding, suspicious silences—having begun all this and having lingered for nearly seven decades to supervise from her porch, and from her kitchen, and from her little potato patch up on top of the hill, and from the driver's seat of that season's car—having overseen life's ever-unreeling enlargement and complication, Edna L. Daugherty, on October 29, 1992, departed it all.

One more detail: she lost two children during all this as well. "A son, Paul R., in 1987; a daughter, Bonnie Ann." I had not known of this. Nor had my father. To learn of it was for both of us a moment of confused sorrow.

"Visitation," her obituary concludes, "was on November 1, interment on Nov. 2." That's All Saints Day, then All Souls Day. Mother of a huge family now dispersed all over the eastern part of this state, great-great-, great-, and grandmother to nearly fifty children, solid neighbor of me and my family, neighbor of all on Greenbrier Ridge, Perry Township, Monroe County, Ohio, Edna L. Daugherty contributed her share of saints, her contribution of souls—and hers was more, much more, than a woman's usual measure of both. And now, on a

Seven Times Seven Sons

cedar-lined lane outside Graysville, Ohio, where everyone knew her and her family and all of her children, she rests. The landscape is arranged, in a way, all around her; as I think of her there, she is at its center. Like her life, this landscape is uncapturable; it is a landscape of infinite detail and iteration, of billions of leaves and pine needles and stalks of grass and the veins of the feathers of all its thousand upon thousands of birds, and of all the hooks and burrs and spines of all the seeds of every plant that grows here.

3

Thus I am returned to my dilemma. I have held this clipped obituary for years, making sure it passed from pile to pile, folder to folder; I knew I would come someday to write about it. And now that I have, I do not feel any relief from the great burden of stories and poems and essays I will not write about it. I am oppressed by what cannot, will not, be done. I feel confronted by something akin to what William Heyen reports in "Erika," part of his *Swastika Poems*. "I will always remember speaking to the caretaker at Belsen. He said that he still finds things there. When spring breaks he tills the soil or replaces a brick along a wall or transplants a tree or rakes through the Erika and finds a rusty spoon, or a tin cup, or a fragment of bone, or a strand of barbed wire, or a piece of rotten board, or the casing of a bullet, or the heel of a shoe, or a coin, or a button, or a bit of leather that crumbles to the touch, or a pin, or the twisted frames of someone's eyeglasses, or a key, or a wedding band."

What can we make of such poignant residue, of such a relentlessly-presenting list, which has the sacred and inevitable force of a litany, though it names things associated with atrocity? In remembering, what dare we attempt? In the final estimation, so much more of silence than words arises from a writer's life—from anyone's. How could we name a thing so huge?

I thought our job was to finish what we started, as Hemingway insisted, to bring to completion what was suggested or given to us. Now I am reminded of the coldness of the fact that art requires selection. It is a kind of triage we perform, turning our backs on whole lives and subjects, whole complexities of memory, attention, travail, potential achievement. I am haunted by the sense that I have chosen ill, that what I do write is not what I might have written about, not what the universe most required me to write about, not what the world most needed from me. Even more, I fear that what I have written about Edna is not about her at all; I fear that it is no selfless homage, or dedicated memorial to her, but that this all is mostly about me. I fear that her presence in my life and the presence of her death have descended into mere subject matter. Shame on me.

Thus, though the imagination is capable of great accomplishments, in some ways it remains a cowering tiny thing in the face of the plain facts of a single actual life like Edna Daugherty's. Though from a cosmic viewpoint it was small and brief, moving through a corner of the universe as tenuously as smoke, her life among us, and now her death, is larger with mystery than the most brilliantly clear night sky. What we can know is only part of the story, no more than the points of light in the heavens are all the light. The greater portion is darkness. And try as we might, only rarely can the most desperate heave of our imagination link the disparate stars into constellations that might momentarily stand still and make a kind of meaning for us. Only rarely can such effort bring back, if even in a single, sharp inhalation of wonder and surprise, one breath of a life that has gone.

SMOKED

About twenty-five years ago, I stopped smoking. Because smoking and I had a long and productive relationship, and because it certainly was one of my most earnest occupations, during which I sometimes inhaled forty or more Winstons or Vantages or Newports a day, I missed it terribly. It took four years, actually, to completely quit, though there were long stretches of abstinence all through them. But I hadn't really kicked it until after those four years, when I no longer allowed myself nor in fact even desired a celebratory smoke on St. Paddy's Day or on the summer solstice. (One of the head-tricks I tried to play on myself was to ritualize smoking, making it, in effect, part of a high holy day, like censing the altar at Easter or Christmas High Mass. Oddly enough, it worked, to a degree. I was able to forgive myself the brief backslides, and could count them off, even, as occasions of amnesty and grace.)

Besides, smoking had served as a great excuse for writing for years. If I went up to my study, or if, after I put the boys to bed on Monday and Wednesday nights when my wife was teaching, I went out to the kitchen and turned off the overhead, so that there was only an inviting golden pool of brilliance cast by the lamp on the table to write in, I would light up the first of the chain, and get focused. The writing and the smoking went hand-in-hand: pen and ink, milk and honey, sleeping and dreaming, writing and smoking.

In order to try to break this connection (and it is a breaking, and it is painful) I started to write on the computer. The actual assuming the position of writing and poising before the blank screen was agonizing; a deep anxiety arose in me, because I knew I would want to smoke, smoke a lot—and that I would not, I had promised myself, I would not smoke. For more than twenty years, that connection had existed, reinforced hundreds of thousands of times, in the company of my most beloved thoughts and most intimate friends and lovers, and there I was, trying to overcome it literally overnight. Faulkner said that the raw materials of the writer's trade were food, paper, alcohol, and tobacco. I was trying to throw away half of them at a shot.

Still, I tried. I started what I thought might be a fairly long and leisurely writing project detailing my withdrawal. I gave it the uninspired working title of "Cold Turkey" and each day for a week or ten days, I sat down sometime during the day and wrote at it.

Some of what I wrote was good—that is, it taught me something I hadn't known about smoking, and about writing—and, as is always the case when the writing's going well—something about a couple of other topics I hadn't even suspected I'd been thinking about. Gender roles, for example. And a kid I hadn't thought of for over thirty years.

Though this piece of writing, done in part as therapy during a period of withdrawal, was interesting to me, I somehow lost it. It is gone, flushed down the black hole of the computer I wrote it on, sent back into photons or sticky electrons or reverse quanta or whatever the words on a computer screen become when they go away, and though the kid is mostly gone with it, too, still, there remains a kind of ghost-image of him, quietly standing, smiling, in a haze of smoke or dreamwood another life ago.

We hid our cigarettes—whole flattened packs of L&Ms and Pall Malls, under rocks in the woods out past Mr. Smith's garage where you could hear the radio playing faintly in the distance all afternoon and evening. Our fathers had cleared a thirty-yard run in the second-growth locusts and built an archery buttress for us with a half dozen bales of hay; they had thought to improve us in some way by encouraging us to master the bow and arrow. Actually, we went there mostly to sneak cigarettes. After burning one, we'd hide the packs under slabs of damp sandstone where snakes and pillbugs lurked, and fire off a few shots with our little bows and then have another cigarette.

Smoking in those days was a kind of ritualized ecstasy, always communal. Before our serious addiction, we never smoked alone, and our experience with tobacco was shaped by all sorts of conventions. Never three on a match, for example. It was a rule inherited from our fathers, young bucks not long back from World War II, who had learned that an open light visible long enough for more than two quick ignitions was enough for a sniper to draw a bead on. At least that's how the folklore went. So despite our smoking in an obscure woods on the outskirts of Steubenville, Ohio, far from Nazis and Japs, as our fathers still called them, we didn't linger. The third guy always flicked his own Zippo open with the trademark metallic click, and lit his own.

The first deep drag was filled with an edgy excitement. You knew that within seconds the buzz would come upon you, starting in your head. You grew dizzy first, then a kind of thrill ran out into your arms and legs. You'd feel the woods sway and rock, and you'd spread your feet apart, to steady yourself. Then followed the tightening of concentration, the pleasant oral rhythm of suck and blow, suck and blow, and the camaraderie of the other guys, smoking. The world was good.

I vomited horribly after my first cigarette. It, too, was smoked in the woods, outside Wheeling, West Virginia, at a nature camp I'd been given a scholarship to by the Steubenville Audubon Club. I was eleven or twelve and weighed, probably, ninety pounds. Some delirious miscreant named Jackie Diamond or something like that had flashed a pack of Pall Malls before dinner and whispered, "Behind the cabin, fifteen minutes." I found him there, leaning suavely against a big beech tree and French inhaling like a Parisian pimp. He lit me one off his own, and I closed my eyes and dragged on it. I gagged, coughed, wheezed, and finally, after forcing three or four more inhalations, fell to the ground in a sick green swoon. I got up on all fours and heaved my guts out there on the frowning earth.

So this kid of memory—this kid who may have died years ago, or who may still be going at it in Wheeling or Bridgeport or Woodsfield or somewhere, smoking and hacking and coughing—was he an angel or a devil? So many of the good times I had in college were times when smoking was present. My freshman year, I would go out on Friday night with a fresh pack of Winstons or Vantages or whatever brand I was smoking at the time, and drink draft beer by the mug at places like, well, the Mug Club, or at Shipley's, or The Family Owl. Everybody smoked in those days; bars had a gray haze and stank like quenched house fires. Smoking was a way of meeting girls; you watched until some lovely pulled one from her cute leather bag, and then you stepped forward suavely, offering a light. Smoking was a way of punctuating an argument; Tennyson was never better than when, frowning over the curl of smoke burning your eyes from the cigarette clamped in the side of your mouth, you made one final point, your finger on the bonanza passage in the text. Just standing around on campus, a smoke in your mouth, maybe getting photographed for the candids that appeared in the school paper, was good stuff, and built your reputation as a rake and intellectual.

Those earlier smokes in the woods by the archery range still brought with them a rush of dizziness and nausea, but as our tolerance increased, the queasiness subsided and we could smoke two or three in an afternoon and suffer no apparent effects.

Keeping our smokes under stones in the woods had, of course, some negative consequences. If it rained, for example, they got wet. The printing on the paper inside the cellophane would blur and smear.

The sharp red capitals L and M would slowly disintegrate into blobs and splotches, while the cigarettes inside would dampen and go moldy. Once so ruined, a cigarette, though completely dried out, still tasted like a grass door mat when you lit it. But getting smokes was risky, and we used every one, no matter how spoiled.

We bought them at Mr. Howard's, a front parlor store in a house one street over from ours on Lincoln Heights. Until our neighbor put up a fence, I could cut through his yard and be at Mr. Howard's in ten seconds. The most remarkable thing about Mr. Howard was that he had no ears. I have no idea what happened to them, but their lack seemed to set off in him other lacks as well: he hardly ever spoke, for example. You went in and ordered what your mother had told you to get, and Mr. Howard silently padded around the room (it was really the front room of his house, rigged with shelves reaching to the ceiling, and as ill-lit as a basement) and got your order together in the dark silence. Then (this was just about the best of the strange details to me) he'd write your order down in the receipt book with the stub of pencil—it was always the same pencil, a yellow one, no more than three inches long, which he kept in his apron pocket—licking the point of the pencil in between each item. No, not exactly—what he did was he inserted the entire end of the pencil into his mouth, as if sucking on it briefly, as if to draw out it fullest graphitic darkness, then withdrew it and made his dark, damp entry. It was marvelously strange, and every time I gaped.

One summer as an adult, while I was in one of my many withdrawal periods, I sneaked out to the space between the garage and the fence to my compost pile, where I would smoke. I had noticed months before, in some weird drift of thinking while I slouched smokily next to it, how my compost pile was exactly the size of a grave, and that if I died, my body would fit exactly into it, and could be covered with vines and clippings from my gardens. I thought of myself as compost, and entertained the notion of the ultimate recycling—my body composted, then spread out over the gardens, feeding beans and peppers and tomatoes that my surviving wife and children would eat.

But no such weird, guilt-shadowed reverie occurred that afternoon. As I dipped into my pocket for a match, I looked up to see a piece of notebook paper taped to the garage window:

NO SMKING

I knew immediately that it was in my younger son Brendan's hand. A few weeks before, already indoctrinated by the helter-skelter uncritical but headlong drug program of the public schools, in which nicotine and heroin were lumped together as equally heinous addictives, he had nearly done me in. At Mass one Sunday, after Father had invited anyone who had a special prayer to speak up, Brendan had turned to Pam and whispered loudly, "Should we ask Father to help Dad get off drugs?"

For a time as an adult, I occasionally lived alone in the woods. I rolled my own cigarettes, in an attempt to cut down the chain-smoking. I figured if I had to take all the time and trouble to manufacture each one, I'd indulge myself less. I bought papers and a bag of Bugler's tobacco at Whitacre store, and set out to become a cowboy of smoking. It didn't last long; the intensity of my addiction and the long habit of instant gratification doomed this attempt. Soon I was buying packs of smokes and again unconsciously pulling them out of my shirt pocket and lighting up.

So it was back to the smoke-filled bars. There's still something about the phrase that sets off a warm thrill in me: the eye-burning staleness and stench of such places is difficult for me now, but then, the very smell of cigarettes and beer and perfume was so warmly entangling that to remember it overwhelms me with nostalgia. I smoked and drank, drank and smoked, and in between shot pool and yearned for the wearers of those perfumes.

And isn't it strange, o yes, looking back on it now, to see myself in shorts and a tie-died t-shirt, out in the middle of Clear Fork, fishing, shooting a little spinner in around some likely bass-attracting structure near the bank, a cigarette hanging from my mouth? It's all a picture of rural health and activity, of a kind of oneness with nature, except for that cancer stick sending out its treacherous fairy of smoke, that foreshadowing, that reminder of breath and ghost.

There were girlfriends who smoked, and that was always interesting. At the same time some part of me idolized them, another part of me, lighting their cigarettes, smelling the stale smoke in their hair, watching them, late at night perhaps, after all the carry-outs closed, grubbing up a butt from an ashtray and firing it up, and squinting in the acrid smoke—that part of me wondered what it was we were doing, us beautiful young people, dragging our bodies through addiction and abuse and late hours and all. What did we know? What did we care?

And then I am almost fifty years old; it has been more than a decade since I quit smoking, nearly my whole lifetime since my father quit. Yet here he lies, almost naked, shivering, in a hospital bed in Columbus, Ohio, the pneumonia he suffers from nearly killing him. Was the damage of his youth inescapable? Had those service-issue Lucky Strikes or Camels or whatever they were he so enjoyed while fishing for hammerhead sharks in Hawaii during the War hurt him in some immensely slow way that took forty-five years to catch up with him, but catch up it did?

And his survival of this bout of pneumonia, only to succumb on Christmas Eve, 1996, to the next—was this a result of smoking damage sustained even in the midst of bliss? The last glimpse I had of my father was his body-bagged corpse on a gurney being wheeled out the front door of his and my mother's condominium off Hague Ave. in Columbus—he who had borne me on his shoulders when I was a child, who had sat quietly with me in the woods as I suffered after a divorce, he who must have bought hundreds of packs of cigarettes at Mr. Howard's.

It took my mother an even longer time to die of respiratory failure—it seemed like a long time, there in the room with her and my sister—witnessing her death-struggle, although struggle seems the wrong word for what was a mercifully unconscious suffering, and a kind of extended, slow, running-down to breathlessness. How surreal it seemed. Only a week before she had been fine, planning a trip with my sister, getting ready for her birthday. We all sent flowers, and that may well have been the beginning of her end. She had allergies, exacerbated by her life time of smoking (even during chemotherapy for her cancer she sneaked them). Weakened, perhaps overcome by an abundance of fresh pollen, she succumbed.

Years ago, when I was still chain-smoking as I worked, I wrote a poem about the ubiquity of smoke in my life. Cigarette smoke, the smoke of brush fires across the abandoned strip mine we played ball next to, the smoke of the coal fires that burned still in many home furnaces in old Steubenville, the fuliginous outpourings of the steel mills, even the explosive and cinder-filled exhalations of the puffing bellies—our name for the steam locomotives that pounded through town when I was a boy. Filled with clouds and miasmas, the poem ends, "Smoke's trouble was my trouble./ It still is." And it is still, these manifold deaths and these many years later, these recent Republican environmental backsteps later, these times of "An Inconvenient Truth" later, these times of fracking and mountain-top removal—still true. Only it's all of us who are in trouble now, not just me.

TROUBLE, MESS, DISASTER

Even though I am a terrible curser of things, damning this and son-of-a-bitching that over the drop of a hat, or the spill of a glass of water, or my inability to grasp the toothbrush in my dopp kit, or over anything else that my failing eyes and weakened grip fail to catch firm hold of, and even though I know that all of matter is in conspiracy against me and will try to trip me up whenever it can—the sweeper cord, despite my pains, tangling on the only piece of furniture in the entire room, the garbage can lid sticking so that I drop the whole load of chicken bones and dog shit I'm trying to toss, my shoelace breaking when I'm late for a meeting and have no other footgear—even though I know I will be eternally a victim of Murphy's Law and that if something can go wrong (if there's even the remotest possibility that it can go wrong, it will) I nevertheless cherish trouble, messes, disasters and the other hundred species of foul-ups this flesh is heir to. I cherish them because I know the richness they bring into my life, the unexpected opportunities they present, the utterly surprising obstacles they can throw up before me, making me dance my way through life rather than bulldozing a heedless path through the jungle of disorder.

When I was a kid, sometimes I'd do something that perturbed my dad so much that he'd send me to my room for half the day. I'd mope around for a while, feeling sorry for myself, but then I'd figure out some project to accomplish—working with my insect collection, reading a book about beetles, daydreaming about the Amazon. What would have started out as the punishment for some trouble I'd brewed often turned into a pleasant afternoon of solitary busyness. Trouble transformed, became freshness, opportunity.

Messes—those piles and avalanches and dumps of stuff that life accumulates—also offer rich opportunities, not just frustrating obstacles. For example, there was a dump near the pond we boys often visited. During most of our adventures nearby, we steered clear of that fouled hillside of trash rolling down from where trucks could back up and disgorge their clots and slides of trash. The stuff glinted with dangerous shards of glass, ragged sheet metal, and exhaled the fumes of old paint cans, turpentine, creosote, the ashes of a burnt outhouse. But one afternoon, I surveyed the smoking spill of debris and eyeballed the skeleton of an old Whizzer motor bike, its back wheel still intact. That back wheel with its welded flange became the central component of a home-made motorcycle I built with a friend, and which afforded us several rich lessons about, among some other serious things, tools, work, freedom, power, and perseverance.

Similarly, nearly forty years later, rummaging around in the basement of my wife's pottery studio and gallery in Madisonville, I came across a single Victorian porch post, the bottom foot of which was riddled with termite damage, but the upper six or seven feet of which was perfectly solid, if in need of some major painting and scraping.

The moment I saw it, I knew we could tear off the rotting makeshift deck on the back of our recently-acquired house and rebuild a grand Victorian verandah around this beautiful architectural relic. My wife and I have since spent most of our free time in warm weather on that porch, its posts newly painted, the salvaged one solid at the center of the roof beam.

Even disaster may yield goodness if the gods that day are favorable, or if the sunspot cycle is right, or if we are in a state of grace, or just lucky. When my first marriage collapsed before I was 22, I began a series of summer hermitages in the country, living alone 250 miles from Cincinnati, and getting to know ticks, raccoons, puff adders, tulip poplars, blackberry hillsides and four generations of my Daugherty neighbors. The travails, despondencies, and enlightenments of those difficult days gave me, over years of recollection and recovery, most of two books of poems, half a book of essays, and a dozen short stories. Not a bad haul from what looked more like tragedy than treasure.

And now I see that I've tried to make my teaching more like some of that, too—messier, less linear, not always predictable, and so apt, at least sometimes I hope, to surprise and wonder. I want my students to dance, too, not plow their ways with cold logic and steely intellect alone through literature and life, building high walls against confusion and doubts and sudden turns of luck. I want them—and me—to be a little lost now and then, so that when we do at last find our ways, they will be *our* ways, not someone else's. They will be knowledges and lives we have constructed ourselves, not hand-me-downs already worn out by others. This is not to say that there is no place for tradition in learning; but rather to point up that there is no place for thoughtless conformity to convention in the discovering and shaping of an original life.

Those who never get into trouble, who do not have the gifts of messes and disasters now and then in their lives, live poorly and meanly despite their extravagantly safe existences. They starve on the empty abundance of success while us lucky ones, bloodied, black-eyed, limping a little, emerge from the burning barns of our lives with wild grins on our faces. "Damn," we say, standing up straight once again, knocking the ashes from our jeans, positive that we're the better for having survived. "Damn," we say, "a little more of that just might of kilt me entirely."

GETTING URBANE AT THE ACADEMY

It was at 22 West 7th Street, in the Lancaster Building, downtown Cincinnati. I passed under its coral pink awning sporting the neat white letters of its name while returning from a rare downtown lunch a few years back, and I almost stepped in, but thought better of it and walked on. Still, the place had stuck to me like a burr to a coonhound, and two blocks later, my mind was in full howl.

"An *urbane* academy?" I wondered. "Is it an academy for the urbane? Or is it an academy whose staff is urbane, come like doctrine-gorged missionaries into the outback of Cincinnati to civilize the natives?" (I remembered Mark Twain's insulting desire to be in Cincinnati when the world ended, since everything important arrived there ten years late.) I almost turned back to check it out more closely. But I didn't, and went with my instincts. To noodle this Urbane Academy, to mull it over as pure idea, unblemished by the slightest pimple or boil of mere actuality, would be rich thinking ground, I was sure.

At least once a month I inspect my students' shoes. As they stumble and moon-walk and shuffle into the wrecked barge I've inherited as a classroom, a kind of houseboat dropped like Noah's Ark onto the black-topped Ararat of the school parking lot, I confirm once more a dread that has grown for two decades now. I see Topsiders, mostly, easily slipped on with no need to know knots, even the simplest, let alone such wonders as the sheepshank or running bowline. Or I see loafers of other, even more decadent genres: black pumps that hardly cover their wearers' toes, so that there's a kind of multiple and misplaced cleavage to consider there, four little peeping mysteries between the squeezed and cantilevered flesh. But it is not the brand nor the style of my students' footgear that most deeply feeds my dread; it is the fact that nowhere—not on *one* of their shoes—do I ever see any honest-to-God, down to earth *dirt*.

Where in the world do these students live? (Hick that I am, still remembering that there is life outside the mall, I once asked students to observe a square foot of the grass and weeds in their backyard, noting all the vegetable and insect life there for a week, pondering it a while and maybe even writing a little essay about it. I got this exclaiming complaint: "But I don't have any yard! It's all paved over. You know, to park the cars." Where have these students come from—and how—that they have not had the gut-tingling pleasure of sinking a foot with a funky *sloosh* into a decent mudhole? Are they all, as in some sophomore-fantasy version of *Lifestyles Of the Rich And Famous*, conveyed schoolward in stretch limos so extravagant that they travel only on the toniest freeways, avoiding common sidestreets where puddles and even a bit of scrawny grass upthrust from a little loam might be sighted?

They're all so scrubbed and primped, relatively speaking, that I think they must have all attended this Cincinnati Urbane Academy. There, I imagine, tall handsome men wear English Leather—or whatever the latest version of pheromone-enhancer is marketed to pubescent boys these days— and coral pink ties (to match the awning, of course—"This is the urbane thing to do, my dears.") There, elegant women with hundred-dollar coiffures speak with a such care as to make it clear that "Cincinnat*a*" is for the Marge Schott redneck, while "Cincinnati" is for the urbane sophisticate—for, say, the graduate of the Urbane Academy.

Whenever my family and I visit our friends in Boston, we have a great time using the T—local parlance for Boston's subway and transit system—and we get to feeling quite, well, urbane about being able to find our way to destinations as various as the Aquarium, The Isabella Stewart Gardner Museum, and the Peabody at Harvard. The kids love the delirious accelerations and dizzying decelerations, the clashing, rail-screaming curves, and the flickering lights of the subway. My wife and I love the people-watching and listening that it affords, and in general we thank God that we do not have to drive in Boston traffic, perhaps the most suicidally reckless of any in the East.

So when I suggest to my own students that they take the public transit to the Cincinnati Art Academy or to the Taft Museum or to the occasional coffeehouse poetry reading, I think I am simply appealing to a universal urban habit. Wrong again. "Take the bus! Nobody takes the bus! Do you know what stuff can happen on the bus! Do you know what kind of people take the bus! Do you know how dirty it is on a bus!" In short, it is not the urbane thing to do.

Our foolish entertainment society has fallen almost completely out of touch with nature, even in its most domesticated forms. Last September, during an idle tramp through East Walnut Hills with my students—among them some real champions of scholarship and wit—

in every other block a mockingbird was singing high from a treetop or chimney. "What's that bird we're hearing?" I asked. A selection of their answers:

"What bird?"

"It's a robin, of course. There aren't any other birds around here."

"Probably a sparrow. A sparrow's a bird, isn't it?"

The endpoint of that particular walk was the Ohio River over-look at the end of Ingleside Avenue. When my colleague George Christos and I had scouted this pilgrimage a week earlier, we'd been pleased to watch a trio of black vultures circle at eye-level, catching the updrafts off the hillside above Columbia Parkway. "The kids will get a kick out of this," we said to one another.

But we hadn't counted on their suave urbanity. Not only were they yawningly unimpressed by the buzzards, but within a few mo-ments of our arrival at this vantage point, offering a busy, detailed panorama of the Ohio River valley stretching roughly from down-town Cincinnati to beyond Mount Washington on the Ohio side, and from Covington to Dayton, Kentucky on the other side, most of the students sat with their backs to the view. I saw with dread that we hadn't really made much progress since the early Middle Ages, when pilgrims daring to cross the Alps closed their eyes so as not to see the jumbled chaos of wilderness which so militated against their sense of order and their elaborate theories of the perfection of God's creation. Much too urbane to acknowledge, let alone celebrate, the panorama of complexity before them, many of my students chose self-blinding.

So, as a last ditch effort, when I pointed out, in the middle of the biological desert of our school's parking lot, a goldenrod in full bloom, and, intending to provoke some thought, called it one of my heroes, the students snickered urbanely, not fooled. "It's just a weed," they said, and turned their eyes towards the cars in the lot or the varied fast-food litter on the sidewalk or the sexy gang graffiti scratched on the lightposts at the corner.

With the exception of a few eco-types, earth-firsters, tree-huggers, bless them, my students are quite urbane, and have little desire to get dirty in the woods or wet at the pond or sweaty climbing Buzzard's Roost out in Adams County. I try not to let it bother me, but it is as if they have led deprived lives; I want to take them all for a day and a night into the woods at high summer, when the Milky Way is splashed across the sky, and say: "Oyez! Oyez! Oyez! Your life is hereby and gloriously changed forever." And I hope for them that they will cast off their car insurance payments and their addictions to mall shop-ping and such, and hie themselves unto nature, to listen and watch and learn.

Right. Not.

Still, there's something to be said for resisting ironed clothes and ironed minds. There's something to be said for a kind of pleasant messiness in life. I've never been too comfortable around things that are too clean, too rigid, too righteous.

So, lest the Urbane Academy close in on me and my students, I offer one last batch of bad news, in a genre made famous by a Midwesterer who can't sleep at night, and so tries to make the rest of us laugh at his jejune humor: The Top Ten List of Things They Will Never Teach You at the Urbane Academy.

1. How to write a letter to the Regional Planning Commission demanding the immediate razing of all malls, gambling casinos, professional sports stadia, and amusement parks in Ohio, Indiana, and Kentucky.
2. How to contact sources of free manure for your garden.
3. How to hang drywall by your lonesome—no help—and without a shirt on.
4. How to prepare all the edible plants growing wild in Cincinnati's abandoned urban lots.
5. The top three reasons why it might not be wise to eat more than one pound of catfish caught in the Ohio River per month.
6. The best technique for scooping the poop of your mutt on its morning walk.
7. The best sidewalk-cooked ribs (do not attempt an answer until you have had a chat with and sampled the wares of Mr. Ribs on the sidewalk at Cincinnati's Findlay Market)
8. What alleys, if need be, in which to discreetly upchuck your overload of Hudy Gold beer during Oktoberfest.
9. What Thrift Stores carry the finest selections of second-hand tuxedos.
10. How to cook roadkill possum over a can of Sterno.

If you know—or if you even would venture a guess at any of these answers—you probably should look elsewhere than the Urbane Academy for the next stage in your education. And don't bother to get dressed up. If you're not attending the Urbane Academy, that "Eat the Rich" t-shirt you've been wearing for a week will do just fine.

GUERILLA GARDENING

1

Tax time. Throughout the country, newspaper and TV reports cover the restless queues of citizens lined up at special Post Office depositories, having waited until the last minute to file returns. Their delays are motivated by anger, laziness, revenge. I read a newspaper story in which a woman factory worker blisters the system that makes her work "two days out of five for Uncle Sam." On the TV news a young man squints into the lights and admits to having lost three copies of his form before getting the fourth filled out. Another man, graying at the temples, glares into the camera and mutters, "I'll keep what I owe until the last minute. I'll be damned if they make a cent more interest from me. They've taken too much already."

But on this same day, at least in the great midsection of the continent, thousands of people turn their attention to something more ancient and more important, in the long run, than paying taxes. They have business of another sort, a deep and binding contract with a power larger than any government, more trustworthy and forthcoming than any bureaucratic agenda. From Maryland to the southern Great Plains, roughly, though with thousands of local variations, April 15, Tax Day, is also the statistical date of the last spring frost. Having rendered unto Caesar, folk now turn their energies and hopes to a fundamental relationship whose rewards are more humane (and often more tangible, more literally sensible) than the distant and secret defense struggle. On the Ides of April or thereabouts, cruise missiles give way to Brussels sprouts, B-1 bombers to broccoli. Citizens turn for a time from their anxiety about international violence to the creative issues of gardening. And they do it in convincing numbers: surveys suggest that over 50% of American households produce at least some of their own food.

The sources of this urge to garden are both practical and pleasantly mysterious, almost mystical. On the one hand, gardening can save money. On the backyard scale it is labor-intensive rather than capital-intensive. In older neighborhoods like Madisonville, large yards, railroad right-of-ways, and even a few abandoned lots are under cultivation. If you watch the Walgreen's sales and buy the ten-for-a-dollar packets of seeds, you can have a twenty-crop garden for less than a slice of pizza costs at the mall. In the bargain, growing your own protects you from being poisoned by dubiously fertilized, chemically-drenched and nutritionally inferior food.

But there is more to gardening than economics and nutrition. Something deeper in many of us needs to garden, enjoys it, desires it, beyond the savings that it might bring. Therein lies its greater value. Facts and statistics tax us (the root of "tax" is "burden"). In this light, gardening is resistance against the predictable, the expert and absolute. For gardens can fail. One year, the broccoli produces exuberantly; the next, the plants rot in the rows. Gardens remind us not only of possibility, but also of limitation. They teach us humility, patience, observation, craft, right work, and the respectable meanings of failure. They literally root us to our place, and bind us to the local cycles of weather, sunlight, the courses of the moon and seasons. They teach primordial truths.

None of this, of course, is news. Some of the most ancient myths are built on the vegetative cycle. Human beings have always paid attention to growing things, not only as sources of food, but also as manifestations of the cosmic and the divine. There was, for example, the Roman ritual of "Old Mars," which took place in April, and which was practiced long before Mars had been transformed into a war god. Originally, he was a vegetable king; his name may be related to the old words for both "generative force" and "to shine," thus linking him with terrestrial and solar energies. Mars was the original fertility god, appropriately enough born to Juno after her union with a flower. During his spring ritual, a man dressed as last year's decrepit god was driven through the city, urged on his way by citizens armed with sticks. He represented the spent vegetation; banishing him made way for the new, youthful god and the fresh season's crops.

Even more dramatic are the minutely preserved corpses found all over northern Europe, first popularly described in P.V. Glob's *The Bog People*, then linked to contemporary Irish conflicts in the poetry of Nobel Prize-wining Irish poet Seamus Heaney. In the stomachs of these male sacrifices, scientists have discovered the remains of a last meal, a gruel composed of over forty edible grains. These men were human composts, in a sense, cast in fear and hope into the bogs as warrants that the new season's grain would arise from their deaths.

Dozens of such rituals abound in myth and legend. Nor are our symbolic participations in fertility rites extinct today. Though their deeper meanings may be almost totally obscured, we still engage in plant rituals, as evidenced by such phenomena as the seasonal interests in Christmas roses, Easter lilies, and the lush green shamrocks (not to mention the ecstatic orgies of drinking and wild spring fevers) associated with the equinoctial feast of St. Patrick.

"Man is embedded in Nature," writes Lewis Thomas in *Lives Of A Cell*. The enduring popularity of gardening indicates the degree to which modern folk remain instinctively connected to the natural world. That we find in our region a coincidence between tax time and the commencement of the growing season is a sign nature and society invite us to study. As much as we are obliged to pay taxes to the New Mars, whose weapons of mass destruction threaten us with annihilation, we are equally invited to garden, to pay homage to Old Mars, whose promise of rebirth inspires us with hope. Such hope helps ensure the preservation of the planet and ourselves.

The ancient injunction to beat swords into ploughshares may not be, even in our complex and troubled world, as absurd or impractical as it may seem. "Fishing," George Orwell once observed, "is the opposite of war." I suggest that the opposite of war is gardening. These fine spring days we take up our trowels, so many of us, in the ardent cultivation of peace.

2

Not so fast. I'm conveniently overlooking, for the sake of high-mindedness, self-congratulation, and "literature", the fact that in the name of gardening I regularly trespass on private property, dig holes in it, and plant things, as if in perverse, woefully belated obedience to Lady Bird Johnson, who entreated her fellow Americans in the Sixties to "plant a tree, a bush, or a shrub." Perhaps there was some unconscious desire on her part to make reparation for the inestimable defoliations of forest during the war her husband commanded for a time in Vietnam. And it is perhaps part of my legacy from the disobedient Sixties that, in the name of the higher good, I cling to my guerilla gardening career as steadfastly as the Viet Cong kept hold of the Ho Chi Minh Trail. I organize raids, curse the capitalist dogs, and generally disregard lots of laws. Victory is a garden!

When we first moved here in 1981, my wife and I hardly looked beyond the floors and walls and broken doors of our house. When we finally got the place under control and began gardening a bit outside, we couldn't help but notice the abandoned lot across the street, its rank four-foot weeds, its bedraggled and generally cast-off state. I did a little research and found out that in 1950 it had been sold to the Chessie Railroad, who has owned it since then. CSX obviously felt no need to maintain their property beyond cutting the weeds down around the signal box that stands on the far northeast side of the lot, at the edge of the railroad ballast. For the first years we lived here, the place was completely neglected. A local youth group made a video of the neighborhood around that time; my neighbor Roger Miller and I, to emphasize the state of the lot, knelt down in its weeds. On the screen, it looks like we're on the African Veldt, or in a stand of the original big bluestem grass that grew eight or ten feet high on the Ohio plains in pioneer days. The show aired on local public access; the next summer the city took to mowing the lot once a month.

Not that it helped. They bush hogged it, chewing up beer bottles, papers, pieces of wood, frequently wrecking their machinery. Where I had begun to carefully mow, the blade set high enough to allow continued growth and root formation, the grass was green, lush. Where they bush hogged it, the vegetation was destroyed, mowed so close to the ground that it was, in my father's word, "scalped." It thereafter declined to yellow then brown patches of dead vegetation poxing the whole lot. The bush hogging destroyed the weeds, yes, but it also trashed what could have been there, what diversity might have sprung up. In another weird echo of Vietnam, the city crew destroyed the piece of ground in their intent to save it.

Still, I kept at it. In fact, I think I enjoyed the challenge; there's something satisfying about believing you occupy the high moral ground on an issue. There are people, for example, in this neighborhood who would call the police immediately if they saw someone kicking a dog, let alone a child. But here this lot sits, abandoned, neglected, at times as abused in its own way as any child in need of foster parents. And, of course, no one gets the slightest bit exercised over it but me and Roger and sometimes John Hale, who lives across the street. So it has become a kind of stubborn and ornery issue of mine, the earnest occupation of many a summer morning and afternoon. I have been so angry sometimes that I have considered forcing the Chessie System to have me arrested to publicize the corporate and civil absurdities.

There was a particular term of official abuse of the lot about ten years ago that tells much of the story. I had been complaining for years to the Chessie about their lack of policing and maintenance of the lot, and when, frustrated, I told one of the men I talked to that I would simply keep calling, every day, and bugging them about it, he'd answered, "You can call till hell freezes over, buddy, it don't make no difference to me."

It had reminded me of the reply I'd gotten from the City Engineer, when, shortly after moving here, I had received a notice ordering me to have all my sidewalks replaced. Simpson Street has no curb, and so school buses and parents waiting to drop their kids off at our corner often pull into the green strip between the street and the sidewalk, and sometimes even up onto the sidewalks themselves. It was causing huge ruts that gathered water after rain, and which froze in the winter, heaving the edges of my sidewalks and cracking them. When I told the engineer of this, and then asked him how the city was going to protect my new sidewalks after ordering me to replace them, he said they'd do nothing. "It's just something you inherited when you moved to Madisonville, sir. You'll just have to live with it." That was an astonishment to me — as if moving to certain places in America carried a penalty like Original Sin. "You just inherited it."

At any rate, I embarked on a series of phone calls to various city offices — Litter Control, Health, Zoning, Streets and Sidewalks, to see if I could stir something up on behalf of the abandoned lot. Nothing doing. The buck was passed so many times, became so dog-eared and ragged, that at last I took it out of circulation.

A few months later, as if to show me how little my concerns had moved all these governmental departments, the city staged a Neighborhood Blitz, a clean-up campaign which at first glance looked like a commendable project. Throughout the 45227 zip code area, the city would pick up all dead appliances, haul away all abandoned vehicles. Our neighborhood had a problem with both; we citizens looked forward to the improvement. On the day the Blitz was to begin, suddenly in the lot there appeared four roaring front-loaders, spewing diesel fumes, accompanied by several huge dump trucks. For the next two weeks, the lot became the repository of hundreds of mangled freezers, doorless refrigerators, defunct washing machines, and paralyzed air-conditioners drooling freon into the gravel and dust. A pile of scrap metal rose to nearly twenty feet. From my front porch, through the hanging ferns and baskets of impatiens, I beheld a scene more reminiscent of the county landfill than of a nearly two hundred year-old residential neighborhood filled with Victorian architecture.

A few years later, it was the railroad's turn. Section gangs aboard a work train tore out one of the two lines running less than a hundred yards from our house. They rebuilt the crossing on Simpson. This resulted in a huge pile of rotting ties, stinking of creosote, piled eight feet high and running for a hundred and fifty feet along the back of the lot. A young crazy with long hair and a Bobcat came and for a day selected the best of the ties, steel-banded them in bundles, and hauled them away. He took maybe a hundred of the thousand or so. He never came back. He disappeared as completely as the thugs who by night pull into the lot and download wrecked cars or dumpster-sized piles of construction debris they don't want to pay to dispose of properly.

The tie incident was two years ago. They continue to lie by the railroad right-of-way; six-foot high mulberry trees now grow among them; weeds obscure the edge of the pile. It has become, almost, a part of the topography. I have talked to the man in charge of the maintenance of this section of the Chessie; he is a helpful and sympathetic fellow who shakes his head over his own company's behavior, but he can do little. He did tell me, however, that the railroad had contracted the man with the Bobcat to remove all of them; he fled the commitment after selling the few he selected, and the railroad feels no responsibility to clean up after itself. Nor does the city seem to feel any obligation to make them. When huge corporations and city bureaucracies climb into bed together, their offspring are often, like the lot, bastards of abandonment, ugliness, and ignorance, and those of us in the neighborhood either have to turn our backs on them, engaging in a kind of forced rudeness and ignorance, or we have to take on their care.

Now, it hasn't been mowed this year yet, and we're in the middle of June. Here in humid southern Ohio, where the last frost might be as early as the end of March, that's a lot of growing already. The poison hemlock, seven feet tall, has been in full bloom for about a month, and various grasses nod heavily with full seed heads. I am happy, on the one hand, to see this growth around the edges of the lot, but I know that one day without warning the bush hoggers will come, trash it all, and leave behind bushels of mown papers and shredded plastic pop containers and fast food debris. What was on its way to recovery, and to engaging in its own natural succession, a succession I would love to watch and record, will have to start all over again. It's the equivalent of waiting for a child to grow in his permanent teeth, then deliberately taking up a hammer and knocking them out.

No wonder certain neighborhoods, certain stretches of ground in our cities, decline into vileness. What happens to the self-image of those who live in such places — do they, too, inherit some warped notion that they themselves must be vile? Do they turn to destructive ways of living and thinking because it's in the air, so to speak, around them?

I know what I'm up against: a bureaucracy that in no way understands the notion of advocacy for abandoned lots and industry officials who have long lain abed with city government, and who thus fear no consequences if they abandon their responsibilities to vast areas of railroad right-of-way through the United States, including my neighborhood of Madisonville. (To get the Chessie person responsible for maintenance, you formerly had to call their Corbin, Kentucky offices; now, there's a number in Jacksonville, Florida—talk about absentee landlords!) City agencies and departments are staffed by inept or grouchy overworked people who keep passing the buck, so that a simple inquiry about a litter problem takes up forty-five minutes of a spectacular June morning better spent in the yard, under the sun, in the company of the breeze. It is not lost on me that this habitual laggardry makes it practically impossible for working people—night-shift employees, for example—to contact their government about local issues such as the lot. They simply don't have the time. As a teacher, I do have some time, and in the summer I make phone calls and use up whole mornings or afternoons, and little or nothing happens. I am afraid that such environmental abandonment happens widely; much potential for beautiful and productive land goes unrealized, and hours of human endeavor are wasted.

I was talking to Ed Valeska, department of Public Works today. He had paused at the curb in his marked car and was filling out some form when, like the Ancient Mariner seizing the Wedding Guest, I rushed over and leaned into his window. He turned into the lot and got out, eyeballed the pile of ties, and tried as well as he could to help me, but without much promise of being able to accomplish anything. But he listened, and he was tuned to the environmental and economic issues involved: the ties rotting and the creosote leaching from them into the ground below; the disaster a fire would cause, with choking smoke smothering the neighborhood, and even the possibility of burying them being a no-go, since they would poison the ground they were interred in. He knew about the effects of mobility, too: about how the city mowing crew, having no continuity of memory from year to year, continue to mow down the saplings I'm trying to start. I talk to them when I see them in the spring, yet, as Ed pointed out, "There's such a turnover that they don't remember which piece of ground needs special care or where things might be planted. They just come in and bush hog it to death, indiscriminately."

I appreciated this city official's sympathy and the patient ear he gave my spiel. But I know, and he does too, that he can do nothing. He suggested a class-action suit, or getting a consortium of neighbors to buy the property, or getting in touch with someone in Congress responsible for the oversight of railroad rights-of-way on the federal level. What a waste of resources, this local problem morphing into a Federal case.

3

Not a mile from the lot, up the ridge on whose nearer crest once spread a fine Madisonville farm, sits the Kenwood Towne Centre, a huge mall whose mushrooming enterprises have contributed to the destruction of small community business districts like Madisonville's and whose vast parking lots have contributed to fatal local flooding. Where once there had been forest and field, then small houses surrounded by lots of elbow room, there is now asphalt and glass and steel, and a billion pounds of machinery driving and idling and parking on it every year. The original land lies asphyxiated—but no one calls the police. If someone strangled a child, or an elder, if someone buried a victim alive, folks would stand around clicking their teeth and shaking their heads and wondering what the world was coming to. But when the lot across the street from me gets dumped on or trashed, or torn up by a few drunks doing doughnuts in it at three o'clock in the morning, no one gives it a second thought. When the Kenwood Towne Centre—and its suburban precedents—pave over old forest and field, it's called progress.

So I have taken the old lot to care for it as if it were my own—even more, as if it were sacred ground. And sacred it is; it has survived great suffering, and that it can support anything at all green and growing is a testimony to its and to nature's toughness.

Try to dig a hole anywhere in this lot except along its very edges, where a few trees have stood until recently, and you will immediately strike compacted glass, furnace cinders, spilled oil, gravel, nails, whiskey and Wild Irish Rose bottles, and construction debris. Haggling out a hole big enough to plant an ash tree I'd grown in gallon pot, I had to turn my head aside more than once because of the nasty smell of the stuff I excavated. I laid it aside in a black pile and filled the hole with good dirt from my garden, planted the tree, watered it in, and just hoped that it might survive whatever that black stuff is. Nature, of course, is tough. I remember Annie Dillard's writing of the sycamore trees along Penn Avenue in Pittsburgh, wondering over their survival in what was, in her girlhood, a place of smoke and grit, a place which Charles Dickens had described, a century earlier, as "hell—with the lid off." Annie writes, "It is hard to understand how the same tree could thrive both choking along Pittsburgh's Penn Avenue and slogging knee-deep in Tinker Creek. Of course, come to think of it, I've done the same thing myself."

But there is an exasperating footnote to the story of this ash tree. It survived, with a big red warning cloth draped over one of its branches, for more than a year of heavy equipment and sewer pipes and water lines during a big city job that used the lot as their staging area and parking. (How exactly the Chessie System and City of Cincinnati Sewer District got together in such a way is an interesting question, which no one ever has answered. A tiny sign on the lot says

"Private Property. No Trespassing"; I guess the city is exempt.) My wife had gone over to the lot the day the work crew showed up, and asked them what they were up to, and generally made it clear that we expected the place to be taken care of during their stay. The foreman agreed, promising to replant the grass and to protect any trees we indicated. He'd marked the ash tree himself. About a month ago, the work crew left, leaving behind about twenty truck loads of dirt and broken sidewalk and pavement; it took about three hours' worth of calls to get the city to make them clean it up. That done, we waited for them to return to sow the grass, as they had promised, but they didn't. Most of the lot was a morass of clay mud, corrugated by the tires of the Bobcat they'd leveled it with. Then, as a final blow, the city crew showed up, and before I could sprint across the street to stop them, mowed the ash tree down.

Where I plant something in the lot, I set a stake. Three or four years ago, I made a point of going over to the lot whenever the mowing crew were at work. I'd introduce myself, smile, make small talk, then thank them for being careful not to mow the saplings I'd planted and marked with stakes. I did all I could to engage the mowers in the life of the lot, to give them some ownership, to give them the feeling of a partnership with me in the healing of the ground. Two years later, after the fast-growing hybrid poplars I had planted were ten or twelve feet high, the bush hogger skinned the entire side of one of them, running over it till it bent to the ground, then letting it snap back up as the machine passed over. Stripped of half its branches and bark, the tree is dying a slow and ugly death, great slabs of its bark coming loose and stains of sap running down its trunk, like rust down the side of a battered ship.

Most of the stakes disappear. Kids cut through the lot after getting off the school bus, and break them off at ground level and leave them lying. I watch people, passing by the big perennial shrubs — forsythias, lilacs, Roses of Sharon — I planted by the corner, reach out, grab a branch, and strip its leaves. It used to drive me crazy; now it merely makes me wonder how such weirdly destructive habits arise in us. Sometimes I am tempted to the despairing thought that we are anomalies in nature because our presence so often contributes to the destruction of the environment. In the chaos of creation, the ongoing evolutionary experiment with flabbergastion and flying fish, derring-do and dugongs, are we humans merely an astonishing temporary — and mistaken — development? I watched a man downtown the other day, walking along a city street near Government Square, smoking a cigarette. The deliberateness of his movement on the plotted ground, the high steel and glass-curtained buildings dwarfing him, the self-

inflicted danger of his smoking — these all struck me deeply. We cannot continue this way; in our arrogance and waste and foolish exercises of power, we will edit ourselves out of the text of nature.

4

A long time ago, I answered a call for some local people to get together and apply to the the Civic Garden Center of Cincinnati for
help in building a community garden. Dave Van Dyke, a friend of
ours and pastor of Eastminster Presbyterian Church, gathered folks
for the first meeting. I found myself quickly in charge of clearing a lot
next to Mannino's Market, the neighborhood grocery, and of organizing the garden and recruiting members.

Five or six of us worked on the lot, a deep narrow chunk of urban
wasteland that had three diseased silver maples on it towards the
back. Cleaning it up, we learned quickly to be careful: there were hy-
podermic syringes (if you poked yourself with one, could you get
AIDS?), hundreds of forty-ounce bottles, defunct lottery tickets, candy
wrappers, and the odd detritus that accumulates in city lots: bicycle
tires, hubcaps, old lumber, bits of brick and broken concrete, a billion
shards of glass, pieces of old slate shingles, the occasional penny or
nickel or dime, a grimy set of long-unprayed rosary beads.

Getting it squared away was work good for the spirit as well as
the neighborhood. I found myself imagining an Eden springing up
here, an abundance of flowers and vegetables pouring out of this narrow lot into the community, feeding it and brightening its corners and
edges. You must hold before you, at the beginning of such enterprises,
a vision. It is a fiction, this vision, but it is one toward which you gradually nudge and sometimes rudely shove reality. It is the castle in the
air, this vision, and we sweat in the here and now and the here below
to build its foundation. We put our shoulders and our haunches to it.

I was helped in this endeavor by three women — Miss Edye
Fletcher, a worker in Mannino's Market, the garden's immediate neighbor; another woman who worked in the store, and whose name, sadly,
I can't recall; and Chris Meyer, a young gardener whose future son
Nathan was to become my future son Brendan's schoolmate and close
friend. We cleaned and filled trash bags and pulled weeds, Chris getting so bad a dose of poison ivy that she wound up in the hospital. We
sawed lumber for the raised beds, hammered nails, spaded up the
ground, hauled in topsoil, and generally worked at making something
beautiful of that abused place. We were joined later by some other
neighbors, Jody and Byron Coaston, Michael and Marcia Richards,
and Mary Ann Westendorf, a carpenter by trade then, but now a

Master Gardener and licensed horticulturist, who graciously took on the management of the garden recently. Mary Ann, by the way, has one of the greatest secret urban gardens I know of; her house is at the end of dead-end street a few blocks from ours, abutting Little Duck Creek, and she has installed a pond, and has gentle slopes planted to perennial beds. We once overwintered an orphaned snapping turtle for her in an aquarium in our basement. One warm spring day, we took it over to her place, and watched it disappear under the duck-weed in her pond. Just last week I walked over and as we talked, watched her two huge red-eared sliders sun themselves on a log in the pond; they reminded me of several I had as a kid, rescued from the county fair or benighted carnival where, their backs painted with some silly image of Bambi or ducklings, they had been for sale.

We got about a dozen four-by-ten raised beds built, and invited neighbors to rent them out at a nominal fee. For the first eight or ten years, we ran the garden on a shoestring budget, often no more than 60 or 80 dollars, with which I would buy some annuals and some manure or a hose. Mannino's let us tap into their water, and I'd pay the summer's water bill in Mr. Mannino's tiny cramped office at the back of the store. Now and again I'd see his son John, a former student of mine, and yearly, Purcell Marian students would come out to the garden and get some community service hours weeding, making repairs, or building a shed for our accumulating tools. Mary Ann Westendorf fronted us a couple of hundred dollars to maintain a minimum required balance in our checking account, and so we continued.

Gardeners came and went; Chris Meyer went on to garden in her own yard, and Mary Ann Westendorf, before she returned recently as manager and coordinator, spent years building her remarkable garden at her home. Miss Edye's eyes were going bad, so she gardened by proxy, letting a fellow grow some of his own food in part of the beds she had rented. And Ervin showed up, "Alabama" to the people in the 'hood, an itinerant grass-mower and odd-jobs man who joined the garden just a couple of years before Mary Ann took it over. He was enthusiastic and disorderly, always smiling, and created some real excitement.

One hot midsummer afternoon Ervin staggered out of the garden, smiling his crazy smile. "Hey, Dick, " he said. "How you doing?" His dreadlocks were tied with bright yellow and red ribbons, and his technicolor Hawaiian shirt blared like a jukebox. I could smell the beer on his breath as he approached me. The whites of his eyes were bloodshot, tracked with red.

"Hey, Dick, you know I cut them bushes down, man. Them guys doing drugs was hiding behind them whenever the cops came and I got mad and cut them down. They'll grow back fine. I just cut them down. I was mad, you know, man? They'll grow back."

Ervin always approached in a cascade of colors, verbiage, fragrance. He was an event, a kind of multimedia presence, and it was this, I think, that unsettled many of the other gardeners. He was coming at them on eight or nine channels, and for them, the garden was a place of respite and peace; Ervin was too much.

He'd joined us that spring and his energy was the best—never in the decade of managing it had I gotten so much help from one guy. I'd let him take home for safekeeping the weed eater the Community Council bought us, and the mower my next door neighbor donated. I was grateful for Ervin's help. But he was unpredictable, wild, a constant drinker. I'd find him sitting in the garden like some sort of Calypso Buddha, his open 40-ounce of Red Dog in the dust on the path before him. 'Hey, Dick, how you doin?" he'd cry, and I'd wave and go into Mannino's for the Sunday paper.

I looked to where the privet I'd planted two years before had stood until this morning. Nothing was left but stumps and fresh white cuts. Ervin had so fully and completely gotten rid of them that it looked like he'd swept the ground where they had grown. He grinned and staggered, pointing at where they'd been.

"Them druggies got no place to hide now, hey Dick? We going to clean them out of here."

I shook my head and went back into the store.

"Dickie," Edye said, standing by the register. "That Ervin is driving us crazy. That boy don't know how to sit still. He's always messing with something. Now he's cut your hedges down."

Edye held a grocery bag in the left hand, a lit Kool in her right. Her red hair glinted against her brown skin, and she leaned over, squinting in her own smoke, to fold the bag.

"Dickie, I don't know. I think I might have to kill him." Her eyes brightened and she grinned. A couple other shoppers, all of whom knew Ervin, muttered, "Amen."

Out the big front window, framed by the stacks of charcoal and the leggy houseplants Edye kept growing in the north light, Ervin stood shouting wildly at someone out of sight up the sidewalk. He held a hoe from the garden in his hand; he wielded it like a Moses staff, shouting, raising it over his head with one arm. Onlookers, tough guys all of them, fell back, stepping into the street filled with speeding traffic.

"Out of here, ye hypocrites!" I thought I heard Ervin yell. "Begone from my father's house!" I saw tables turned over, money spilled, skulking Philistines and pimps and addicts fleeing Ervin's wrath, clearing out of the precincts of his holy temple.

A week later, I walked past the garden and saw Ervin there, dead asleep on the shabby park bench, in the shade of the apricot tree. He looked at home; unfortunately, I learned how apt the phrase, for I am pretty sure (telltale signs of food and of bedding, for example, in the hours of dew when I went to work before the heat) Ervin often overnighted in the garden, under the overhanging branches of a huge honeysuckle bush, since cut down to make way for a gazebo.

Sleeping in the garden. It is at once an image of safety and peace, to be in your dreams surrounded by health and abundance. It is at the same time an image of homelessness, of desperation. These are the two threads of the tale of contemporary Madisonville, perhaps of America at large. Families have lived here since the beginning settlement; others arrive weekly like migratory birds, alighting for a month or a season or a year, then abruptly take off for somewhere else, leaving behind no residue of history, no contribution to the culture or the soil, hardly even the memory of their names. I have been struck by the recent idiom for it: it is no longer "Where do you live?" but "Where are you staying?" as if dwelling in a place were like a visit to a motel. It is a rootless human existence, as alien to my way of thinking as my volunteer unpaid work in the garden is absurd to the crack dealers on the street. And yet Ervin's repose brings a charm to the place. There is a kind of abandonment to circumstance in it, a deeper kind of at-homeness, an accumulation of experience, and a leap of the faith and forgiveness necessary to commitment to a place. If this garden can be slept in, something is well.

5

We have arrived, it seems, at some millennial moment of the big trees here. Several ancients have died or been cut down in our time here, some of which I have already mentioned. Roger Miller and I both lost big silver maples, mirroring each other across the street, a couple of years ago. His neighbor lost an elm that had survived the blight somehow; it turned up leafless two springs ago, stood for a year, then was taken down. Great lengths of its unsplit trunk still lie on the site. Once, right after moving here, as I was sitting talking with my sister-in-law in the parlor, I watched as the huge silver maple across the street silently lurched over and fell into the front of my neighbor's house, tearing off half the porch.

Still, there are surviving prodigies, if not on so grand a scale as trees. I walked over to the lot this afternoon with a couple field guides in hand: here's what grows there, beyond the things I have planted: seven feet tall, a huge stand of poison hemlock, "juices very poisonous," my Peterson says, growing at the base of an old maple stump.

When we first moved here, I saw a sparrow hawk eat a house sparrow in the top of that tree. Chicory, plants four feet tall, at this time of the summer covered with blue flowers. My Peterson notes that they are "alien," meaning they, like most of us, came from somewhere else to settle here. They are tough, growing along country roads, or, as they do here, settling waste land, this "brownscape" in the city. Later in the summer, if the city mowers do not come, there will be primroses along with this chicory, and blooming goldenrod. Goldfinches will congregate by the half-dozens, foraging for seeds and sweeping up out of the brush when I walk the dog in the morning. For I have left the grove of trees and shrubs; I have allowed rows of natural growth — burdock, Queen Anne's Lace — to thrive between the hybrid poplars that spring up as volunteers. I have done so for several reasons: the sight lines now are broken; crazies like the one I confronted last summer in his mustard-yellow ATV, who would appear occasionally to do careening doughnuts in the lot, raising horrible dust clouds that fouled our porches and windows, leaving ugly black ruts in the struggling grass that took years to heal, and raising the blood pressure of people like me, can't see clearly enough now to jump the curb off Simpson, cross the sidewalk, then plow through the lot. It's safer now from that kind of urban vandalism. The natural succession is fascinating to observe; I would love to see if any native trees can make it even in the most poisoned middle of the lot. Many more birds are now evident: every time a freight train highballs through, a dozen mourning doves shoot out of the grass and weeds, fast as the train, flushed by the sound of its whistle as it clears the Simpson Street crossing. Grackles hang out in the tops of the two poplars done in by bush hoggers; and robins, and goldfinches, and purple finches glide over and through the brush. The buzz of insects has increased, and the clumps of blooming chicory and the drying grasses and the russet flower-stalks gone to seed create a pleasingly complicated visual texture. Finally, and most importantly, this growing stuff improves the soil; after a century or two, topsoil will accumulate, more plants will thrive, and one might never guess that it was a former dump.

My friends Anthony Corder and Jason Haap and I, several years ago, sat at a table at Arnold's Bar & Grill, the site of the planning of the river trip decades before by Jimmy Quinlivan and me. We brainstormed another adventure, an interdisciplinary course called The Tree. It combines religion, literature, ecology, and folklore; it's been offered several times now, and is one of our school's more popular electives. The hope is that anyone coming out of the course might look at a lot like this one, with its recovering diversity, and see a future in which really big trees, like the magnificent tulip poplars at Dysart Woods in eastern Ohio, to which Anthony and Jason and I made pilgrimage in preparation for the course, might someday stand there.

6

There is no ending yet to the story of the lot. It is an ongoing essay in local ecological stewardship versus civil and corporate bureaucracy, patience versus expediency, the spirit of the law versus the letter of the law, adventure versus routine, hope versus a kind of crackpot realism.

Neighboring this piece of ground—and I mean "neighboring" not just as a spatial term, but as a verbal action, as in "fathering" in "fathering a child"—has been one of the two most difficult challenges, most earnest occupations, in my life here, a stretch now of more than two decades. The anger I have felt when people knock down a tree, the temptations of despair when all my work, and Nature's, is ruined in fifteen minutes' reckless mowing, the guilt over the curses I've loosed at the lot's despoilers, the mutterings under my breath as I picked up the three hundred trash bags full of litter over the years, the insanity of the very thought of keeping all those bags of litter somewhere and occasionally dragging them over there and piling them along the edges of the lot, with a big sign saying, "Thank you, neighbors" glaring out over Erie Avenue—all of these have been a moral cost to me, a failure of virtue. I have been exposed to the spiritual and psychological occasions of sin, and I have given in, dreamed the violent dream of putting a sledge hammer though the windshield of the big tractor-trailer parked over my saplings, its huge tires tearing up the slowly healing ground. I have given in and called my fellow human beings pigs. This is not living peacefully or nobly in the world, and I know better.

But I feel something Ahab must have felt when he was brought up against the mystery that was embodied, for him, in *Moby-Dick*. And try as I can, I cannot always Zen myself out of the same ire Ahab felt at the inscrutability of things: I too have raged at the unfathomable ways of people who trash the lot, trash their neighborhood, trash their own homes, trash their own families and hearts and motherland. But unlike Ahab, I cannot make war against them, plunge my heart's hot iron into their souls, and so feel avenged. I make furtive sallies, gathering trash and litter, sneaking around among trees and shrubs, refusing to fall behind in my little silly green repairs. It's a guerilla action I pursue, and, despite what I have said at the beginning, not always a very effective, admirable, or pure one. Despair is for quitters, I know. But for all of my work and momentary joy, I am afraid that I can't be sure whether or not I, nor the tiny lot, is any the better for it. Sometimes not sure at all.

Ice Time

> Nor need we trouble ourselves to speculate how the
> human race may at last be destroyed. It would be easy to cut
> their threads at any time with a little sharper blast from the
> north. We go on dating from Cold Fridays and Great Snows;
> but a little colder Friday, or greater snow, would put a pe-
> riod to man's existence on the globe.
>
> —Thoreau, 1854

I sneaked out around lunch time today and walked the four long
blocks from school to the river overlook at the end of Ingleside Avenue. It's late December, the wind roaring, temperature falling: a lean
day with its skin barked off, raw and stinging as a bare-knuckled
punch. I could see that the river was up after several days' rain, and
under the glowering gray of the sky, it looked much like T. S. Eliot's
Mississippi, that "strong brown god." The Ohio was massive, broad-
shouldered, muscling its way through the hills. The wind had raised a
chop on it which I could see even from my height and distance, and a
tangle of big logs heaved and rolled in the middle of the channel. To a
giant tow of coal or gravel and sand, these great soggy dangers would
mean nothing. The bows of the barges would loom over them for a
second, then under the logs would go, moiled and churned, booming
along the metal hulls, then they'd be afloat again, scarred by the pro-
pellers, maybe — and the barges and boat none the worse for the wear.
But to a pilgrim in a canoe or a john boat, such drift would threaten
destruction. "Sawyers," they were called by the old river pilots, for
what they'd do to the flimsy wooden hull of a shallow draft sidewheel
packet built of little more than sticks and paint and bunting. I imagined for a time the sudden breaking loose of those logs in a high creek
somewhere in Pennsylvania or West Virginia. I imagined that they
had been seedlings a couple of centuries before the First American

Regiment came downriver to guard the surveyors of the Seven Ranges of the Northwest Territory in the old Fort Steuben, on the site of my home town. As mature trees, they had fallen, maybe forty years ago, washed downstream on the Allegheny or Monongahela, the Kanawha or Big Sandy, and snagged in a choked bend. There they had lodged for years, maybe, then, a week or two ago, suddenly they gave way, and six or eight of them washed out at once, and began a seaward journey that had begun when Shakespeare was alive.

A third of a century ago, during the first of two successive brutal winters in the Ohio Valley, the river froze from shore to shore. Here in Cincinnati, daredevils walked across it; some rode bikes, and I even heard rumors of attempts to drive across in cars. One day I was ice-walking along the solid sheets close to shore, noting the crushed canopies of ice lower down the banks like the one weighing over a thousand pounds that had collapsed and killed a boy just a week before. I lifted my eyes and saw what I mistook for fungi growing at the same height from almost every tree. I doubted that all those trees could be dead; just the summer before I had veered and stumbled through them, my fishing pole tangling in the undergrowth. It couldn't be fungi. On closer inspection, I saw that those elephant-ear-like protuberances were instead tongues and filthy hat brims and ragged ledges of dirty ice, and that they marked the high water of that frigid winter. There was freshly scraped bark on many of the trees where great rafts of ice must have crashed against them during break-up. Even more amazing to me was that none of the trees had been taken down. As the river fell and the ice broke up, a chaos of grinders and slicers and crumpling sheets had rumbled south, crushing a legendary local riverman's workboat against the Markland Dam and sinking it. Back up the bank, walking to my truck, I noticed graffiti on the building at Turkey Ridge Park: "Jeannie Odell is a fox." "I love and dig James Chaplin." But they were summer scrawlings, made in the heat of passion and bright steamy days. Nowhere could you see, "Ice here in the winter of '78," and underneath it, a cold, brown, final line.

The ice, back in the old days that helped shape the Ohio's course, worked its way south, too. The air at its advancing edge must have felt much as this air today, sharp, heatless, a kind of invisible form of danger from which the body shies as it would from a charging bear. And if you turned your head just right, so that the breeze didn't roar across your ears and drown it out, you could hear the sound of the ice advancing, a little pebbly clatter at its leading edge, mixed with the deep, continental grind of its rock-clogged heart, holding boulders so tightly they carved yard-wide grooves along a thousand feet of bedrock. You would almost think the ice was speaking, and you would shiver with dread for not knowing what it might tell you — or for intu-iting, suddenly, exactly what it said.

What the ice said, of course, was that your world was not stable, not even in a geological sense. Impermanence rules. Even the very landscape you have come to know your way around in, to feel at home in, can be ground away, utterly obliterated. You are a small, small thing, the ice announces, tiny in your fragile hut of bones, and you will not live to see my retreat. You may not even survive this annual winter I bring with me; surely you will not survive the epochal winter I portend, an era of darkness and cold as long as a hundred of your generations.

But this is all academic. Although recent discoveries are chal-lenging the conventional wisdom, it is still perhaps reasonable to claim that there were no human beings on the continent at the height of the last ice age. Such a profound and absolute absence of the human in the landscape is almost utterly impossible for us to comprehend. Let us imagine the absurd notion that we have been taken back in time to about 11,000 years ago, when the last of the Scioto Lobe retreated, but with this one exception: the outerbelt freeways around the Cincinnati metropolitan area, I-275 and I-471, somehow already exist. On either side as you drive, there is nothing but tundra, boulders strewn here and there, and kettle bogs — small ponds formed by melting blocks of ice — dotting the landscape. Here and there a kame — a little hill of de-posits left by a stream running under the glacier — wanders across the landscape. If there is any living movement at all, it is far distant — a mastodon, or a giant beaver, or a loose skein of storm-blown passen-ger pigeons flung across the sky. For all your life, if you imagine your-self in this world, you will hear no car horn, no airplane droning over, no recorded music. You will hear the wind; you will hear thunder, maybe; you will hear all summer the ceaseless roar of the frigid glacial rivers pouring out from the edge of the ice; all winter you will hear almost nothing beyond the crackle of fire close up as you hold your hands out over it to warm them in the star-crazed empty night.

There is a deep loneliness in all this, and in the vastness of the world around you. It is a world fit to its own size, silent in its own silence — not altered, patched, plotted, intersected, developed, subdi-vided, malled. If you want to hear a human voice, it will have to be yours. What are you going to say in all that vastness? What are you going to offer it in words by way of introduction?

Thus the time of the ice is, I would guess, the time of the first poetry, for only poetry dare approach and try to give voice in the presence of such magnitude and power. The pioneer North Ameri-cans came across the Bering land bridge at about this time, and they brought with them the memory of that far northern crossing, the vastness of the sea, the presence of the ice, the unceasing hiss of the wind.

How stupid to make small talk into the profound human void of continental North America. Those firstcomers must have felt the challenge of that fresh and unworded world, and they must have felt that what they spoke into it should be worthy, and, as best as they could manage it, in scale with nature. For nature's steppes, there must be language as large and with equally broad horizons; for nature's boulders, those erratics left behind by the retreating ice, there must be words that stand as solidly and largely and that build meaning in solitary and in sedimentary ways, single pronouncements as startling as pyramids or complex layers upon layers accreting and accumulating; for nature's fishes and fowls, there must be poems as fluid and as free as the milky streams roaring from the foot of the summer glacier or the wind off the winter ice face.

In 1928, Henry Beston, having spent a year alone on the great Outer Beach of Cape Cod (itself the product of glaciation—in effect a huge stratified pile of sand and gravel left behind by the ice), summed up his experience there: "The world today is sick to its thin blood for lack of elemental things, for fire before the hands, for water welling from the earth, for air, for the dear earth itself underfoot." I can't help but think that he is still right. And I think of how, in this new millennium, we have lost the first poems said by our ancient brothers and sisters. We have forgotten even how to speak and listen to their language. Much is irrecoverable.

So remembering the Ice Time may be a useful exercise in renewing our sense of where we are, in time and place, and of avoiding any false sense of security, conquest, or entitlement. Yes, we and our PCs and laptops and iPhones and stock markets and Pentagons and Kremlins survived Y2K, recovered from 9/11, and we have not been completely undone—yet—by fracking, mountain-top removal, and Gulf oil spills. But those were entirely man-made threats. The ice may return, in spite of—or, in the marvelous unpredictable permutations of chaos, eventually because of—global warming. And if it does, it will change everything. Everything.

Nor are we exempt. Our cleverness and our wealth and our planetary power thrown at the ice will not turn it back. All of our most earnest occupations in defending ourselves from it will be to no avail. We are a part of nature, not apart from it. When—if—the ice returns, it will have us.

A Day and a Night on the Late Big Bone

1

When I was a boy in Steubenville, my grandfather often took me fishing at a secret place he'd marked with a few drips of tar on a rock. To get to it required a slippery descent down a steep bank from the railroad tracks below the foot of Logan Street, followed by a stumbling progress through a waist-high blackberry thicket, then a last, panting lunge through tangled willows to a sandy beach no more than a few yards long. It was a formidable journey for a boy. But it offered, in small, a sense of the river's large past, a sense of wilderness plunged into, of silence and a forgotten solitude—a kind of paradise regained.

There, insulated from the noise and acrid smokes of the city, we fished long afternoons, seated on driftlogs and rocks. The smells—my grandfather's pipe, the river, the ripening bait—were fundamental, pure. Facing the water, surrounded by foliage, the drone and tick of insects, the hot weather chatter of grackles, I imagined us on an island unknown to anyone but ourselves. It was an ancient place, a place of ghosts and tales and adventuresome solitude.

Growing older, I became all the more haunted by that imagined island. The place where my grandfather and I had fished was long gone, drowned beneath the deep pool raised behind the Pike Island Dam, but images of that scene, and its earnest joy and magnificent privacy grew more brilliant in my recollection. At last, one summer free of teaching presented itself, and my friend Jim Quinlivan and I decided to spend a week on the river, to recapture, if possible, something of another similarly suggestive place.

*   *   *

2

The night before we arrived, we camped up Gunpowder Creek, on the Kentucky side. We had to paddle the canoe, an eighteen-and-a-half-footer, a good ways upstream from the mouth before the trailer-crowded, manicured banks gave way to willowed bends and deep reaches where orioles sang from the treetops and bass flashed in the coves. After taking out on a grassy flat shaded by maples and locusts, we made supper and sat on the bank till the fog wandered down the hollow, and a barred owl, high in a crosscreek sycamore, warped its strange call through the darkness.

Forget the florid haggler who, at supper time, roared down the gravel road above us in his red Camaro. Attended by his stern, unspeaking wife and two kids dressed in identical orange shorts and t-shirts, he claimed ownership of the land we'd made camp on. Forget his peevish reluctance to allow us our adventure despite our guarantee to leave the place cleaner by far than we'd found it. And forget the good old boys who came later, at two or three in the morning, flashing the lights of their pickup, whooping and cursing till we grabbed knives from our packs in the tent and lay sweating an hour after. Forget the intrusions, the noises, the upsets ashore. Remember the call of the barred owl, and the trill of crickets in the reeds, and the gauzy light of the morning. Remember Big Bone Island, where we got to.

Two days before, when Jim and I put in at Shawnee Lookout, up from the mouth of the Great Miami, we'd had in mind a leisurely tour of the towns and islands between Cincinnati and Madison, Indiana. Of the former there were many: Aurora and Rising Sun, Rabbit Hash and Patriot, Vevay, Ghent and Milton. But as for islands, there were only two: Laughery and Big Bone. Though the river towns attracted us, and though we envisioned lazy afternoons spent exploring muddy waterfronts and drinking beer with the locals on the banks and levees, deep inside us there dwelled a steady hunger for the islands.

We'd scouted Laughery ahead of time. Several weeks earlier, standing in the late afternoon shade of sycamores and cottonwoods in a trailer camp at the mouth of Island Branch Creek, a few miles downstream of Aurora, Indiana, we'd gazed out across the channel at Laughery, silvery gray in the haze, and dreamed of the silence and peace to be found among its distant groves. There, we imagined, history stood still, and the island's untrammeled beaches, strewn with shell-bits and drift, might be as they were in the old days, when only passing parties of Shawnees stopped to fish or dig mussels in the bars. For we were out to gather some past, to steep ourselves in the slow pace of another time, a time made of natural days and natural nights on the river. We felt that the islands were where we could find it.

We made Laughery in the late afternoon of August 15. Paddling nearly half its length before we found a landing place, we took out on a shady beach stretching a dozen yards between clumps of overhanging willows. The channel lay on the far side of the island, so our afternoon and early evening were disturbed only by a handful of waterskiers flashing by behind the deep-hulled whalers whose sudden, high bow waves, we had learned, were more dangerous to canoeists than the wakes of the most powerful tows.

Within the trees that lined its shore, Laughery enclosed, in part, a narrow meadow where high ironweeds, Queen Anne's Lace, patches of burdock and blackberries grew thick. Hundreds of white cabbage butterflies fluttered and lit on damp spots beneath the vegetation. When Jim and I walked through it, clouds of flies, wasps, and glittering beetles buzzed and hummed around us.

Later, we found abandoned camps up and down the island's length — muddy wooden picnic tables, their legs set in concrete so they wouldn't wash away, peeled locust poles set up for hanging tarps from, even an old metal porch glider, its cushions split, its iron scalded with rust. But all these reminders of the present faded when evening came and twilight softened on the meadow and the shore. We sat among the willows on the bank, imagining the place a hundred, two hundred years ago.

As the last light dimmed, we fished from a small clearing just upstream from our camp. The river gradually darkened from its sunset green to a night-dark indigo. In the willows, the katydids grew more insistent; a few late crows cawed above the farmlands on the Indiana shore; a mockingbird warbled and trilled high in a snag behind us. But as the unlit, lonely night of the past began to descend in earnest, as the ghosts of fog started to rise up from the river and their pleasant haunting to overcome us, the troubled murmuring of a distant engine came against us, grew, and took unnatural shape.

An awkward, snub-nosed houseboat — little more than a trailer on a barge — drifted past, just yards from our rod-tips. A fellow in a bright t-shirt emblazoned with the slogan "Shad Busters" leaped ashore from its stern. After hasty greetings, during which Jim and I struggled unwillingly up from the still depths of our solitude, we learned that our visitor was a college biologist, come down the Wabash River from Depauw University. He and his mates were in the temporary employ of a regional power company. Their project involved conducting population surveys of fish in the Ohio below the Great Miami.

"They use our findings in legal actions taken against them," he said, lighting his pipe. "Don't ask me exactly how."

Jim inquired about their methods, how they counted the fish, how big their nets were.

"Oh, no," the visitor answered. "We don't use nets. We've got a generator aboard. We send an electrical charge through the water. All the fish in the area are stunned, and they float to the surface. We count them by species then move on. We keep very precise records."

"Are the fish killed?" Jim asked.

"Hardly at all. Some of the smaller ones, sometimes."

"I see. So what you do is kill more fish to find out how many fish have been killed."

"Not exactly," the visitor said. "I'm afraid you don't understand."

"Me too," Jim said.

Our chat took a different, less contentious direction after this, and at last faded out, like the ash of our visitor's pipe. The Shad Buster made his way down the island to where the houseboat had put in, and Jim and I fished a while longer, without much hope. But there were other pleasures to enjoy. All up and down the darkened shores of Laughery, tree frogs were singing. Close above us, one would strike his note, then another, further away, would answer, then two or three would pipe at a time. Then there would come a silence, in which the wash of waves ashore would seem momentarily to cease, then the frogs would sing again, weaving solos into duets and duets into great crazy choruses in the dark.

Later, out of beer, we broke our unbreakable rule: never go out on the river under the influence of drink. Feeling our way into the canoe, we drifted out into an absolute and moonless dark until we heard voices to our left and saw the faint light of the houseboat's window. Making a line fast to the Shad Buster's stern, we clambered aboard. Inside, we crammed ourselves into the bunks — equipment covered every other available seat — and made small talk into the morning.

The short paddle back to our camp was an adventure in error and luck. Weary and awash with the Shad Busters' Beaujolais, we fell into the canoe, fumbled up the paddles, and launched ourselves into a darkness as impenetrable as stone. After what seemed a motionless hour, despite our uncoordinated and frantic efforts, I murmured from the stern: "We're going to drift forever. They'll never find the bodies."

Somehow Jim saw the scoured log that marked our beach. Neither of us felt the need to note aloud that although the houseboat had been downstream, we undeniably had come from upstream to our landing. But when we crawled into the tent, zipping the mosquito netting behind us, our bleakest visions, haunted by the sudden ghost-gray presence of the bow of a swift tow bearing down upon us, gradually faded away.

The next morning came clear and quick. Moving as best we could in the shattering morning light that glinted all around us like a broken bottle on the beach, we broke camp. Regaining the current quickly, we shot past the Shad Buster and headed for Gunpowder Creek.

Thus we had camped on our first Ohio River island. We had shreds of a sense of the past to show for it: the solitude, imperfect and brief as it was; the wilderness meadow full of butterflies; the tree frogs' chorus; the night journey back from the houseboat. But something was missing still. Laughery had become too busy with the arrival of the houseboat, too populated and too modern, packed with equipment and cold, scientific voices. What we wanted more than ever was an uninterrupted quiet, a perfect solitude, a complete and primitive simplicity in which we might understand the lonely largeness of the river's past.

Nor did we fully experience those things up Gunpowder, either. True, the night raid of the good old boys had brought us close to something of the terror that early explorers must have felt when Indians descended upon them in the darkness. And later that day, we discovered another clue.

Stopping for lunch at Kirby Rocks, a mile or so below the mouth of Laughery Creek, we explored the shore. Later, sitting on the sand, we found a musket ball lying among the shellbits and gravel. Checking the notes that I had made on our river charts before the trip, we found we were directly across the river from the scene of an Indian battle. On August 24, 1781, Colonel Laughery, or Lochry (for whom the island and the creek were named), landed his party for a rest. They were on their way to meet George Rogers Clark, who was gathering forces at the Falls to attack Detroit. What happened that afternoon was recorded matter-of-factly in the journal of Lt. Isaac Anderson: "Colonel Lochry ordered the boats to land on the Indian shore...we were fired on by a party of Indians from the bank...they killed the colonel."

Once again, then, we felt something of the river's history. Later, standing atop Kirby Rocks, handing the ball back and forth, we imagined the scene, heard the snap of musket fire, saw the puffs of smoke from their powder-pans, saw the white man fall, and the Indians dissolve again into the woods. Piece by piece, shred by shred, we were getting hints of the past, yet the whole picture still eluded us.

But our hope grew stronger as Big Bone Island came within reach. The whole region surrounding it—the famous salt licks whose mam-

moth fossils had so fascinated Thomas Jefferson and drawn early naturalists to it from the East, that had been written about by the Englishman
Thomas DeQuincey, that had been explored by Daniel Boone himself —
was rich with legend and possibility. And we had heard that river pi-
rates had used the island for raids on tradesmen and travelers. Big Bone
was our last great hope for a sense of the past we had come for. Laughery
and Gunpowder Creek, we saw clearly now, had been mere rehearsals;
we meant to go to Big Bone, to linger in its rare and antique airs, and to
draw from it, however indirectly, however imperfectly, the secrets it
conserved. We had come to learn, and to remember, on Big Bone.

3

August 17. Two o'clock, a brilliant Friday afternoon. We paddle
the length of Big Bone Island, taking out on the wide and treeless bar
at its foot. Sitting on the sand, we can see far downriver to the town of
Patriot, Indiana: a church steeple, a few gray and red brick buildings
shimmering in haze. Behind us, the thick trees of the island offer shade,
but this place in the sun is pleasant.

Jim and I look at one another, grin, and nod. The river makes
small waves on the shore; bits of shell tinkle in their wash; a heron
glides low and clear across, far downstream.

I get the paddles from the boat, and a tarp, and rig a sun-shade
where I can sit and work in my journal. Lounging on the sand with
my shoes off, I recopy a passage from a favorite old book, Clark B.
Firestone's *Sycamore Shores*, an account of an earlier river trip. "A
river flows into the past and carries you with it into some forgetful-
ness of present things." Yes.

In the humid warmth, lulled by the soft lap of the water and the
drone of cicadas, tiger beetles, and flies, I drowse. Suddenly I am awakened by Jim's return from his scouting of the island. He has bad news.
At the head of Big Bone, two houseboats have tied off to some trees,
and a party of kids, dogs, and parents is headed our way.

Before I can shake off my nap, the shore is crowded with shouting people. A lanky Irish Setter barks once and hightails into the river,
chasing a stick. A huge, painfully sunburnt woman in a pink bathing
suit stands over our canoe. "Look, George. How cute!" George, a pot-
bellied, bandy-legged man with a black goatee, takes a slug from his
bottle of Calvert's, frowns, and turns toward us. "If they had a motor,
it'd go better. They'll wind up getting killed. Can't go on this river
without no motor."

Two kids with inner tubes run past us into the water. The bar
we're on extends twenty or thirty yards downstream off the end of

the island; it's an ideal swimming place. Before long, Jim and I are surrounded by a dozen people busily setting up lawn chairs and tables with bright plastic umbrellas over them. Somewhere up the island, fireworks crackle in the trees. Dogs bark, children yell, and from a fancy radio with a ten-foot antenna, propped up in the sand a yard from our canoe, Frank Sinatra, backed by horns and strings, croons sweetly out over the river.

Jim and I wander back and forth along the beach. Three more houseboats arrive, tying off on bending trees with heavy knotted cables. Another group comes down the beach towards us. Angrily, I rip the tarp off the paddles, and a small Pekingese, yapping, appears out of nowhere and squats in the center of it and urinates.

Jim opens a beer, raises it high to the crowd, and says, "Welcome to the past."

Later we pack our gear and paddle around to the Kentucky side of the island. There, the trees and brush at the water line discourage the bigger boats' landing, and we regain a little peace, though we have to pitch our tent on a sloping, drift-ridden patch of sand stained with oil from the channel.

Salvaging what we can from the wreckage of the day, we turn again to the journal. From the *Gage Correspondence*, a collection of letters written during the 1766 expedition to chart the Courses of the Ohio, there's this: "There were about one hundred Iroquois and a considerable number of Delawares and Shawnees. . . the entire party with its baggage filling seventeen canoes." But it offers little consolation. Though sheltered from the sight of the houseboaters by the trees, we are not delivered from their noise. Radios blare, and the whine of high-powered runabouts shatters the quiet.

Around six o'clock, the noise lessens as the houseboaters convene in their galleys for supper. Jim and I cook a pot of stew. As we eat, balancing mess pans on our knees, we watch the tows labor up the channel. First to pass is the *Nancy Sturgis*, shoving gasoline barges, and later, the *Lelia C. Schaefer*, shoving coal. The boats are prodigious, spouting blue-gray plumes of exhaust, but their graceful names redeem them. As they disappear upstream, beyond the head of Big Bone, their wash batters the shore at our feet, and the green-gray smell of the river fills the air.

At seven o'clock, sitting on the bar at the foot of the island again, Jim and I philosophize on the perils of searching for the past. We agree that we have been naive, that our quest is probably futile, and that our imaginations, rather than the actual environs, may have to provide us with whatever feeling for the old days we hope to gain. Digging our feet deep into Big Bone's sand, as if to take root and suck history from its heart, we keep a keen downriver watch, entertaining shimmering delusions that some antique scene might yet be spread before us on the gilded water. And in a day full of surprises, another gradually appears.

Jim is the first to notice. Far downriver, in the channel off Patriot, faint as the distant glint off a belt buckle or shell, a regular flashing commences. He squints and points.

"It's a wet log, flashing in the current."

"No. A man in a johnboat rowing across."

"Very like a whale."

But as we trade guesses, it becomes clearer and clearer to us that it is indeed what we have hoped for: a kindred spirit, an adventurer, a fool like us. For as we watch, the flashing resolves itself into a paddle blade, rising and falling in the rhythm we have learned, and soon we make out the canoe itself, black against the background of sunset-flashing water, and at last a figure, seated high, too high, in the stern.

The canoe is a hundred yards downstream, now fifty, and we see that there are two aboard: the stern man perched high, and in the bow, without a paddle, a slighter figure, hunched and attentive, trailing a hand in the water.

Jim and I stand and help pull the canoe ashore. It's a seasoned craft of dull, battered aluminum, loaded heavily with pine boxes bound with half-inch hemp. Its stern is covered with a sloping makeshift deck, from which the paddler, a boy of seventeen or eighteen, nimbly leaps. In the bow is a slight, sandy-haired boy of thirteen. As he steps out, he thanks us for our help. The other splashes out of the river and shakes our hands. He has a powerful grip.

"Name's John," he says. "This here's my brother Frankie."

Here at last is a character from another time, from the past we have been seeking. Sunburnt, his reddish-blond eyebrows nearly invisible, he has a pair of dark blue, almost purple eyes, full of orneriness. He wears a sleeveless buckskin shirt over a pair of shorts cut from vintage trousers that hang as loosely as potato sacks on his thighs. A piece of rope holds them up. He wears no shoes. The tops of his feet are sunburnt and peeling. He motions to his brother, and they unload.

"This here's the kitchen," Frankie says with a grin as they pile three boxes on the sand. "And this here's our other stuff."

Their gear ashore, John unties one of the boxes and pulls a leather pouch out. Carefully unfolding it, he reveals a long red clay pipe and a flat can of coarse tobacco. Intently, with the steadiness and concentration of a person for whom life is a series of simple right-nows, he packs the bowl full, takes a match from his shirt pocket, strikes it on the zipper of his shorts, and squats on the sand with his back to us, facing downriver. Shortly, he is sending out thick and fragrant clouds of bittersweet smoke.

During his brother's ritual, Frankie is smiling up at us, curious and excited. Later he will show us one of his school books that contains an engraving of Clark's Army gathered at the Falls. Now, he scratches his feet in the sand. Jim and I smile at him. Then John stands and taps the bowl of his pipe against the canoe. He turns to us and says, "If you fellas haven't eaten yet, we got plenty for everybody."

Within moments, it seems, dark falls. Upstream, the yellow lights of the houseboats patch the water, then one by one go out. Behind us, in the woods of Big Bone, over the pleasant drone of John's stories about the paddlefish he and his brother saw on the shore below the Markland Dam, and the time he fell out of the canoe at night in the middle of a fog bank, June bugs buzz in the brush, frogs trill in the willows, and now and then a big carp splashes out in the channel.

Later, supper and stories done, and Frankie's fire keeping the mosquitoes at bay, there is little need for talking. John, propped up on one elbow, is reading Conrad, and Jim and I are lying in the sand. The past is as close as the great circle of night that surrounds us. We lie awake a long time, listening as the river, like an old man already turned in, mumbles darkly past, talking in its sleep.

4

I wake early, before dawn, in the tent. Lying still, feeling Big Bone Island firm and whole beneath me, I can see stars through the nylon of the roof, and can hear the muted swash of waves against the shore. Society is far away, an undiscovered country of fevered business, tantalizing confusion. In the drowse of half-waking, it is easy to imagine whatever I desire. The damp air, heavy with the river, fills the tent, and I separate its smells, one by one, and linger over all the images that stream across my mind. Now I smell the rankness of shell middens, six feet deep, downwind from some Mingo Town where thin hounds haunt the camp in darkness, gnashing split bones for a smear of marrow. I catch the scent of shad and catfish, lying in the bottom of a dugout. And now, the sweet smoke of a hickory fire, up some willowed cove, where men who speak a language I've never heard wrap their blankets tight around them and do not wake. Smoke. Fish. The smell of men:

I will arise and go now, go to Innisfree.

My God, I think, *this place. This place.*

Somewhere, years and years behind me, wrapped in fog, a small bird in a thicket on some perfect, unfound island warbles in the darkness, dreaming in my dream.

5

That was Big Bone Island. Jim and I woke the next morning to the sound of the houseboaters' circus, and said farewell to John and Frankie. We snapped a picture of them as we pulled out into the river — Frankie with his arm raised over his head, John with his hands in his pockets, clay pipe in his mouth. In the background, the tiny piece of island we'd camped on, thick with willows and locusts, glowed in morning sunlight. In the course of our search for the past, we'd found many such fragments, vivid and suggestive as potsherds at some ancient ruin, but never the picture entire. We discovered more, downstream, on the levee at Madison, Indiana, where our trip ended with an afternoon of tales among a group of old rivermen, whittling cedar sticks in the shade of cottonwoods and sycamores. But as we drove back to Cincinnati in the late Indiana night, we talked most of Big Bone, and promised ourselves to return, earnestly reassembling the past as best we could, accomplishing our occupation, however fragmentary, of a piece of the Ohio's history.

We waited too long. The next March, paging through the Cincinnati *Post*, I came across a brief story with the headline "Picknickers Need New Bone to Chew On." Astonished, I read it through. Winter floods, ice jams, and most of all, the raising of the pool behind the Markland Dam, had contributed: Big Bone Island, described as long ago as 1766, a place where the ghosts of history still lingered in the late-night silence despite houseboats and Sinatra, was gone.

In his journal, Thoreau reminisces about his ancestor Ulysses, a fellow wanderer. His mind leaps to the pitch pine before his door, and he calls it "symbolical" and "significant" — one of Nature's later designs. "There it is," he cries, "a done tree. Who can mend it?"

So it was with Big Bone Island. Now it is gone. Who can bring it back?

In *The Unsettling Of America*, Wendell Berry writes, "By understanding accurately his proper place in Creation, a man may be made whole." Time too is a part of Creation. And it was time we had journeyed in, trying to understand, earnestly exploring the fragment of time past we had found. Now the place it adhered to, the place that grew its trees and leaves and butterflies and bird nests as parts of time's incarnation, is gone, and with it is gone the chance to study and to learn something of our "proper place." As with the secret shore I fished from with my grandfather years ago, all that's left of Big Bone is a haunting, a swirl and eddy in the river. All the maps and charts, all the tales and journals, are at last faded, placeless memorials.

THE COURSE OF THE RIVER

A few years after the summer Ohio River canoe trip Jim Quinlivan and I took from Cincinnati down to the now-disappeared Big Bone Island, I was standing by the open window of my classroom. I don't remember exactly what was going on—the students were taking a test, maybe, or praying intently for me to be raptured suddenly, gone forever from them. But in the silence I heard it—the long, high, distantly sweet moan of a steam whistle—the Delta Queen's.

A few kids looked up. The whistle sounded again, echoing up and over Columbia Parkway and the East Walnut Hills bluffs and finally sighing its way down Hackberry Street. It was a moment of connection, and I looked around for some sign of acknowledgment in my students' faces. In me, it caused an entire complex of emotions: nostalgia for the life of the river, which Jimmy Scanlon and some others of my own ancestors had pursued in their shantyboat days; the forbidden temptation to run away from it all and hang out along the banks for the rest of my life; the desire to share something of the river and its characters and stories with my students; sorrow that they might never experience the river richly, its lore, its physical presence, its flooded history of beauty and destruction, even though native Ohio River valley dwellers they were, all of them.

Soon the moment passed; the students had not been impressed and went back to their work. In my mind's eye I watched the boat labor upriver past St. Rose's Church, past the East End Water Works, past the mouth of the Little Miami, past Coney Island. Later, as I sat in a shrieking basement lunch room eating sandwiches I'd unwrapped from damp wax paper, I imagined her locking through Meldahl Dam, her calliope shooting steam and melody, awakening the brilliant autumn air.

One of the many great things about teaching where I do is that it is close to the river—close enough to hear the Delta Queen's whistle.

For a reasonably fit class, the banks of the Ohio are a fifteen minute walk away, and it's all downhill from here—cross Madison Road, down Hackberry to William Howard Taft, right at the bottom of the hill onto the precipitous Collins Avenue, cross Eastern at the foot of Collins, and we're there.

We gathered at the river last week. "We" includes our students and Nicki Hewald, third-year teacher, Purcell Marian science department, and me, thirtieth-year teacher, English department. Several months previously, I'd sat across from Nicki, a slender, vivacious former college volleyball player who was enjoying the end of her second year of teaching. In the faculty room over lunch and conversation I got from her a kind of informal resume. I learned that she held dual degrees from John Carroll University, English and science, and some wheels that hadn't turned for quite a while began to revolve again. During a short experiment with quarter-long electives in the early Seventies, I had taught a little course on the river. The boys in the class (Purcell was still an all-male institution back then) collected songs, read some stories and poems. One especially enterprising fellow interviewed the wife of a river captain and made an oral history tape. It had been an enjoyable teaching and learning experience, and I regretted that the experiment had been so brief. I kept my notebook from the course, and every once in a while looked back over it, remembering the boys and our studies. So there in the faculty room, a few other teachers at the lunch table with us, I said to Nicki, "How about us teaching a river class together? You do science, I'll do literature and history and folklore." Nicki was all for it, and since the call for interdisciplinary classes had been sent out by our principal Jan Kennedy, we got the go-ahead. Over the next couple of days, we wrote the course description, and speeded it into the latest course selection catalogue— the crucial step, so that students could sign up for it for the next school year. We did not worry about planning out all the details of the course beforehand; we knew that innovation often requires fluidity and speed, not inflexibility and heavy-handed deliberation.

What a pleasure it was to draft that course description. At the beginning of any enterprise, there is a sense of adventure, an anticipatory delight that, after everything has been in place for a while, wears off and can hardly be recaptured. When Jimmy Quinlivan and I were planning our Ohio River canoe trip in 1976, much pleasure arose from talking about it all winter over beers at Arnold's Bar & Grill downtown, a place that has been in continuous operation since the lag-end of the glory days of steamboating here in this river city, and where I once had an evening-long conversation with Captain Jim Coomer, whose book about his days on the river is a valuable contribution to the literature of the Ohio. Jimmy Quinlivan and I also had followed a course of reading, studying maps, imagining what we might see, building and refining itineraries, their details scribbled on napkins and menus, all the while knowing that the river would not, could not, be put down on paper, and that we would have to wing it and change our minds often during the trip.

Similarly excited, Nicki and I built a list of possible science topics involving several realms: ecology, biology, botany, physics, chemistry, engineering. As for my part of the course, I already had a literature reader, *Down The River*, an anthology of Ohio River Fiction and Poetry, published by Always A River, Inc. here in Cincinnati, and edited by the late University of Cincinnati professor and writer, Dallas Wiebe. I had served on the book's editorial board during the Year Of The River when the National Endowment for the Humanities and all six of the Ohio River states' Arts Councils collaborated on a multifaceted celebration. I was pleased to be able put the book to classroom use. Besides the academic content, we were excited by the prospects of regular field trips, and of doing river-related community service, including water quality monitoring for Green Acres, a private environmental group, and working in various river cleanups as they appeared on the calendar.

So down we went, two teachers, sixteen river rats, including three game young women, Erin Qualters, Alicia Vargas, and Shannon Simpson. Eric Rosemire, a former student at Clark, one of the first Montessori high schools in the country, confided that he knew about a secret beach. We padded through his old school's parking lot off Eastern Avenue, threaded our way on a dirt path through a green tunnel of honeysuckles along the chain-link fence, turned left, and descended a set of hidden concrete steps down to the river.

I do not think this world in all its variety and surprise offers anything much better than a late summer river's banks when it's at normal pool. The scenery is always excellent, water flashing in the sunlight, the wooded opposite shore soft and green, the sweet wash of waves at your feet, and the smell of the river, its funky perfume compounded of mud, fish, rain, oil. For the artist's eye, there are the shards of polished blue and green and frosty white glass, mixed in with the buffs and tans and umbers of sand and gravel, and, more vividly, the pebbles of crushed red brick; for form and mass, there are bigger, older loaves of glacier-fetched granite or sandstone, which I knew as a kid in Steubenville as "river biscuits." In addition to all this, there is the movement, the constant onwarding, of the river itself. Life is motion, it reminds you; life loves movement, change, and is constantly transitioning from chaos to form, from amorphousness to pattern, and then back again. The polymorphous design of things is hardly more apparent anywhere else than at the side of a river: the textures of cottonwood bark, the million flashing and expertly grown cottonwood leaves, all so much alike, the sprawl and dance of willows along the high-water line, the pearly arrays of mussel shells, the heavy installments of stones, even the astonishing assemblages of junk and debris—all are accomplished in intricate detail and abundance, gorging the eyes on complexity, and brought to you, for free, by the forces of nature. Even the ribbony swirls of eddies are a wonder. To one not sleepwalking through life, a river bank, as well as being a sensual smorgasbord and a scavenger's delight, is a theological event.

There's more, too: the river is a great collector and re-distributor, forever leaving wonders along its length for those lucky enough to catch sight of them. On a recent trip upriver to California, Ohio, at the foot of the wistfully named El Dorado street, we found, among other things, the carcass of a beaver—what in the world was it doing there, within humming earshot of the huge I-275 bridge, and less than twenty yards from a low, frowning concrete block building with an Iron Horsemen sign over its door? We also discovered a great rusty square of heavy sheet metal, upon which a few of us assembled an arrangement of stones, driftwood, and bones for some other pilgrim to stumble upon in surprise. It later came back to Purcell Marian with us in an art project, the base for a sculpture by Nick Christen that became, for a season, a part of the Course of The River Collection. You never know what gifts will be presented by the ever-presenting river. During our canoe trip down the Ohio from Shawnee Lookout on the Great Miami in the pre-gambling-boat towns of Aurora and Patriot and Lawrenceburg and finally Madison, from out in the middle, on a high sunny day in August, Jimmy Quinlivan and I had watched a bald eagle, nearly unheard of then in those parts, fly with us, parallel to the shore, for nearly a mile. And on our trip that afternoon, decades later, to the beach behind Clark Montessori, Drew Dempsey and Dane Baumgartner stumbled upon a message in a bottle.

Dear Finder,

My second grade class at Crosby Elementary is learning about oceans. Scientists use messages in bottles to study currents. My name is Marina Annunziata. I am 7 and a half years old. I have a little sister named Kylie. She is five years old. My favorite food is pizza. My favorite color is green. I love animals. Please recycle this bottle.

Sincerely, Marina Annunziata.

What a gift! A child whose name might be ocean — *mar*, or something close to it, linguists tell us, is the Indo-European root for "sea," and provides many Indo-European words, including such English cognates as marine, marsh, and meershaum. Here, along this river whose ultimate destination is the sea, a girl named Marina studies the ocean, and leaves a message for us to stumble upon and wonder over. Here, along this river which is ever-renewing, ever-appearing before us, appears a girl whose last name remembers the annunciation, when the angel told Mary she would bear the son of God — and which would lead, a few months later, to the Epiphany — that revelation of the divine in our own time and space. If such a set of coincidences were set forth in a novel, no one would believe them.

Our educations often overlook the local — as if there could be no such wonders as this annunciation of Marina Annunziata — nothing of interest or significance or historical or geographical importance — in our own place. As if all adventure were always somewhere else, and not at our own doorstep. As if art appeared only in museums — a finished thing, hung on the wall, displayed on pillars of marble in high-ceilinged galleries. As if there were not a thousand occasions of poetry and drawing and photography in every river walk. Marina Annunziata's little note is a reminder that creation is ongoing — *now* — and if we are to be present for the show, we have to keep our eyes and our minds open, and keen. I am continually delighted by the connections that happen in this big small town of Cincinnati — people who know people who know people who know just about anyone you need to know, families interrelated over generations, the same surnames showing up in the honor rolls of high schools for decades. In the upcoming fall elections, no less than five graduates of the high school I teach in are among the candidates for mayor and city council. Two I had in class; the incumbent mayor I missed having in class by three months — he graduated in June of the year I started teaching in August. My wife's mother and father were born and raised here in Cincinnati, and shopped and ate ice cream and went to the movies in establishments within a three-minute walk of where we now live. My pastor back at St. Peter's in Steubenville, Cronan T. Molloy, was a graduate of the old Purcell High School, most certainly sat in rooms I have taught in, and was even a visitor in our present house, half a century before we bought it. You never know: the very word "adventure" means "what is to come" — it's more a question than the name of a sure thing.

There are, I think, slow adventures and quick adventures. Quick adventures are those like the exploits of Odysseus or Beowulf, with climactic moments of intense passion and consequence — will Odysseus survive Poseidon's wrath and make it ashore one more time? Will he outwit the demi-goddess (and overcome what I imagine to be his own ambiguous lingerings as Calypso's love-slave) and escape? Will Beowulf defeat Grendel, or will his short career as hero be snuffed? As metaphors for the kinds of trouble life tests us with, these are fine enough indeed. But I think what I want to call slow adventures may be equally valuable, and perhaps even more indicative of how the universe works, and of our purpose in it.

A slow adventure takes place over the scope of your entire life. It may begin without your even noticing it: a day in flood-time, for example, when you're five, and walking with your grandfather between the rails of the Pennsylvania tracks at the foot of Logan Street in Steubenville, Ohio, near the headwaters of the Ohio, just across from West Virginia. The river is so high you're sloshing through it, stepping from tie to tie. Then, just ahead of you, a carp, a great golden one, is slapping and thrashing, trying to escape the water between the rails. It flips over into the flood, and is gone. Part of yourself, attached instantaneously in that shared moment of vision, voyages the river with it, in the fluency of dream, all the rest of your life.

But you do not know that on that day, something of your life began to unfold, to effloresce outward, and that it would involve the rest of your years to pursue it and to explore its meaning. It would send you into the river in a small narrow boat, downstream, paddling hard through storms and dark. It would bring you into a small river town in southern Indiana, on the day that Elvis Presley died, and teach you something about American culture through the tears of the waitresses in the little diner where you ordered lunch. It would bring you into contact with other wanderers in time and space along its banks: with Harlan Hubbard and Reuben Gold Thwaites and Clark B. Firestone and the extravagant Constantine Rafinesque; with John James Audubon and Micajah Harpe and Tim Russell and John Knoepfle, and all the other warriors, heroes, poets, scamps, scoundrels and plain good men hanging out during, or after, or just before the battle of life in the wine-bottled willows where they cook their driftwood-smoked hashes and catfish stews and wait to see what's going to happen, or not happen, next.

The river is one of those slow adventures. Its influence is gradual, subtle, unconscious. Its first advances into the spirit are like the basement seeps in houses too close to the water, houses that are adventures themselves, erected in hope one season but liable to being swept utterly away in the next. As the river comes up into those dwellings, so it rises in the house of the spirit. Sometime later, it may rise in flood, and a book you've read, or a day you've spent along its shores, or a foray you've made to the river museum in Marietta, brings it brimming over into consciousness: suddenly you know what it is you are doing. You are answering the river's call to life. It presents you with a hundred potential stories, an abundance of settings, settings as exotic as tiny islands and as mundane as gob heaps steaming on its banks. It is ever-unreeling, like that famously lost panorama, painted on a canvas an entire mile long, wrapped carefully around upright drums and unrolled before rapt audiences as a kind of early motion picture. Depicting the entire Mississippi and Missouri River banks, it was created by George Banvard, an Ohio River boy from Louisville, and was exhibited, reports claim, "all over the civilized world."

Teaching, of course, is another slow adventure. The patient instilling of habits—using a dictionary when reading, proofreading an essay or poem carefully, rereading and noodling difficult passages until they make sense, casting and recasting a sentence until it sings—none of these comes quickly. There is no equivalent in the classroom of a last-minute winning shot in a soccer match, so the kinds of gratification are more subtle, more slow. But they do come—students do respond, as beans and potatoes do, to cultivation. I use the metaphor deliberately, if a bit humorously. It was Wendell Berry who said that a community's most important commodity is the minds of its students, and that the cultivation of those minds is of supreme importance to a nation. But this kind of work takes time, and the gratifications are gradual, like the slow rises and falls of a summer river, like the frosty ripening of persimmons.

The Course of the River has been, like its subject, unpredictable, sometimes difficult. The various levels of enthusiasm and commitment of the students have made our job more challenging than in some other classes; the absolute necessity of getting our students out on field trips is often unwieldy—our short school bus dedicated to field trips is pretty much crammed when we all climb aboard. The readings in both science and literature are often demanding, taking some of our students to the limits of their comprehension. Finally, there is one of the most difficult frustrations that teachers deal with—the difference between the level of our own hopes and expectations, and the reality of our students' commitment and achievement. But through it all, there is one affirming constant: the river remains, ever hauling the past before us for study and reflection, literally presenting us with the present, and ever promising the future, just downstream.

Far below our observation post on the bluffs overlooking the river at the end of Ingleside Avenue, four blocks from school, we can see, set on concrete blocks and almost completely hidden by a grove of cottonwoods, an old boat, maybe twenty or twenty-five feet long, wooden, with a windowed cabin and the name *Rock And Roll* painted on its peeling bows. Nicki and I and our students have gazed at it during each visit, imagining fixing it up, dropping a new engine into it, and launching forth on river voyages daily.

It might happen. But even if it never does, the idea itself is the source of a calm delight, as the anticipation of any desired journey is delightful, almost as good as the trip itself. The river calls, in the haunting whistle of an old-time steamboat, in the lilt of its summer green waves ashore, in a note or a poem left by one of its thousand pilgrims. And though we may travel it mostly in the imagination, it nevertheless is a place inhabited by the real, whose beauties and marvels still awaken and refresh the mind that lingers for an hour, or an afternoon, or the best part of a lifetime, as I have, beside it.

BOX TURTLE

I had three of them one summer, a quarter-dozen lumberers. They were all Monroe County turtles, kin to the rain-walkers we'd see trudging Greenbrier in wet weather, crossing the road to whatever richer pastures or riper berry-patches lay down the other side of the ridge. Their purposefulness was impressive, and we'd stop either to carry them over to the brush along the gravel, or we'd plunk them in the car, where they'd take refuge under the back seat, hindmost out, and where later they'd hiss, pull in, and grow stubbornly heavy when we tried to get them out of there and turn them loose near the trailer on the knob in our adopted neck of the woods. And some, like the three I remember, we'd take the ninety miles home to keep for the summer in the yard, not out of some wicked acquisitiveness, I hope, but out of a desire to have Greenbrier neighbors up there in Steubenville.

Watching one we helped off the road and into the lilies along the way in the country was like watching a ship set out on a long and mysterious journey. There was something of the same nostalgia, the same mixed desire and sorrow that attends all adventurous leave-takings, even by the noble unnamed. Like the coracle of the Welsh and Irish, the box turtle seems a bit unseaworthy, a vehicle too prosaic, too clunky, for the demanding passage it pursues. We'd often come upon one overturned in the road, spun by the glancing tire of the local oil tanker or milk truck, clamped slightly shut, and, we imagined, holding its breath until the world got right again.

As a boy, I had known of box turtles kept tethered on strings in back yards. One end of the string would be tied to a stake, the other knotted through holes drilled in the rims of their carapaces. There they would be, ceaselessly tugging, digging up little divots of turf with their implacable claws. The sight depressed me. At our house, we kept them penned in a relatively spacious enclosure of chicken wire whose perimeter was buried six inches in the ground. That way, they had at least some elbow room, and they couldn't dig out. Box turtles are, like many low-slung animals, expert excavators. They know their ground.

One summer, after a trip to the country, my father brought a couple to Madisonville for our boys, and so extended the ritual into the next generation. I built an extension onto one of the garden's raised beds, installed a shallow pottery bowl in the center for water, and plopped the pair in. From the beginning, it was clear that they were individuals; each had its own personality. The female was not to be penned; within two days, she was gone. Surly and distrustful—unspoiled—she had, I figured, simply clambered up the back of the male, then stretched and heaved herself over the board and out.

The male, on the other hand, showed signs of domesticity. He had not shut himself in when Patrick and Brendan picked him up for the first time, nor did he shy, retreat, and hiss whenever someone walked by the pen. Maybe he'd been another's pet, snatched from a ditch a year or two before by some boy in the country, and had been dandled and fed until tamed. Within three weeks at our place, he actually perked up when humans were near, and by the end of the summer, he'd respond to my younger son Brendan's squeal by crawling up from his shaded hole, head and neck extended, with something of a lap dog's attitude of anticipation.

He ate roughly sixty slugs, all of them champions, three-inchers at least, twenty nightcrawlers, a couple of apples, and a pound or two of cherry tomatoes. That's what we fed him—what he scrounged on his own, I cannot say. But he was healthy; often we'd see his substantial droppings in the pen and be satisfied that all was well. When the serious heat began, and the drought deepened into July, we rigged a board over one end where he could rest in the shade all day, and that's when he dug out his cellar, a fist-sized depression that he fit exactly into, like a stone.

But I worried about the other one. There had been no rain to speak of for six weeks; the front lawn was a crisp of dust and stems; the street beyond the driveway gate was delirious with summer traffic. There are a hundred feral cats in the neighborhood, several felonious dogs, and even a family of raccoons, the patriarch of which I'd surprised on the back porch bird feeder one early autumn morning just after moving here. I hoped that neither Patrick nor Brendan would find the turtle smashed into the pavement, dead and gnawed in the hostas, or rolled stiff against the fence, stinking and ashiver with ants and maggots.

Not to worry.

One afternoon in late August I stepped out back for a moment, and glancing down the sidewalk toward the back gate, I saw her.

Head and neck straining forward, she presented the classic profile of the box turtle in full — if such a word is allowable in turtle lore — *gallop*. She was traversing the sidewalk, intent on the southwest corner of the yard where a huge spirea spreads beneath a twenty-foot pussy willow. There are lots of snails in the leaf-littered dampness beneath them and I suppose she had caught a promising scent on the wind.

Stupidly, I put her back in the garden pen with the other, and lavished slugs and tomatoes on the both all afternoon. The next morning, she was gone again.

And as I thought about her, and especially about her invisible presence all through the worst of the drought, I grew more and more amazed. There is no water in the yard save for the bird bath, three feet above the ground. Yet this turtle had actually flourished — she was still spunky and wild — and this through the most dangerous summer in years. Displaced 250 miles from her native upland territory in the center of Wayne National Forest, she had somehow adapted to this flat and smoggy place of lawn mowers, school buses, and sewer assessments. Certainly our yard supports plenty of cover for a turtle, and the compost pile spontaneously generates every fortnight a gallon of slugs and earwigs and crickets, and volunteer cherry tomatoes spring up wherever compost has been dug in to feed sunflowers or clematis along the fence. Yet the fact of her thriving on an urban lot, during such hard weather, was something to ponder.

When I was eight or nine, my father brought home a tiny snapping turtle, hardly larger than a half-dollar. Its plastron was still marked with the scar where its yolk-sac had been attached; it couldn't have been more than a few weeks old. I kept it in the shed, beside my snakes, in a high square box half filled with sand, a small pie pan filled with water to one side. I fed it gobbets of raw hamburger, pieces of boiled egg, live redworms and whatever else I thought it might eat, and the summer passed. Then a hard frost struck suddenly in October. I'd already released the snakes, but I had overlooked the snapper. Taking the box down from the cabinet where it sat, I saw that it was empty. I mourned guiltily, and then as winter set in, forgot about it.

The next spring, I was moving things around in the shed, and knocked the box over. There, moving sluggishly, still alive in the pile of spilled sand, was the snapper. Dug in, it had survived the winter. I did not know what to think, how to square its plain toughness with what I, mufflered, mittened, well-fed and warm through that cold season, had come to know about life. I recall how my wonder over the turtle gave way to a kind of wary distrust, a superstitious dread. The world and its wild things was stranger than I had ever thought: it spooked me.

And at the same time it fascinated me. What was this place I lived in, this neighborhood of sycamores and strip mines, this Ohio, this baffling, snapping turtle world? What utterly other beings dwelled in it, hidden just below or just beyond my weak eyes? I began, literally, to crawl about, hunkering down beside creeks I'd formerly leaped across, burying coffee cans with their openings flush with the ground to trap beetles in, clambering rockfaces in mingled hope and fear of finding a copperhead or rattler. There were secrets out there, and I wanted in on them; I wanted to participate in the details of a sowbug's day, I wanted to find a salamander's eggs. I wanted to live, if it were only possible, like a wren or field mouse or cricket.

Strange and wonderful furnace, a child's imagination. In it burns the fuel of wonders and possibilities rich and strange, before education and that smothering monster, sophistication, damp it and reduce its heat. Silly and superficial textbooks begin to take the place of visions; facts crowd out the dreams; curricula pluck us out of field and thicket, out of the rich and open solitude of the day. The further we go in school, too often, the more distant we travel from our own home place.

We end up either knowing too much, or too little. We become doctors unaware of ethics, economists ignorant of weather or disease, citizens blind to history. We become grotesque parodies of box turtles. When the rumbling thunder of a new idea (or even worse, an old idea that's still as true as ever) races by, we are spun haplessly butt-over-toenails aside. We clamp ourselves shut until the hassle blows over, or seems to, or until the election is won, or the revolution lost. And when the all-clear sounds, we take off again, headed for the old familiar corner of the world where we can eat our plain meals, sleep our plain sleep, and be untroubled by troubling dreams. Or are we simply plucked up by forces we don't understand, only to find ourselves plopped down again somewhere else, strangers in a strange land? Do we run, or do we cope, learn, adapt? Or do we give up?

"Parodies," I said. For the box turtle, the genuine article, is more at home, more intimately attuned to its world than the most profound of human naturalists. Certainly it doesn't know where it is in any human sense, but neither do many of us really know where we are, beyond the superficial data of careers and addresses and zip codes, or beyond the secret treasure maps that tempt us deeper and deeper into specialties that reward us with kind of gilded idiocy. But to get inside, to imagine our ways into the head—and into the world—of a common box turtle, might be a thing to desire. Or to fear. Whichever, it would be an adventure.

And it is that kind of adventure that I now realize my earnest occupations with, and meditations upon, box turtles must be based. I have learned something about my immediate neighborhood, my yard, the Earth House Hold, that we all are a part of here. It is important knowledge. The place is apparently healthy, unpolluted enough (and far enough away, I hope, from the horrors of the local superfund site known as Fernald Feed Materials), to actually support a wild turtle. Like the miner's canary, whose continuing health was a sign that the air in the pit was good, and like the praying mantis that lords it over the basil patch all summer, and like the butterfly larvae that feed each season on the fennel I plant just for them, even like the slugs that burgeon and multiply in the secret corners of the garden, or in the niches of our old rubble-filled cistern, the box turtle in its wildness and survival, in its tough and resistant otherness, is a warrant, an assurance. The health it implies does not show up in the equity I have in the value of the house; it shows up in the spiritual equity that accrues in our dwelling together here. There is more than the physical in the nature of a healthy household. There is wealth that cannot be measured in dollars. The box turtle, after its fashion, and I and my family, after ours, gather it in, and are glad.

GREAT WINDS

I don't know whether it's an inheritance from the Depression-era generation that brought me up, or an innate disposition toward pessimism, or some Calvinist expectation of doom seeping past my Catholic resurrectionist upbringing, but I often can imagine much more vividly the darker sides of things than I can imagine heavenly delight. Terror, Dread, Foreboding: these are spiritual cousins of mine, and sometimes they occupy a room so close by that I can hear their groans and curses under the routine murmur of the day. Their presence in my life intensified after I became a father; I tended to over-protect my toddler sons because I could imagine the worst scenarios for the most benign of circumstances. If Patrick were playing in the yard, I'd be visited by sudden fears of huge branches plunging from the ash tree and striking him dead. If Brendan were coasting his bike down the driveway, I'd be certain that he would fall, bust his noggin, and be bound to a wheelchair the rest of his days. In my seventy and more years now, I have begun to learn how to control this psychological quirk, but it has never gone away completely, and I can still suffer flashes of near-panic, most often translated into anger, over minus-cule events.

My mother had a habit of collecting disaster. She wrapped herself in stories of death, disease, and doom as others wrap themselves in a comforting quilt. It was one of her most earnest occupations, and in a way it sustained her through life, as if misfortune were a vitamin. Now it's true that my mother had every reason to dwell on darkness; her own grandfather was killed in the act of tossing his child, my mother's mother, to safety at the last moment as he was run down by a train. My mother's brother, the son of that tossed infant, died in his early twenties of tuberculosis; his little sister, my mother, was devastated. My mother's only sister, a half-sister, really, since that tossed infant's first husband eventually did die on the railroad and was succeeded by Henry Heights, my mother's father — my mother's half-sister then, Betty, dearer to her than could be counted, died instantly, along with her daughter Linda Lee, my mother's favorite niece, in a brutal head-on car crash outside of Steubenville while returning from the rehearsal for Linda Lee's daughter Tracy's wedding, which was to take place the next weekend. The wedding gown was retrieved unharmed from the trunk of the demolished car — and the ceremony, mixing grief with joy, went on.

Whenever I went home from college, or visited later, one of the central themes of my mother's talk would be trouble: who had fallen ill, which of my high school classmates had died, who shipped over to Vietnam, whose son was in jail or stricken with a fatal disease, which great auntie or uncle was probably going to pass away next.

If there had been a calendar of her heart, each month would have had blacked-in days remembering Brud her brother's death, or her father's death, or J.C. Hague's death, or Grandma Heights's death, or the day my father died, or the day my mother herself underwent a huge chemotherapy dose and almost died herself, and so on, until hardly any light would be left in the year. But rather than depressing my mother, this set of bleak anniversaries gave some sort of order to her life. She tended these memorials as one would tend a family graveyard — one of those up on a hill somewhere, off a bit from the homestead, with a great ancient oak growing in the middle of it, and all surrounded by a wrought-iron fence. My mother would putter in that little place of the heart almost daily, and it seemed somehow to please her.

So maybe it's to be expected that I am often tempted, when people ask me, "How are you?" to answer, "I'm not sure" or "Hell if I know," or "Terrible, but it'll pass." Often I feel like Melville's Ishmael before he took that great cathartic voyage with Ahab; when I see a funeral procession I want to take up my place in it; I want to knock the caps off hipsters passing on the street.

A person with a permanently sour disposition, though, will not get much accomplished in the lines of work I've come to pursue. I had better know how to laugh and how to find optimism when plunged into the welter of human nature my work as a teacher and husband and father and urban neighbor involves. And truly, by trusting in some force greater than I have any control over, I can encourage people whose lives may be more intricately dangerous and dark than Hamlet's, or as apparently purposeless and directionless as Gogo's and Didi's in *Waiting For Godot*.

I say all this by way of suggesting it's counter to my nature and nurture to be optimistic, yet I find myself, in my official capacities as teacher and mentor and gardener and neighbor and colleague, more and more behaving as if all will be well—or at least as if all that *is*, is well, even if in the short-term it looks disastrous. I know that the world is tricky and strange; I know the Holocaust and Pol Pot and mad cow disease actually inhabit history; I know too that evil has a camp in my heart as well as whatever good intentions I invite to bivouac there.

So when I was asked by some students to speak at the Communion Breakfast part-way through the last week of their senior year's events, a week loaded with pressing issues and tensions of all sorts, and, underlying it all, an understandable if not articulated fear of the future, I sat down to think about all this pessimism business. I wanted to try to say something encouraging and helpful without sugar-coating the world and its ways, and to affirm the better part of myself, and to encourage myself, by encouraging my students.

Here's what I said:

"I want to talk to you briefly this morning about one word. It is a word handed down to us from the old language of the Catholic religion, from the Roman tongue that the Mass was celebrated in since roughly the Fourth Century A.D. It is a concept embraced by the early great teachers of the Church, derived from a compound of two Latin words, one of which means 'completely' and the other of which means 'glad.' Glad completely. Completely glad. The word is 'exhilaration.'

"Though we will hear, and already have heard, talk of the journey we are about to finish, and of the new and larger and more difficult journey we are about to embark on, we rarely hear straight talk about how hard school has been, and how hard college or job or the military or motherhood or fatherhood will be. Many of us, still reeling or still-to-be-reeling from final exams and Exhibitions, Life Philosophies, graduation details, last-minute reviews, proficiency test hassles, and a hundred other pressures and complications, are limping along, a bit wounded, a bit worn out, maybe even a bit discouraged. Our spirits are down, but we can't put our finger on what the problem might be. As they say in some parts of the country where horses are still understood, we've been rode hard and put up wet. Uncomfortable. Unsettled. We don't know exactly how to feel. Shiveringly unclear.

"And it hurts us. The glitter and promise of the future is clouded over by the murky mess of this ending that is not ended yet; it is haunted by an uncertain dimness of something—who knows what—not yet arrived. We are in a kind of limbo, neither here nor there, neither finished with this nor started with the next.

"It's a strange place in life.

"But it is an important place. It is the threshold, the place where we are gathering ourselves, getting ready to step over, preparing to go through. It is a holy place, charged with potential energy. Our whole life is a holy place, but this in-between place, this place that is neither here nor there, now nor then, past nor future, is especially holy.

"For what can be sown in us in this preparation ground, this temporary waiting place — is exhilaration. Gladness complete. Exhilaration that will lift us off our feet and sweep us into greatness, if we welcome it, if we face it and meet it with courage. It is the exhilaration that comes from realizing we are not the center of things; that the world is larger than we ever imagined, larger even than the stunningly beautiful pictures from the Hubble telescope have captured, larger than the vast star-making cauldrons of the cosmos. It is larger than the deaths at Columbine High School; it is larger than the recent hurricanes in our part of the world, it is larger than the huge genius of Michelangelo and the bank roll of Michael Jordan. And its largeness is grand and awesome — exhilarating, in a word — and the exhilaration sweeps over us when we realize, when we believe, when we accept, that we have a place in its grandness and its awe. We have a place there. There is a room prepared in it for us.

"Amazing. We will become history. We will be what the human world is for the next fifty or seventy years.

"We *will* be, we will *be*.

"So exhilaration is one of the names of God. Exhilaration is one of the names for the best kind of learning, where discovery and surprise are still alive, where little is handed to us and much may seem hidden, but wonderfully so, excitingly so — and the finding of which is exhilarating. Exhilaration is the name for the best state of living. Though we may not be able to achieve it every moment, every day, still, it is the fuel of all that is good, the center of all that happens that has potential for good. Gladness complete. Complete gladness. It was exhilaration that carried Mother Theresa smiling through Calcutta's bleakest slums. It was exhilaration, a grand dark awesome exhilaration, that shook Leo Szilard, the physicist who first realized that atomic fission could be induced, and that it could lead to a bomb. It was exhilaration that dictated to Shakespeare the words that became *Hamlet*. It was exhilaration that raised the arm of Moses and parted the Red Sea.

" 'Sometimes I go about pitying myself,' says an exhilarating passage I found recently. 'Sometimes I go about pitying myself, and all the time I am being carried on great winds across the sky.' Discard pity. Find exhilaration. Gladness complete. The sky it means to carry you across is your life. And right now, the winds that will carry you are rising."

Many years ago, noting this phenomenon as I was working on some of the essays that became my first prose book, I wrote in my journal: "Sometimes my writing is smarter than I am." I meant that in the process of making words make sense, I revise and straighten out my own thinking. Really, writing often takes me to the healthier, the tougher places in myself; it develops and exercises both sense and sensibility; it clarifies what might have looked bleak and monstrous from the vantage point of unarticulated sloppy thinking and feeling. It invites me to accomplish difficult but rewarding interior work that I might not otherwise do. It makes me a steward of the garden of my own mind and spirit. It is the healthiest addiction — and the most earnest occupation — I have.

STILL LIFE WITH SHOVEL

In the heap of rubble next to our garage—rubble that was considerable when we moved here—I have discovered hundreds of strange items, relics of the lives of unknown predecessors on the land our house occupies. At first, the pile was an above-ground midden of old bedsprings, broken crockery, rough-sawn lumber. I had to remove a section of chain-link fence to even begin reducing it, and dug out the huge bolus of concrete that the corner post was set in. Then I battered my shovel blade against a deposit of fist-sized stones: coarse gravel someone—or some garbled upchucking of geology—had deposited there who knows how many years ago. Once the fence was down, I hauled away two pickup trucks of scabbed iron, wood, refrigerator parts, bones, rocks and bushels of flaking orange chips of spalled brick.

Things turned interesting then. I had gotten to ground level, and any further removal required my digging down along the garage, opening a trench like an archaeologist's at some ancient site. The first treasure I uncovered was a clutch of antique marbles: they lay in the ground like smudged eggs in a nest, and at first I was reluctant to disturb them, half-entertaining the notion that they were about to hatch. They blocked my clean-up, though, and I scooped them out of the ground and carried them across the driveway to the garden faucet where I washed them off. Wet, they glistened pertly, though I noticed with interest the nicks and scratches that marked them, as if during their stay in the earth they had not rested motionless but had been rattled and cracked and shunted about by obscure subterranean heavings.

Once the marbles were saved, I went at my removal with renewed vigor: metal pipes came up from their graves like resurrected arbors; huge boards—once the girders of what I suspect was the original garage or carriage house—revived as well. They were incredibly heavy with moisture, but after a day or so in the sun they simply collapsed into musty splinters, as if their souls had been dampness and drying out had swiftly bedeviled them to dust.

One day, my shovel struck metal that rang like a bell. It was a small thing like an overturned cup, and was attached to a rusty length of metal as curved as the antler of a deer.

The antler was really the handlebar of a bicycle — a Schwinn, I was later to learn — which had been buried upright, pushed down into a trench and covered up still standing. The rubber of its tires was rotten and came away in great shabby lengths as I pulled. From the end of my driveway it must have looked as if I were harvesting adders from the darkness.

A man I know, who lives in the country 50 miles from the nearest criminal, buries all his money. During the late Twenties, he cashed his paper in for gold and silver and sealed it all up in wooden nail kegs. These he planted at random in the pasture behind his house, relying on memory to find the bank when he needed it. The last time I saw him, the money was still there, but his mind had been assaulted by a series of strokes. He sat with a blanket over his knees on the back porch, staring out over a lost El Dorado, his fingers counting slowly a fortune in phantom coin, an intangible mist of dream-gold, gone.

Time, to revive the old saying, is a robber. It takes our parents, our lovers, our children, our own penny-bright youth. But it's a hoarder as well, and that grubby vice partially redeems it. Armed with nothing but a shovel, fueled by a weekend's long-delayed chore, we blunder into its vault, and like a Schliemann agog, face the mystery of the past.

I think of the child whose Schwinn that was, of the cool air of an October evening half a century ago, when the bike perhaps lost both its rider and speed at once, and became a strange still life in the earth. Standing again in my sweat among roots and shards, I am chilled by its duplicate meanings: *Here we are*, the wrecked bike and the cluttered soil mutely witness. And here, too soon, I must be.

WINTERING OVER

The winter solstice has long ago come and gone. Days lengthen, but in the lag of climate, grow no warmer. During the occasional thaw in late February, we worry that the forsythia will awaken its delicate blooms and be wasted by another Arctic blow. Here and there in the border garden, bulbs hurried in too shallowly and too late last fall heave from the soil, their crowns blackening. The goldfinches on the thistle feeder still wear a winter dinge, their feathers not yet worn enough to blaze up in summer's breeding plumage.

T. S. Eliot's poem "The Waste Land" originally began, "February is the cruelest month." The revision that made it April, though more pleasing to the ear, is perhaps less true. For there is an ugliness to February that lasts grimly, some years, into March. Rotten leaves thaw and stink beside the walk; the compost pile along the garage goes alternately juicy with thaw then sharp and hard again with frost; the roof gutters' old scars open to leak a black and dismal brew. The sooty and polluted snows along the streets take the shapes of corpses lying face-down in the alkaline bitters of their own fluids. The heart needs the promise of love that St. Valentine's Day is. Without it, we would all go crazy with a desperate grief this time of year.

Luck will out, though: luck and the world and its lives. For, this frigid morning, we watch the sparrows.

The full meaning of sparrows is most dramatically manifest in these sorrowful end-season days. During the green explosions of summer, against the foliage of our backyard maples and mulberries and ash trees, sparrows are dusky nonentities, itinerant chatterers in garage eaves and ivy thickets. The eye is drawn to flashier tribes: loud grackles with their purple helmets, their iridescent feathering and yellow-rimmed eyes. Saffron finches bob across the garden toward the grassy hillsides below the old cemetery, and there are the quieter ash-of-rose subtleties of the mourning doves down from the graveled wastes along the railroad.

But when the leaves have fallen, and snow has dusted the tough kale stubs of the winter garden, the sparrows come to the fore. Contentious as congressmen, they crowd the feeder hung from the porch, and we are reminded that despite the frost and drifts, there remains in winter a vitality, a vitality which daily observed might help sustain us through the bleakness of the months.

Even more powerful a reminder of life is the sight of a flock among dead leaves. In a mysterious synchronicity, sometimes a dozen birds will freeze at once for a moment, confounding the eye's efforts to pick them out from their background of buff and rust and tan. But then they move again, and it is as if the leaves have come alive, animated with some superb notion to fly.

This restless durability is bracing. In the static weeks of cold and darkness, sparrows exist like embers deep in Nature's banked fire. The coldest northerly blast only fans them to a more persistent glowing, and through the ports of our eyes, their tiny warmth enters, keeping hope liquid within us.

THAT TIME OF YEAR

That time of year thou mayst in me behold
When yellow leaves, or none, or few do hang
Upon those boughs which shake against the cold,
Bare ruin'd choirs, where late the sweet birds sang.
　　　　　　　　　　　—Shakespeare, Sonnet 73

It's suprised me this year, the fall. Suddenly the backyard walk that runs from the porch to the street is shrouded with leaves, and the potted impatiens are losing their red petals, littering the concrete with a thousand sad hearts.

Last year around this time, my neighbor George Frost died. I'd joked with him the evening before, and he had grinned around the cigar he always wore in the corner of his mouth like an extension of his smile or a wordless, ever-ready celebration of the little joys in life. He'd looked well, stout and powerful, his green workman's clothes fitting his dark bulk, as moss fits a grandaddy oak.

So his death sneaked up on me, too. I somehow slept through the life-squad's siren at two in the morning, and when I backed out on the way to work a few hours later, his car was still parked at the curb as usual. His brown pickup waited in its hood-first readiness at the top of the driveway. It wasn't until I came home that afternoon that I learned he'd passed on; over the next few days his Alabama kin gathered, and my wife, small sons and I offered cherry tomatoes through our shared back fence to the children of his children.

There's something in the light and in this end-season heat that can't be trusted. Day gives way too quickly to shadow; the mugginess has the scent of decay to it, unlike the relentlessly green and fertile humidity of high summer that ripens tomatoes and sets the peppers swelling and making seed. At this time of year, I keep looking over my shoulder, as if there's something stalking me. Out of the corner of my eye in the late afternoon, I sometimes think I see a stranger in dusty overalls, his red-rimmed eyes unblinking among the drooping quince branches. The crickets rasping under the broken sidewalk sound a warning. Few birds sing.

So I know it won't be long: It happens every year. A week or two before Halloween, I'll be sitting on the porch just past dark. The wind will rise and I'll have to zip up my jacket. The last yellow leaves of the ash tree will clatter down against the steps. And then something white and cold will brush the back of my neck with its icy hand. Instinctively, I'll lurch forward, the bow of my spine like the bending stalk of a sunflower struck black and stiff by first freeze.

Evening in the Garden

She lives in a green world populated by beings known as "Early Girl," "Big Boy," "Delight," but she is oblivious to them. Through her eight eyes, who knows what colors they are, or how greatly their planetary loomings affect her. Her body, though much smaller, is intricately dazzling, decorated with a brilliant gold calligraphy over a velvety black. For the past week I have studied her, trying to decipher those messages scrawled upon her, yet she remains silent, unyielding of the mystery. Often she is motionless from sunrise to late afternoon. Yet she is busy enough. In stillness is her living; in vibration and a moment's wildness is her continuance.

Daylight fades. The sun over my garden in Madisonville now drops behind the high oaks and maples across Simpson Avenue. Shadows slant; I feel the rocking of day into night. Pima Indians tell this story: Earth Doctor created the world from a handful of dust. As he danced and sang, the world expanded beneath his feet, and he created the sky. But the earth continued to tremble and stretch until the sky did not fit properly. Earth Doctor created spider to spin together the sky and earth so that the world would be stable.

In Madisonville, the shadows grow, stabilize, are still. So is she, spider, perfect in her place. Drawn subtly into her, the humid evening air is gently fanned across the multiple leaves of her book lungs, in my imagination tiny membranes like the pages of a volume thumbed loosely open. Her breathing I cannot see, of course, but I know it is happening. I am seeing with my mind, my knowledge, as well with my eyes. Such seeing often doubles the vision, makes of the observed moment a larger event, the larger and larger, until, if I am lucky, this particular place loses its distinction from Everywhere, and this particular time loses its distinction from Always, and I am placed in the All.

Not so tonight. Something is happening here, happening now, and that is just as good. A faint humming hangs in the air, hovers and whines, high-pitched, at the edge of my hearing. In the dusk I cannot see keenly enough to discover its source, but I know it is some small insect, roused by the cooling air and growing dark. It comes from its resting place in the fold of a leaf or the white tongue of the fading Siberian iris that droops along the house. I turn my head. The sound moves toward the garden, passing within a foot of me; suddenly everything changes.

The humming abruptly ceases; a moment of silence weighs on the air, like the silence just before the first distant rumble of a storm. Then, just as suddenly, the whining begins again, this time higher. A shrillness, a sharpness colors it. I lean forward carefully to see.

Yesterday I leaned in much the same fashion, but not at dusk, and not to witness this. I rose early and came outside to take my place by the garden bed to watch her engage in another kind of work. I had watered the tomatoes too vigorously, smashing her web. I knew she would labor all night, performing the task which gives her that uncommon common name: Golden Orb Weaver. I knew that I would see, in the morning, only the last finishing touches applied to her work — three short, right-angled connectors that cross-hatch the longer radii, which, in turn, attach to the basic framework of the web.

That I saw. Her movements were exact, precise, preordained. She did not think; never had thought; never would. Nor, for that matter, do the stars think out their courses through the universe, nor the dace in the creek up the street think out their two thousand perfect scales. But that such things are instinctively, unthinkingly accomplished does not make them less beautiful. I saw her move inward toward the center of the web, the apparently hectic activity of her legs and the dabbing of her spinnerets in reality quite efficient, economical. She wasted no movement. All was for a purpose. And then she settled into motionlessness once again, and soon it was almost easy for me to forget she was there, a foot and a half off the ground, floating in the warm morning before me.

But by this evening, all has changed. When the insect strikes her web, she leaps from her shadowed bunker, the network vibrates wildly, she darts to the source, the frantic humming abruptly ceases — and then a whiteness, a shrouding, an engowning with the finest luxurious silk, a pallid embrace of the cloudiest, most appalling gossamer thickens, draping and entwining the bitten prey.

Her poison, as always, has acted quickly. The death-throes of the victim have, as is all thoughtlessly planned out, only entangled it the further; the greater the struggle, the more suffocating the choking embrace. She injects through her fangs a chemical that dissolves the inner tissues of the insect, making of it a kind of instant soup, gnat-gruel, bug-broth. This she extracts, sucking the husk dry until it grows almost transparent beneath its shroud of silk. Hers is a potent, practical digestion, a kind of reservoir system that allows her to metabolize the nutrients from her prey very slowly. She will not have to eat again for days, even weeks.

So simply it is over. She takes her place again near the center of the web, grows still. Again she disappears into the background of garden soil, yellowing tomato vine, weed stem, curl of withering leaf. I relax, feel night coming on like a pleasant coolness rolling down my back, slowly, just between the shoulder blades. Aloft, a nighthawk's beeping reminds me, for a moment, of my grandfather, and then of the intense and fragrant heat of the neck of a girl years ago in high school, and then the smell of wine, then hay. I do not struggle with these thoughts that appear, without fanfare, and in no particular order, like stars gradually emerging in the slow letting-go of day. They, and other thoughts, varied and shifting as the curtains of the aurora, flow over me and enfold me and then fall off me successively and silently, like garments of air.

Shifting position slightly, I notice that here and there the growing coolness has drawn earthworms to the surface. Of the many common beings in backyards and gardens, earthworms are, though taken for granted, perhaps the least appreciated. Trying not to overstate the case, Darwin wrote of them, "It may be doubted if there are any other animals which have played such an important part in the history of the world than these lowly creatures." Watching one slowly emerge from the ground beneath a broken tomato, its body alternately thickening and contracting to drive its bristles against the walls of its tunnel, I remind myself again to see not only with my eyes, but with my mind, with what I know.

Darwin's claim becomes believable. An English naturalist estimated that the earthworms in a single acre process eighteen tons of soil every year. The "processing" involves the digestion of organic materials, the earthworm's casting of which mixes and helps release nutrients into the soil. Their tunnels aerate the ground, allowing airborne minerals as well as water to percolate deeply into the earth, helping keep the soil loose and providing maximum root growth. All of this, of course, is of great interest to any gardener, and in turn, to anyone who relies on a garden for food, which means the vast majority of human beings, if you allow that any farm is a large-scale garden. It is not too much to say that the history of agriculture and thus all subsequent human civilization is contingent on the earthworm's contribution to healthy, productive soil.

A sudden vibration, too faint for me to feel, causes the worm to retreat with surprising quickness. I move again, the sleeves of my shirt dampening with dew. Next door, my neighbor's light goes off.

It is fully dark, deep into evening. In the porcelain-berry vines and Virginia creeper that cover the fence, katydids call in their interrupted clicks and buzzes. Under the garden bricks, crickets rasp. A single nighthawk beeps over the railroad tracks, fluttering and gliding as it catches insects attracted by the lights on Prentice Street.

At last I struggle up. I walk stiffly toward the back porch, and pause by its cinder block foundation. Covered with warped and rotting boards, the foundation encloses the old cistern, a brick vase three feet across at the neck and widening as it descends six or eight feet. Over the years, previous inhabitants have filled it with rubbish and debris: old tongue-and-groove flooring, beer cans, aluminum pie plates, parts of several lawn mowers. There must be organic debris in it, too, for it harbors immense slugs, including a finger-long champion, a dogged slime-tracker whose dried mucus trails I see in the morning when sunrise glints off their silvery paths that cross the boards, descend to the foundation, and skirt the edge of the sidewalk.

Tonight he is again on the prowl. I mark his dark moist form moving almost imperceptibly toward something on the sidewalk. I cannot see him clearly now, but I know that he and his kin are beautiful:

SLUGS

Always the last guests
at the banquet, arriving
from cisterns and plant-heaps
long after dark,
you mark your trails
neatly, wandering laces of slime
of interest to crickets and house cats.

I watch you, five inches long,
patterned like tigers or pike,
nose the round bits of potato
into evening's senescence.

I admire your delicate eyestalks,
the fluid contentment of your bodies,
the way you go back where you came from
saying nothing,
gleaming and muscular as silence.

Of course, I am not unaware of the great damage slugs can do in my garden. Slowly and patiently, they gnaw neat-edged oval holes in the ripe shoulders of my tomatoes; they drill the slick hulls of bell peppers; they mar the red half-moons of radishes showing above the soil. But this one, this giant, attracts me. I cannot bring myself to salt its back and watch it shrivel and crisp like a pork rind, nor can I imagine employing the old folk cure of attracting and drowning it in a shallow saucer of beer. In a sense, its being here casts a spell on me, a part of the power and silence of night.

I turn at last. Half-entranced, I think again of what John Burroughs calls "this book of Nature," and the tiny portion of it I have seen tonight—the hieroglyphics of the spider's back, the unseen scrawl of the worms' trails in the earth, the slug's silver signature on the sidewalk. All of them write a language I have yet to master. On my knees at the garden's evening edge, the sky high above as spangled with stars as the spider's brilliant back here below, I learn the alphabet of the world by tracing the sounds of its letters on my own mind's dampening ground: *slug, spider, earthworm, soil.*

ACKNOWLEDGMENTS CONTINUED

I thank the editors of the following anthologies, magazines, exhi-bition, and journals, in which these essays first appeared, sometimes in slightly and sometimes in substantially different forms or with dif-ferent titles:

"A Day and a Night on the Late Big Bone" (*Licking River Review*, re-printed in *Nowhere Magazine* and *AlcaLines: Journal of the Assembly on the Literature and Culture of Appalachia "Reflections on the River"* issue).

"The First Hundred Thousand" (*Appalachian Journal*, reprinted in *Ohio Magazine* as "The Elegant Redneck").

"Working Back To The Old Place" (*Big Brick Review*).

"Guerilla Gardening" (*Isotope: A Journal of Literary Nature and Science Writing*).

"Evening In The Garden" (*Earth Beneath, Sky Beyond: Nature and Our Planet*, ed. Whitney Scott, Outsider Press).

"Sycamore Country" (*Every River On Earth: Writing From Appalachian Ohio* ed. Neil Carpathios, Ohio University Press).

"Smoked" (*New Southerner Literary Edition*).

"The Elegant Redneck" (*Ohio Literary Homecoming, A Bicentennial Cel-ebration of Ohio Writing at the Thurber Center and Ohioana Library 2003*).

"Wintering Over", "Volcanoes, Gardens, and Resurrection Lilies" (titled "The Hunting of the Snap Bean"), "The Elegant Redneck", "Skirmishes And Sallies", "Working Back To The Old Place" (*Ohio Magazine*).

"Back Doors" (*Ohio Writer*).

"Trouble, Mess, Disaster" (*Pass/Fail*, ed. Ruth Kleidon, Red Sky Books).

"The Course of the River" (*Still: The Journal*).

"Learning The Tongue, Teaching The Ear" (*Teachers & Writers: The Bechtel Issue*).

"Breaking In"; "Trouble, Mess, Disaster", "Getting Urbane At the Academy" (*Word Magazine*).

"Getting Urbane At The Academy" (*Hackberry: Purcell Marian's Liter-ary Magazine*).

"Wilding The House" (*Heartlands Today*, Bottom Dog Press).

Excerpt from "Norway Parents Puzzle on Baby's Name" courtesy of the Associated Press.

Excerpt from "Study: Name May be Key to Getting Job" courtesy of *Pittsburgh Post Gazette*.

About the Author

Richard Hague is a native Appalachian, born in Steubenville, Ohio, just across the river from Weirton, West Virginia. From his boyhood on, he visited and later summered occasionally in Monroe County, Ohio, on Greenbrier Ridge, Perry Township. He taught for forty-five years at an inner-city high school in Cincinnati, while also working now and then at Edgecliff College, Xavier University, Northeastern University, The Appalachian Writers Workshop in Hindman, Kentucky, Radford University's Summer Highlander Institute in Appalachian Literature and Writing, and Thomas More College, where he began as Writer-in-Residence in 2015. He has conducted workshops, lectures, and readings in the East, Midwest, and Appalachia.

Winner of four Ohio Arts Council fellowships in poetry and creative nonfiction, he is a member of the Academy of American Poets, the Appalachian Studies Association, the Southern Appalachian Writers Cooperative, The Mercantile Library, The Literary Club of Cincinnati, and the Irish Heritage Center of Cincinnati.

His *Milltown Natural: Essays and Stories from a Life* (Bottom Dog Press) was a National Book Award nominee. For *Ripening* (Ohio State University Press) he was named co-Poet of the Year in Ohio in 1985. *Alive In Hard Country* (Bottom Dog Press) was named 2003 Poetry Book of the Year by the Appalachian Writers Association, and *During The Recent Extinctions: New & Selected Poems 1984-2012* (Dos Madres Press) won the Weatherford Award in Poetry. His latest collections are *Beasts, River, Drunk Men, Garden, Burst, & Light: Sequences and Long Poems* (Dos Madres Press, 2016) and *Studied Days: Poems Early & Late in Appalachia* (Dos Madres Press, 2017). He has also edited two anthologies for Dos Madres, *Quarried: Three Decades of Pine Mt. Sand & Gravel* (2015) and *Realms of the Mothers:The First Decade of Dos Madres Press* (2016) He continues to live in Cincinnati, and to operate Erie Gardens, a small urban organic farm.

He is married to Pamela Korte, Assistant Professor Emerita of Mt. St. Joseph University. They have two sons, Patrick and Brendan, both of Cincinnati.

BOOKS BY BOTTOM DOG PRESS

HARMONY SERIES

Earnest Occupations, by Richard Hague, 200 pgs, $18
Pieces: A Composite Novel, by Mary Ann McGuigan, 250 pgs, $18
Crows in the Jukebox: Poems, by Mike James, 106 pgs, $16
Portrait of the Artist as a Bingo Worker: A Memoir, by Lori Jakiela,
216 pgs, $18
The Thick of Thin: A Memoir, by Larry Smith, 238 pgs, $18
Cold Air Return: A Novel, by Patrick Lawrence O'Keeffe, 390 pgs, $20
Flesh and Stones: A Memoir, by Jan Shoemaker, 176 pgs, $18
Waiting to Begin: A Memoir by Patricia O'Donnell, 166 pgs, $18
And Waking: Poems by Kevin Casey, 80 pgs, $16
Both Shoes Off: Poems by Jeanne Bryner, 112 pgs, $16
Abandoned Homeland: Poems by Jeff Gundy, 96 pgs, $16
Stolen Child: A Novel by Suzanne Kelly, 338 pgs, $18
The Canary: A Novel by Michael Loyd Gray, 196 pgs, $18
On the Flyleaf: Poems by Herbert Woodward Martin, 106 pgs, $16
The Harmonist at Nightfall: Poems of Indiana by Shari Wagner, $16
Painting Bridges: A Novel by Patricia Averbach, 234 pgs, $18
Ariadne & Other Poems by Ingrid Swanberg, 120 pgs, $16
The Search for the Reason Why: New and Selected Poems
by Tom Kryss, 192 pgs, $16
Kenneth Patchen: Rebel Poet in America
by Larry Smith, Revised 2nd Edition, 326 pgs, Cloth $28
Selected Correspondence of Kenneth Patchen,
Edited with introduction by Allen Frost, Paper $18/ Cloth $28
Awash with Roses: Collected Love Poems of Kenneth Patchen
Eds. Laura Smith and Larry Smith
With introduction by Larry Smith, 200 pgs, $16
Breathing the West: Great Basin Poems by Liane Ellison Norman, $16
Maggot: A Novel by Robert Flanagan, 262 pgs, $18
American Poet: A Novel by Jeff Vande Zande, 200 pgs, $18
The Way-Back Room: Memoir of a Detroit Childhood
by Mary Minock, 216 pgs, $18

BOOKS BY BOTTOM DOG PRESS

Bottom Dog Press, Inc.
P.O. Box 425 / Huron, Ohio 44839
http://smithdocs.net

www.ingramcontent.com/pod-product-compliance
Lightning Source LLC
Chambersburg PA
CBHW022128080426
42734CB00006B/279